Published by BookSurge Publishers
5341 Dorchester Road, Suite 16
North Charleston, SC 29418

Based in part on *The British Butler's Bible*, Mansion Publishing, 2001and *Butlers and Household Managers, 21st Century Professionals*, BookSurge Publishers 2002.

Ferry, Steven M.
     Hotel Butlers, The Great Service Differentiators
ISBN 1-59457-443-X

BookSurge, LLC North Charleston, SC
Library of Congress Control Number: 2004107390

Books are available at discount for schools and libraries or when used to promote products or services. Please contact the publisher at the address listed above, or author services at:
411 Cleveland Street, #234, Clearwater, FL 33755, USA
www.modernbutlers.com
1-813-354-2734

Cover design by Words & Images, *www.words-images.com*
Cover photograph of butlers at Nemacolin Woodlands Resort & Spa (*www.nemacolin.com*) by Words & Images, Copyright © 2004

HOTEL BUTLERS
THE GREAT SERVICE DIFFERENTIATORS

By Steven M. Ferry

HOTEL BUTLERS
THE GREAT SERVICE DIFFERENTIATORS
By **Steven M. Ferry**

Foreword

In the increasingly competitive and mechanistic world in which we live, service is often the only differentiator between one hospitality provider and another. This means the competition is also focused on improving service, so how does one differentiate one's own property in the minds of the guests?

Smart owners and managers, recognizing that butlers represent the pinnacle in service, are considering instituting butler service in the knowledge that they will bring value to the bottom line.

Hotel Butlers, The Great Service Differentiators assists owners, managers, head butlers and hospitality employees who want to develop butler service in their hotel, spa, resort or private villa.

Every hotel is different, but the basics of butling remain the same. This book has been written, therefore, to provide these basics in a way that each hotel, spa or resort can either adopt them fully or adapt them to their particular needs.

The original industry text, *The British Butlers' Bible*, was adapted to include the needs of the American market in *Butlers and Household Managers, 21st Century Professionals*, but both books described the life of a butler in a private estate and so were not on-target for butlers in hospitality venues.

Hotel Butlers, The Great Service Differentiators corrects this shortfall, jettisoning the duties of the traditional butler in a private household that were not used by butlers in hotels, and adding those particular skills that hotel butlers need and which do not apply in the private household environment.

The many checklists in the book cover every kind of situation a butler deals with and are designed, in conjunction with the chapter they supplement, to walk a person successfully through those situations and so increase his or her confidence and ability to perform.

Beyond the Book

While *Hotel Butlers, The Great Service Differentiators* can be used on its own to initiate service, the road forward is much smoother when accompanied by on-site training. The best results are obtained when that training includes four key elements as follows (the initial step being to select the most service-minded among the employees to undergo training):

1) Teaching the mechanical actions, the skills that butlers need, such as how to clean shoes, how to greet guests and tour them around their suite, how to arrange events for their stay, etc.

2) No amount of copying actions mechanically will make a butler, however. It is necessary to understand the point of view of the butler to then be able to handle any given situation as a butler would. This requires knowing and adopting the psyche or mindset of the butler. It is a truism that in order to do something effectively and with conviction, one has to be able to *be* the role that one is playing fully. Unless a butler has this as a starting point, he or she will never be able to carry off the role convincingly or handle guests and even fellow staff with the aplomb that makes butlers such quintessential service professionals.

This is why training has to include the history, rationale, characteristics and communication skills of the traditional butler, and enough drilling-in of these elements so that when the novice butler is faced with a tricky or embarrassing situation, he or she is not left tongue-tied, upsetting guests, or proving that he is not the smooth, low-key character that guests expect in their butlers. In order to achieve this, the butler needs some understanding of the mind in general‹such as why people get upset, what is happening when guests act irrationally, etc.‹so he can eliminate elements that tip guests over the edge, or help them back over it into a happy frame of mind. When it comes to communication, the butler needs to know the basics of communication, starting with the ability to be there comfortably in front of another person, and actually listen to him or her without spacing out or interrupting. These skills come from drilling, not discussion or being told that they need to be acquired.

3) Having covered the theory and done copious drills on applying the skills in a classroom environment, the trainer needs to move out with the butlers and expose them on a gradient to guests in the actual areas where they will be providing butler service. By gradient is meant the trainees start out using each other and then senior staff as guest guinea-pigs, move up to servicing known-to-be-easy guests, and from there on to servicing VIPs and known-to-be-difficult guests. The trainer should correct them on an internship or apprenticeship basis until the trainees can confidently do their duties.

4) For training to be practical and workable, it needs to tie the general actions of butling into the specific hotel environment in which they are being instituted. This means the trainer has to work with hotel management and butler trainees to adapt existing SOPs (standard operating procedures) and propose new ones that align with existing SOPs. These SOPs would be developed during the training and then drilled and corrected and used during the apprenticeship period and then fine-tuned. The result would be a butler manual that would be referred to regularly, and used to train new

staff to be butlers—as the program will probably expand and there will always be some attrition.

The end result of such training should be employees with high morale who competently carry out their duties, wowing guests and resulting in 100% occupancy, a very high rate of return visits, and the opportunity to increase rack rates while enjoying stellar word of mouth.

Hotel Butlers, The Great Differentiators, will help you decide whether a butler program is desirable and feasible for your property, and having made that decision, will compliment the training of your butlers and serve as a continued reference thereafter to keep the butler program on track.

Please feel free to call (USA) 813 354 2734 with any questions or concerns, or to contact me via *www.modernbutlers.com*

Steven Ferry

WHO LIKES TO STUDY?

May I recommend to you a fine procedure for studying successfully, which isolates three key difficulties students experience when studying, and how to overcome them? The information is quite new, and is given in *http://www.appliedscholastics.org/learn_barr.php*. The three difficulties or barriers are linked from the top left of the page.

We have all attended schools of one kind or another and some of us are pretty sure we know how to study, while others have not enjoyed too much success.

If you consider your own studies for a moment, you may have to look long and hard for any instructions on *how* to study. Plenty of times you were told to study, no doubt, but how many times how to go about it successfully? There is a right way to do most things, and plenty of wrong ways. One usually finds the right way by studying or being told. Did anyone ever tell you *how* to study, or give you a manual on how to study? Did anyone ever tell you that study has certain liabilities connected with it?

Maybe you went to school during the last twenty years in the United States and were told to guess the meaning of a word from its context. This is a very unworkable study method.

Another habit readers can fall into is ignoring sections that do not make sense. The problem with this approach is that one inevitably ends up skipping whole chapters and then throwing away the book as "useless." I would hate for you to raise your hopes about a possible new career or instituting a butler program at your facility, and then throwing it all away just because you ran into a study barrier without knowing it.

A quick review of the web page above might give you new tools that work.

For those eager to review the business end of what butlers do to make guests feel they are being serviced in a way they have never experienced before, please feel free to proceed directly to Chapters Four and their related appendices onward. But do not forget to come back to the first three chapters, wherein lie the mindset that enables butlers to win the hearts and minds of guests.

ACKNOWLEDGEMENTS

I would like to thank the many people who have contributed to this work: my mentors, who passed on the basic knowledge, fellow butlers, trainers and consultants, past employers, clients, staff, and students, all of whom have provided the raw materials and inspiration for this work, and Mr. L. Ron Hubbard, for his insights into human nature. I also want to thank Ms. Katie Hurley and Mr. Jeffrey Landesberg, both of whose input has been invaluable, and Mr. Werner Leutert of the International Institute of Modern Butlers, who every day keeps the profession alive and relevant in a world that continues to change at a frenetic pace.

HOTEL BUTLERS
THE GREAT SERVICE DIFFERENTIATORS

TABLE OF CONTENTS

ADDENDA

END NOTES

ABOUT THE AUTHOR

PREFACE

Butlers have been a rare breed, too thin on the ground to form a union or warrant a university degree with accompanying texts; so standards and definitions have assumed no identifiable form beyond capsules of dictionary thought that struggle to cram into one phrase, the entirety of an evolving and disparate profession. By nature, butlers themselves are low-key and unwilling to make possibly controversial statements; so they have written few books.

There is, as well, a certain mystique to being a British butler, living in the shadows of the rich and famous, which may come into too sharp a focus through a down-to-earth analysis.

The cinema and various books create stereotype butlers whom we find amusing for their restraint and biting wit in the face of monumental stupidity; and endearing for their willingness to work behind the scenes while their employers blithely strut across the stage, playing out their own pre-ordained roles.

The handful of non-fiction books that have been written over the last two centuries hardly bring the butler image down to earth, detailing as they do only some of their duties and skills. None were so presumptuous as to claim such a thing as a butler psyche, or to trumpet its value in our society, where moral values slowly erode into a grand canyon that was once the solid ground of trust and dependability.

This book is therefore an attempt to detail the skills and scrutinize the persona of the traditional British butler and apply the key points of that personality to today's world. Whether answering the telephone or dealing with difficult situations, there is something about the serenely aloof British butler that many find fascinating and possibly worth emulating. Hopefully, this book will provide the necessary insight.

Hotel Butlers, The Great Service Differentiators talks of butlers as professionals, for professionals they are, requiring a wide range of skills and know-how in order to provide the high-end service that employers are looking for in this fast-paced, high technology world. It's not a profession for everyone, but for those who like to serve and who have a desire to excel, life doesn't get any better.

If more butlers are found in the hospitality industry as a result of this book, if the profession becomes that much more accessible and standardized, then the time spent huddled over piles of papers, clutching a stubby pencil, will have been well spent.

Steven Ferry

CHAPTER ONE
OUTSIDE HOLLYWOOD, WHAT IS A BUTLER?

For most people today, butlers are amusing mannequins on the screen, sometimes starchy, sometimes scathingly sarcastic, but forever symbolizing the discrete pleasures available to those who have arrived.

For me, a butler is a frame of mind rather than a status or a series of duties. It is a mindset that anyone can adopt in any situation in life to very satisfying results, because it is founded on the truths that it is better to serve than be served, and that life can be rational and serene when one assumes responsibility for all things. In almost every person, there is a penguin-suited figure dying to emerge, to bring order and happiness to the lives of those around him or her. This book may focus on the traditional duties of the British butler, but between the lines and chapters you will discover a mindset that anyone can apply in life—much along the lines of the movie, *Being There*—to bring a surprising level of equanimity and happiness to those in their vicinity.

Officially, according to dictionary consensus, the butler is "a male servant and head of the household." The Oxford English Dictionary breathes some life into the word with the tidbit that "buticula" meant "bottle" to the Romans. Presumably, after enough bacchanalian orgies, the bottle became synonymous with the person bringing it around to the average reveler; and even though the word evolved from Latin, through French and into its current English form of "butler," the idea has remained essentially the same: a butler is a person who caters to the needs and pleasures of the wealthy.

Like the huge vats and dusty bottles of claret and malmsey that he so lovingly looked after in the cobwebbed cellar, the butler has matured over the centuries into a richer, rarer and more complex figure in the household. This maturing process is best illustrated by reviewing the development of domestic work as a whole in England.

Two thousand years ago, a steward cared for the master's animals. It took less than a thousand years for the master to realize that he could also use some attention himself. So by the Eleventh Century, the steward had been promoted to supervising the domestic affairs of his master's castle, such as the service at the table, directing the staff and managing

3

the finances. At that time, the butler, under the steward's direction, was still only responsible for the wines.

During the Middle Ages in England, most domestic staff were men, usually themselves of "gentle" birth, working for the nobility as part of their training for court and other activities. The only women who worked were washerwomen, nurses and "gentlewomen" who waited on the ladies of the castle.

By the Seventeenth Century, a major shift had occurred in domestic work with the emergence of a middle class. These merchants, officials and professionals had enough wealth to employ domestics, but were obviously not appropriate employers for gentry on their way up in the world. This middle class thus drew their household staff from the "lower classes" that they treated poorly, affording them little of the respect shown their more educated and refined predecessors.

This new middle class also began to employ more women in their households because they were cheaper and easier to control. The taxing of male servants from 1777 onward reinforced this trend away from male domestic employment: to raise money for the war against the American colonies, even the powder men used prodigiously in their hair was taxed!

Although unusual, women were also employed as "butleresses." The first female butler on record appears to have been named "Bunch," and employed in the vicarage of a Reverend Sydney Smith, who said of her, "I...put a napkin in her hand and made her my butler. The girls taught her to read, Mrs. Sydney to wait and I undertook her morals. She became the best butler in the county."

According to E. S. Turner in *What the Butler Saw*, "In the Eighteenth Century, the duties of butler, *valet* and footman were not so sharply differentiated as they became in the Nineteenth Century. They also included some unusual responsibilities, such as in the story of the eleventh Duke of Norfolk, known as 'the dirty duke,' who regularly drank himself insensible. This gave his servants their only chance to wash him, for he could not face soap and water when sober."

"A manservant, whatever his nominal title, had to be ready for all sorts of informal duties which could not well be defined in a handbook: guarding his master's clothes when he went swimming; bleeding his master; holding him down for the surgeon; dragging him from under the dinner table and putting him to bed; depriving him of the means of suicide during attacks of hypochondria; lifting gouty guests into, and out of, carriages; and so on. At election times, if filled full of liquor, he would be ready to bay (shout) at any candidate who held views in conflict with those of his master."

During the Industrial Revolution in the Nineteenth Century, the middle class expanded still further. Whereas wives had worked in the house alongside the maids, a new expectation grew amongst the middle class: that the wives should not soil their hands with work. These housewives sought to prove they were ladies by acquiring and running the largest staffs their husbands could or could not afford. At the same time, poorer women who had until then subsisted by cottage industries (e.g. making clothes at home), were undercut by the opening of factories and were thus forced to either work in those factories, or enter domestic service. The result was a burgeoning of the female domestic workforce, so that by the beginning of the Twentieth Century, fully one third (1.3 million) of all women were employed in households other than their own, where they out-numbered the men by 32 to 1.

By this time, the lower rung of the middle class had been redefined in London to include anyone who could afford only three servants. The butler had risen to prominence as the male servant, acting increasingly as the go-between for the employers and the rest of the staff. His phlegmatic approach to resolving the various crises generated by staff and employers alike earned him increasing value in the household.

Working as a domestic at this time varied from the huge households of the aristocracy, with three or four hundred staff, down to those able to afford only one domestic (who had to do everything from scrubbing the floors to cooking the meals).

On large estates, there existed an elaborate hierarchy amongst the servants and an opportunity to advance oneself up the ranks. An errand boy, over time, could become a butler or house steward. A scullery maid (dishwasher) could work her way up to cook. And a chambermaid could rise, in time, to the post of head housekeeper. Those at the bottom of the domestic servant hierarchy often served those at the top.

The butler was responsible for the hiring, firing and the organization of the rest of the household staff. His duties included organizing special functions like dinner parties or receptions. He would manage the household accounts and deal with contractors or any other outside personnel, supervising their work. And he would, of course, also be responsible for buying wine and organizing the wine cellar. The butler would deal with all vendors of goods to be delivered to and used by the household. These butlers acquired their expertise by apprenticeship and learning on the job.

The fixed ideas about classes of people, combined with the lack of real understanding of how to manage people or what made them tick, resulted in repressive and petty treatment of staff. Maids in some households, for instance, could be fired (resulting in no references and thus being forced into prostitution) for being seen after midday—the time by which all their cleaning should be done, and the family free to enjoy the house without hint of servants.

This state of affairs was frequently exacerbated in middle class households by the restricted lifestyles of the ladies of the house, who were able to find little worthwhile to do with their leisure time other than sitting on top of their servants. Having recently arrived, they maybe felt the need to assert their superiority over their servants. The very wealthy, who already *knew* they were superior, had different problems, developing the usual stable of peccadilloes and eccentricities that characterize those who do nothing worthwhile in life, even having their hair parted by others. The aristocracy and church had a tradition to draw on, and in the case of the gentry, sufficient wealth; so they were more likely to treat their servants with some small dignity and give them some measure of primitive comforts (providing a bed, for instance). Although humanitarian employers certainly existed, the net culture that arose was one of harsh and unrewarding drudgery and petty tyranny that was pleasant for neither the servants nor, ultimately, the employers.

When laborsaving devices were invented in the Nineteenth Century (mainly in the United States), the British middle-class employers retarded household modernization by between fifty and one hundred years with the attitude that these devices were not needed when servants existed to do all the drudgery. They were cheap, after all—a month's wages for a scullery maid in 1900 was little more than ten shillings, the cost of a good dinner at the best hotel. So, it's not surprising that many of the staff they retained were the ones who were willing to be drudges. When domestic robots (metal ones like the two made famous in the *Star Wars* movies) were envisioned in a space-age fantasy in the early Twentieth Century, they were seen as the solution to the lack of intelligent and reliable domestic help.

A number of factors acted to reduce household employment after the First World War, significant among which were the increase in the legal minimum wage for most domestic workers and social security and worker's compensation programs, all of which conspired to raise the cost of employing domestics. After the Second World War, households of forty or more staff—with butlers, valets, first, second and third footmen, steward's room boy, hall boys, chauffeurs, stable staff, gardeners and a full complement of housekeeper and kitchen staffs—all but disappeared in England, together with some of the families and fortunes they had served. Education had improved the employment prospects of men and women alike, and the war had forced them out of the household into other occupations. The end of the war saw few returning to a life of underpaid drudgery.

The many middle-class employers who had created the huge demand for a domestic workforce a century before were anyway no longer able to afford the higher wages and so finally resorted to doing the work themselves, using labor-saving devices. The wealthier employers, who had let their large staffs go to war, had been forced at the same time to curtail their life style by the rationing of such as fuel and food, thus reducing their need for so many staff. Buckingham Palace, with over three hundred and fifty staff, is one of the few surviving examples of what was once the status quo in wealthy Europe.

Within the last fifty years, the domestic scene has contracted further to the occasional housekeeper or cleaning lady, a driver or more often, gardener. Domestic staff still refers to those who perform the more menial tasks and who continue to be drawn from the poorer and (relatively) less well-educated segments of society. Their numbers have dropped as most wealthy people live in smaller mansions and their staff use modern, laborsaving appliances. Those who choose to afford a traditional butler or his modern American equivalent, the household manager, are generally employing well-educated and increasingly trained service experts.

More than economics, however, the major problems with household work around the world have been inadequate or no training and an incorrect frame of mind—both issues applying to employer and household staff alike.

From Slave to Servant to Staff—Changing Perceptions and Attitudes

Perceptions and expectations of the wealthy and staff alike have changed. No longer is it acceptable to work twenty-hour days, seven-day weeks, and all for $200 a year. The vestiges of feudalism have disappeared.

Additionally in the last fifty years, media attention on the rich and famous, together with increased education levels and exposure to more cultures, has deflated the mystique the common man held toward those with the power to employ him or her. The British royal family, once the bastion of the upper class and its philosophy of master/servant, has been secularized in the public eye by the media. Ever salivating for a story, which the royals are by definition, the media have barraged every drawing room with familial scandals and financial revelations that have shown the royals to suffer from problems quite the same in essence as any of their subjects, but on a grander scale.

The Christian ethic, that all men are born equal before God, has an important corollary: that some are born more equal than others before they get to meet God—and there is nothing new in this condition. What is new is the understanding that we are all mortals playing out different and transient games on a blob of rock somewhere in a vast universe. Where there is respect for the royal family by the British, it is not based on peasant-like awe at the family's innate superiority, but on their good deeds over the years toward the people they serve, as well as the continuity they provide to those things that the British consider to be their essence. For domestics in particular, wealth, power and status of employers may impress, but ultimately it's only because the wages are paid and they personally can get along with their employer, that they agree to serve.

Mention "domestic service" to most people today, and a negative response usually follows. As described earlier in this chapter, domestic work has developed a reputation for poorly remunerated drudgery and tyranny. The reasons are simple, as is the cure. There was a time when domestic work was an honored profession, and there is no reason it cannot again be so.

The rich and powerful have had others take care of their domestic chores for centuries. While the Romans used slaves for domestic work (their word for servant actually meant "slave" and the word "free" meant anyone in the household who was related to the head of the household), this perception of servants persisted among the less bright of employers in later centuries. They were plagued with staff problems, naturally, because no slave ever willingly volunteered anything, nor really cared for his or her owner's welfare, nor stayed longer than he had to.

Such slaves were purchased either on the open market, captured during battle, sold by their families or "bred" from existing stock. Slavery of Moorish and Asiatic boys still existed in the British Isles up until the end of the Seventeenth Century. During the Eighteenth Century, it became quite fashionable for the wealthy to be served by young, black boys or Blackamoors, dressed in fine silk costumes with turbans and plumes. They were often sent to school, instructed in the Christian religion and baptized. This was quite different from the treatment of black slaves in America. It was another 150 years before black slavery was discontinued in the United States.

Looking further at the roots of the culture of bondage in US households, one finds the system of indentured servants first appearing in Virginia during the Seventeenth Century. Penniless Europeans sold themselves to ships' captains in return for a sea passage to the New World. The captain would then sell them to settlers as indentured, all-purpose servants. These men and women were bound by strict indentures for a fixed term of years (depending upon the size of the debt to be repaid) and could be compelled to do any and every job indoors or outdoors. During their term of indentureship, they were forbidden to enter taverns, marry without permission, stay out at nights, traffic in goods or seek another place of work.

The system had most of the stigmata of slavery, and indeed many Negro slaves were treated more humanely than indentured whites. And not all indentured servants went into this service willingly. If a child's parents died on the voyage to the New World, he or she was indentured until the age of twenty-one. Some were unwary individuals in seaport towns who were either seduced, knocked senseless, drugged or kidnapped and then sold to ships' captains bound for the New World. But, if such a servant were tough and resolute, the system offered him a road to independence. By the 1870s, domestic servants became wage earners in the United States and in most European countries. Domestic service had finally evolved from slavery into paid household staff—albeit poorly paid—but still with the lowly status established by its heritage. It is no surprise, therefore, that the most common refrain to be heard among household employers was: "It's so hard to find good help these days."

Emily Post couldn't have said it better in 1922, in response to complaints about servants, when she wrote, "Perhaps a servant problem is more often an employer problem. I'm sure it is." (1)

In 1949, Dorothy Marshall researched the subject thoroughly and brought a sigh of relief to all maligned domestics with the following:

"Every generation considered itself badly served...each generation of employers was convinced that its particular griefs were peculiar to itself, and that the golden age, when servants were everything that they ought to be, was only just beyond its own memory.... It is a pure myth that the majority of servants in the past stayed for years in the same place; most of them were as fond of change as their Twentieth Century counterparts. In practice, also, good servants were rare and their employers terrified that they might leave...thus...the very dependence which most people have upon their servants gave them a bargaining power." (2)

Increasing democracy, free markets, legislation and education have given domestic staff even more opportunity to avoid oppressive employers. But in some undemocratic cultures, no such freedoms exist for some servants who are locked in, abused and even raped without recourse. This kind of employer can count on little staff loyalty while holding the lowest opinion of staff.

You reap what you sow, as the saying goes, and the few employers who treat their staff well are (and were) generally rewarded with loyalty and good service.

It is an interesting question, of course; what is the proper way to treat staff and keep them?

For the last several hundred years, employers have wanted to regiment and control their servants, while treating them with needless humiliations, giving them unnecessary tasks and capricious management, providing poor living and working conditions and low pay. Small wonder that their servant turnover has been high and that domestics developed a culture of unexpressed resentment, finding ways to covertly repay in kind unpleasant guests or employers for indignities and meanness. Employers have generally wanted robots as domestics because they failed to make the servants and their operating climate sufficiently intelligent to function sensibly. A Lady H., whom I was visiting to determine if we were suitable for each other, presented me one day with a mind-numbing list of actions to do at a precise time each day, such as when to draw which curtain. She had obviously compiled the list in an effort to counteract the omissions she had experienced with former employees. As she showed me round her estate, we came across examples of obvious negligence, such as her own bed unmade at 5.30 p.m. Only two bedrooms and beds needed to be serviced in the house, yet she had several maids scurrying around the house looking worried and busy. She spent the entire interview bemoaning the lack of quality staff and their inability to do the simple actions they were paid to execute.

When I spoke to Lord H, whose businesses employed 75,000 people, he felt I would be unlocking the secret of handling personnel if I could find out why they did not perform the duties they had been instructed to perform. The Lord and Lady in question were so convinced all servants were robots that they were unable to see their own attitude and approach to handling their staff had created that very robot culture. The tradition that the butler is haughty and aloof with inferiors is born of the same out-dated mindset that actually prevents a household from running efficiently and smoothly.

If staff members were properly instructed in the requirements of the house, given principles and rules that they could think with, as well as checklists of actions to undertake, they would undoubtedly fulfill their duties. They would be able to observe and evaluate different situations as they cropped up, and resolve them intelligently. If employers expected the staff to take pride in their work and left them free to do so without continual interruption and recriminations, then the staff would grow gradually into a happy, caring and efficient workforce. They would show initiative within the boundaries set by the employer, and provide the employer with real assistance.

It comes down to the difference between owning a slave, controlling a servant, and employing a staff member.

This attitude problem is not limited to the English; the Americans have their fair share of it, ably described by Desmond Atholl in his book, *At Your Service*.

The Butler Today

In response to shifting demands in the marketplace, several different types of butler job-descriptions exist today, each one as valid as the other when the butler understands and adopts the "mindset" that is unique to the butler.

The very wealthy will always want a formal butler figure, if only for the status symbol he represents. But people of more modest means can also make excellent use of a "butler-combination" to enhance their lifestyles. Any professional family could afford one, as in the television series, *Who's the Boss?* and *Mr. Belvedere*. He might be called a houseman, a butler or even a house manager, depending upon his duties. Whatever those duties, if he understood the purpose and ethic of the British butler and the standards required in the household, he would be a butler rather than a glorified cook or maid.

The classic concept of the butler is one who answers the phone and door, introducing or screening callers; he looks after the wine cellar, serves the drinks and sometimes lays the table and serves the food. This is a formal and limited role.

An expansion of duties can be found in the butler who acts as the manager of the house and the staff: supervising staff, including hiring and firing; purchasing, and supervising suppliers and contractors. He looks after the needs of the family, from serving morning tea in bed to organizing dinners and events, and acting as a valet.

"Major domo," literally "chief of the house," is the Sixteenth Century Spanish and Italian term for the equivalent of this butler administrator. The English used "major domo" to describe butlers or house stewards in wealthy homes abroad, and this term is the one often used in California, with its strong Spanish heritage. The house steward used to perform these same functions in larger estates in England, while the more-lowly butler was assigned them in smaller homes. As the number of large households declined, the steward disappeared and the butler-administrator gradually became the senior male servant. Mr. Hudson, as seen in the TV series, *Upstairs, Downstairs,* approximates this kind of position. As the profession has developed in response to changing social and technological conditions, the term "butler administrator" is being replaced gradually by the term "household manager."

A butler might also take on the duties of a *valet* or *personal assistant,* organizing his employer's personal and social life, traveling with him or her, acting both as a business secretary and social secretary—in other words, the "gentleman's gentleman." In the Sixteenth Century in England, factotums (literally, "does everything") managed all personal and household matters for their masters, and were perhaps the precursor of the Twentieth Century personal assistant. The famous Jeeves would be such a character. In America, "personal assistant" is the term generally used for the female equivalent of the gentleman's gentleman, and certainly describes in more modern terms the functions of the job, no matter the gender of the holder of the title.

A houseman is a modern day synthesis of the factotum and the Victorian "single-handed manservant." A jack of all trades, he emerged in the 1930's as the answer to general domestic needs in private houses and hotels: he would cook, clean, drive, serve at table, look after the children and generally perform all the work that a staff of forty used to perform in England. Such a Man-Friday butler, or houseman, might have a housekeeper, chauffeur and contractors to share in some of the work.

All of the above functions can be mixed, according to the needs of the employer, but it would be impossible for one person to cover them all consistently. If one is busy all day cooking, it is hard to also handle the driving, or the arrangements for the champagne cocktail party for two hundred that weekend.

Some corporations employ butlers, mainly to manage conventions, banquets and meals, but also to run private hotels for their executives and clientele. Along the same line, some hotels, spas, resorts and private villas have butlers who tend to be a cross between their waiters, the concierge and room service. Where their duties cover a broad range of services, they have added value to the guest's experience and thereby enjoyed increased profits and reputation. Another potentially large market for the butler, rather untapped at time of writing, is servicing high-end condos in tower blocks that are often annexed to hotels, being in the same tower. With price tags of a couple of million and owners often seasonal, there is a definite need for a butler to care for the property in an owner's absence and to assist their arrival, service them during their stay, and help with their departure. When this butler is shared with others on the same floor, the fee for his service is relatively low, while he provides the style of life that these condos call for.

A critical element for butlers in "public service" is that they do not serve one or a few individuals, but a series of guests. This creates its own dynamic, benefits and difficulties when compared to butlers working in private estates. The subject of tips, for instance, while of no big concern to highly remunerated private-service butlers, is strong in the minds of hotel butlers, who expect to make a good portion of their income from tips. Those who do their best, of course, understanding the true nature and value of a butler, inevitably make the most in tips for the very reason that they focus on providing stellar service, not collecting tips. Private-service butlers are able to develop a close relationship over time with the individual or family they serve—which has its pros and cons. But good hotel butlers can also develop relationships with many guests who keep coming back for more of that superlative service from their favorite butler. The tips for these butlers can be most generous.

A brief phenomenon that occurred in the hospitality industry at the turn of the 21st century was the degrading of the image and service by calling anything that offers superior service in some small area, "a butler." Some hotels have launched forth with "bath butlers," "fireplace butlers," "technology butlers," "baby butlers," "dog butlers," "ski butlers," and "beach butlers." This short cut to creating a reputation for superb service amongst guests cannot succeed and is nothing short of a gimmick.

There is another category of butler: the freelance butler, who hires himself out to families and corporations and provides any of the services listed above. Apart from the work performed, he also provides the cachet and mystique of a butler to help create a special occasion or event.

And lastly, there is the butler who works as a consultant to families who have recently acquired great wealth and need to be shown how to spend it in establishing themselves and their household, while avoiding both miserliness and ostentation. With ninety percent of the millionaires in America being "new money," there is quite a need for such a service. He or she also consults businesses and corporations on matters concerning quality of staff performance, such as at restaurants, hotels and cruise ships; the presentation of a corporate image; or the production of an event, such as a convention or conference.

The butler can take on additional duties, such as those of toastmaster at large functions, and more recently, as a bodyguard.

How can one claim these widely differing roles are all butlers? Formal butlers of the old school would probably have a discrete apoplectic fit at the idea, while asserting that they were, and are, the only true butlers!

There is a middle ground, however, which is very easy to walk as soon as one defines the essence of butling. Those old-style butlers will go the way of dinosaurs and troglodytes, and the cardboard butlers in the catering businesses will go the way of all cheap imitations, unless they grasp the essential points that make a butler, and apply those to today's (and tomorrow's) markets.

A butler exists essentially to smooth the lives of those he or she serves by performing many functions they would otherwise have to perform themselves, thus freeing them up for more worthwhile pursuits. But a butler is more than an extra pair of arms and legs. He commits himself to his guests and cares enough to exceed their expectations and create extra-special moments. Good service is only the starting point: it is the creativity in bringing about the moments of exquisite pleasure and happiness that is the butler's true mission.

A thousand years ago, butlers had to know how to make and care for alcoholic drinks. A hundred years ago, not only did they have to know how to serve the wine and food, but also how to care for the silver, how to valet if required, and even how to run the whole household.

The simple matters that we take for granted, such as packaged products, did not exist back then; they had to be made, grown or raised on site. Toothpaste didn't arrive in tubes, nor did other cleaning supplies. Wine did not arrive in bottles ready to serve. Refrigerators did not exist. Ice cream wasn't provided but took hours to churn. Clean-burning, self-cleaning ovens were something a cook could only dream about as she stoked the fire and sweated over the soufflés at the start of an eight-course meal for thirty guests. These large estates achieved the conveniences of modern day, pre-packaged luxuries that many people now enjoy, by employing large numbers of staff who made the products themselves and learnt their trades by apprenticeship and working their way up from the bottom.

In time, changing household needs resulted in the butler taking on more and more duties, so that he might be called upon to do what all the other staff used to do. Today, butlers are used according to the perceptions and needs of their employers. In every case, the idea is that they perform household and personal duties that free up the employer or guest.

Today, living is a technological and bureaucratic tour de force that has resulted in heavy specialization. We hire someone to fix the TV, but he can't or won't clean the swimming pool nor do our taxes. One way to combat such a phenomenon is to hire and train technocrat butlers, who combine the character and personal service of the traditional butler with sufficient skills in the myriad systems we use in servicing guests. Such a flexible yet well-grounded individual can be a real asset in the hotel environment. The ethic and rationale of a butler stand on their own and have value in modern society, quite apart from the traditions he keeps alive.

As a side-note for any who expect a book on butling to descend into titillating gossip about bosses, such as the British royal family, you will not find it in this book. Maligning anyone, especially an employer or guest, would be a most un-butler-ish thing to do. A butler is not part of the family he serves, yet he or she works intimately with one, even in a hotel environment. He will see members of the family with their hair down and social graces turned off. The attitudes and characteristics required to deal with this phenomenon successfully are in part what make the butler so unique and so prized, and are covered in the next chapter.

CHAPTER TWO
ESSENCE OF A BUTLER

Gone are the Eighteenth and Nineteenth Century ideas of a butler as one who had worked his way through the ranks from hall boy and knew his position: as long as he could hear, see and above all, say nothing, he would probably do.

In the Victorian heyday, considerate employers were rewarded by a staff that was loyal and who stayed with them for decades. The majority of employers, however, did not know the first thing about managing people and so suffered from a regular turnover of staff, quite contrary to the popular image portrayed of the doddery manservant, loyal to the end.

Despite the many books written at the time, none were able to isolate the attributes that really mattered, so blinded were the authors and readers by social standing, the minutiae of "correct" procedures and a lack of people skills and understanding of the human mind. As a result, butlers had no clear role models and employers had no way of recognizing a butler worth his salt.

The social and economic changes that reduced household staff to mainly housekeepers over the last century could have been successfully countered, had the real values and uses of butlers and other household and personal staff been properly established and applied to the changing condition of the household.

There is an identifiable set of characteristics that allows an outsider to successfully interact intimately with another family. This, coupled with expertise on the mechanical actions of the profession, can re-create the household and hospitality industry as a job-market for many, while providing many with the kind of personal service they value.

Until recently, no real consideration, beyond supplying a few rules of conduct, has been given by existing books and courses to the mental and social skills needed by the household and hospitality employee. Yet this is the very rock that staff, employers and agencies keep floundering on. This is all the more true today, as a deteriorating school system turns out a large percentage of illiterate graduates who have not only been made unresponsive by street and psychiatric drugs, but have been carefully taught that morals are passé. Apart from the damage being done to society by the replacement of a real education with psychiatric programs of behavior control, it makes it harder to find employees who are capable of caring and acting responsibly. The conclusion is far from bleak, however. When one finds a person capable of freely and openly giving selfless service, and they definitely do exist, one should cherish and train them.

A Good Butler's Basic Attributes

1. Trustworthiness is the most basic characteristic that makes a butler. A guest relies on honesty and reliability when he places his family, finances, and possessions in the temporary care of a butler. He doesn't want his possessions disappearing, chores left undone, family sickening from food poisoning or funds being diverted.

2. A guest would not want to be talked about behind his back or slandered to family and guests, nor to see his name in print via the butler—so loyalty is another key ingredient.

3. A guest does not wish to be upstaged by the butler, or big emergencies made out of small ones. So the butler is always in the background, smoothing things over and seeking to make the guest's life as pleasurable as possible. To "butle" successfully, one has to be willing to cause things quietly and let the guest take the credit; or conversely, take the blame in public for a guest's goof without becoming defensive. One is, in essence, an actor on the stage playing a part to perfection. As long as one keeps that in mind, the occasional indignities become part of the script and not a life-or-death matter.

4. The guest would like to feel that his butler really cares for his welfare and that of his family. He wants his butler to be helpful and willing—a "can-do" type who wants things to work out for the family and who helps them wherever possible.

5. The butler has to have some social graces—tactful when confronted with tricky situations so that the guest and his or her family are not made to feel uncomfortable. He knows and follows the accepted manners and customs; he keeps track of likes and dislikes of the family and obliges them accordingly; he treats each person individually and with equal dignity, no matter how bizarre they may appear.

6. Six hundred years ago, the "age of discretion," (the time when a person was able to discern that there were other players in life who needed to be included in any decisions made) was set at fourteen years old. This status meant a person was able to keep his or her own counsel and remain quiet about something until the right time and

place to divulge the knowledge presented itself, rather than flying off the handle. Sir Winston Churchill's advice to diplomats has some applicability: "A diplomat is a man who thinks twice before saying nothing." Discretion is not something one sees in most teens or even adults today, but it is a vital requirement for any butler to work successfully within the bosom of a guest's family.

7. In time, the butler becomes almost as well loved as the rest of the family, but only when he conducts himself as if he isn't; because there is an invisible line that he cannot cross. The upstairs and downstairs (or "back" and "front," as it used to be known in country houses, in contrast to smaller, city dwellings) division reflects a familial boundary, more than a societal one. Caring toward the guest and his family is therefore felt and shown, but always with a certain measure of decorum. Familiarity breeds contempt in the long run, so a butler maintains a professional demeanor at all times. It is a matter of actually caring, while maintaining a certain friendly formality in his actions. Being chummy and being impersonal are two extremes, neither of which work for a stranger allowed into the closeness of the nest.

8. By keeping track of the guest's penchants and moods, the butler can predict or anticipate and provide the item or the *environment* that the guest needs or will want before being asked for it. The butler's attitude is: "I am going to do whatever I can to make the guest comfortable and happy." It is a game he plays and the rewards are pleasing to both himself and the guest. In essence, the providing of service is a given for a butler. It is the starting point, not the finish line. What marks the real value of the butler is that extra perceptiveness (unobtrusive observation to build guest profiles from which one can anticipate needs), inventiveness toward creating "exquisite moments," and caring that allow him or her to create those extra special moments for the guests, and indeed, even other employees and vendors.

9. A fundamental distinction is that a good butler serves, but is not servile. He is there to provide a service that he enjoys. He is willing to accept criticism, and if not justified, to let it ride, or correct it where and when appropriate. But he no longer owes his continued existence to the guests and so can walk tall, if discreetly!

10. Whereas he is flexible about the amount of time he works, a butler is most punctilious about timing, never being late.

11. With regard to other staff, the butler is friendly without being too familiar. He is firm about the amount and quality of work done by those who help him provide service to the guests. On the basis that

they are all teammates, the butler cares for the staff — that their lives are running well — because their performance impacts his ability to service guests.

12. The butler is a good organizer, who can manage many people and activities according to a schedule, while keeping up with all the paperwork.

13. The butler pays great attention to detail so as to achieve high standards and so essentially communicates an aesthetic message to guests. For instance, breakfast could be some greasy eggs served on a cracked, cold plate by an unshaven, unkempt butler with a cigarette stub sticking from his lips and a body odor more in place at a zoo. Or it could be a plate of perfectly poached eggs, bacon, mushrooms and grilled tomatoes as the third course in a breakfast that is served on a sunlit balcony by a butler in morning coat and pinstripes. He offers more hot coffee and the morning's newspapers and all the while, music is playing softly in the background. That's the level of creativity the good butler deals in: the making of beautiful moments to put guests at ease and increase their pleasure.

14. At the same time, the butler has to deal with the raw emotions of upset staff, imperious family members, discourteous guests, indignant bosses, shifty contractors and the best-laid plans falling apart at the last moment — all the while maintaining his composure, his desire to provide the best possible service, and ensuring events turn out satisfactorily. He is much like the proverbial sergeant in the army — the one who organizes the men and actually meets the objectives, sometimes despite the commissioned officers.

15. And at the end of the day, the good butler still has the energy and humility to ask, "Was there anything I could have improved about my service today?"

There is a bit of the butler in everyone — the honesty, the creativity, the caring, the social graces, the phlegmatic; it is rare to find someone with all these qualities who is able to keep them turned on day in, day out, despite all the reasons not to. All of which reinforces the value of the butler in all his various manifestations.

These qualities are not the sole preserve of men — there are many women who could make excellent butlers, too. Unfortunately in such a heavily tradition-oriented occupation, butlers have almost exclusively been expected to be male by those who employed them over the last two thousand years. A valid job requirement, perhaps, in AD 50, but not necessarily in the year 2000. I know of only a handful of "butleresses," and they do a fine job. We could use many more in the profession and the hospitality field is an ideal environment to increase their numbers. In fact, quite a few guests will be found to prefer female butlers.

It is worth pointing out that the butlers most people see on the silver screen do not usually demonstrate many of the qualities listed above. When Black Adder makes disparaging and scathing remarks to the Prince of Wales' face or behind his back, he may be funny, but he is not being an honest-to-goodness butler that any employer would keep for very long — possibly because employers are never quite as naively daffy as they are made out to be.

To be sure, a butler will meet many a situation that challenges his idea of what is sensible. Does it need to be said, however, that a sensible butler will be sensible in dealing with such incidents? The next chapter describes the kind of embarrassing moments anyone can run into on occasion, and the way a butler would deal with them smoothly for all concerned.

CHAPTER THREE
BUTLER ETIQUETTE AND STICKY WICKETS
Managing People and Events with Aplomb

Asticky wicket is a term derived from cricket, describing a ball that is hard to hit for the batter because the ground it bounces on is slick. It refers, by extension, to a situation that is tough to resolve. Butlers obviously are confronted with sticky wickets, and it is the smoothness with which he resolves them that is a hallmark of good butling. He is never confrontational, opinionated or judgmental, rather preferring to put all parties as much at ease as the situation will allow.

It may be that guests are involved in illegal activities and this is condoned by the owner or management—perhaps because the guests are celebrities, or high-fliers, or the hospitality venue is owned by mobsters; in this case, it is best for the butler to hand in his resignation and keep his own counsel. If serious crimes are being committed, then he has to follow his own conscience. That would be a worst-case scenario, as few owners and managers are like this.

If a butler is asked to do something illegal or immoral by a guest (such as procuring a prostitute or drugs), it would be better for him to keep his nose clean, and hopefully the guest's, by declining politely and gently. "I hope you don't mind me mentioning this, Sir, but I really cannot oblige you in this matter," would be one way of ending it right there.

Heated have been the discussions with hotel butler trainees about where to draw the line and the potential loss of a good tip source. It is not my intention to enforce a moral code on anyone, but a definite line exists when it comes to illegalities. If it is illegal to procure prostitutes, then don't go down that road. It will not only endanger your job but also put the hotel at risk. Supposing the guest contracts a disease, from VD to AIDS, as a result of your suggestion? Supposing he is mugged or even murdered while following up on your lead? Supposing he is an undercover cop?

If a guest were doing something illegal that could compromise the hotel, it is important in any case to alert the manager. If of a minor nature, or a matter of morals rather than law, then the butler could keep his own counsel.

In principle, the butler should be willing to take the blame publicly for any goof by a guest so the guest does not lose face. But this should not extend to doing anything that is illegal and has to be played by ear according to the situation, the guest's situation and the relationship between butler and guest. If it's a matter, for instance, of the guest continuing in an unethical pattern, such as visiting with ladies of the night, then that's not something a butler should assist, and certainly not cover up for (or become involved with) when the guest's wife finds out. Lying and doing anything illegal is odious to anyone, most especially a butler. But there are ways in which one can inventively make clever excuses and provide assistance to protect the guest in a situation where he (or she) finds himself genuinely and uncharacteristically embarrassed—on the basis that the better the guest does, the better the butler does.

While the butler is always honest and upright, there is room for a judgment call when the guest's vital interests are at stake, as long as this view is tempered by the butler's responsibilities to the rest of society. For example, in the case where a butler is also assigned chauffeur duties, then taking the rap for a manslaughter charge when the guest takes the wheel and causes an accident, is not the same as having some points added to a driving license. And if the guest would as soon feed the butler to the lions as play another round of golf, then no tacit understanding exists upon which the butler can safely draw in helping a guest out of a jam and then expecting assistance from him afterwards to resolve the matter.

Another possible area of friction is when a husband and wife are at loggerheads. In this case, it is vital to remain neutral, taking neither one side nor the other. Hospitality venues being what they are, a butler is quite likely to witness or know of an indiscretion by one party that is being withheld from the other. If the butler is then asked if any such indiscretion had taken place, he has to answer the question without really answering it: "I really couldn't say, Madam," "Not to my knowledge, Sir," or "If anything were to occur of a similar nature with yourself, I am sure you would expect me to respect your privacy, Sir," would most likely answer the question without answering it, or at least put an end to the questioning. If the person insists on confirmation, the butler would be better off sticking to his guns.

If any member of a guest's family feels that you cannot be trusted, then the basis of your relationship as an outsider is undermined. The idea is not to become involved, as such family problems generally exist to one degree or another and will not resolve by your taking sides.

This non-involvement refers only to the husband and wife or long-term common-law relationships, where both are frequent guests. If the common-law relationship is only short term, and the guest asks the butler about the other, then the butler could suggest that there might have been some indiscretions (if there had been), but he would prefer to leave the matter at that. Then, if pressed, he could comply with the guest's demands for more information so that he or she might be appraised of the true character and risks of the other party.

In the event of indiscretions by children, it would be sensible to note the problem but make no mention of it. Only if the butler notices a pattern or habit forming might it be appropriate to confront the child or teenager in a way that apportions no blame, but which consults his understanding and increases his control over the peccadillo. In this way, the child will not regard the butler as an enemy who must be avoided, and may even seek out the butler for help when in trouble. However, if the behavior does continue, and it is of a serious nature such as the taking of drugs, it would be wise to ask the parent or guest who is paying for a moment of his or her time, and make the facts known.

There are quite a few tricky situations that can occur in caring for guests, the more so as they can often be prima donnas requiring kid-glove treatment.

Theft of a valuable item by a guest has been known to occur, especially in high-end venues that often use antiques or designer items for décor. In this case, it would be possible for the butler to tell the host/paying guest that "(Guest) accidentally/absent-mindedly put (item) into his/her pocket." The hosting guest may let it ride, but if he/she would like the item retrieved, the guest could be approached as follows: "Excuse me, Sir, I understand you were going to have the (item) cleaned/repaired, but we have someone coming tomorrow to do it, so could I please take it off your hands?" Spades are not called such by butlers, as you can see; non-accusatory euphemisms and white lies are employed overtime to keep the social intercourse running smoothly for family and guests alike. While the butler would be more direct with the hotel staff, he would still be courteous and skillful enough in his communications to keep the erring staff member on his side. Whether or not he managed to retrieve the item discretely, the butler should inform management of the event.

On one occasion, a host called the butler to the head of the table during a large private banquet and asked him to remove a drunk and disagreeable guest from the room to avoid further embarrassment for all present. Rather than drawing attention to the host being the instigator of the guest's removal, the butler played at bringing the host an extra condiment from the sideboard. Once outside, the butler summoned and briefed an assistant of the same sex as the offending guest, returned to the dining room and told the offending guest: "Excuse me, Sir, a telephone call for you." When outside and out of earshot, the butler apologized for his ruse, explaining that there had been no phone call. The host had asked that the guest leave so as to avoid causing himself and the other guests any further embarrassment.

The guest was at first belligerent, so it was appropriate to have the extra staff member to hand, but as events turned out, the guest calmed down and became remorseful. The butler then asked for the guest's car keys, as there had been no valet service that evening, and asked if the guest wanted a coffee before leaving. The butler then sent the staff member to the kitchen to order a coffee to be brought to the side room, and to bring the guest's car around. When the staff member returned, and another had brought the coffee, the butler returned to the dining room and whispered in the ear of the guest's partner that the guest had been taken slightly ill, and would she like to stay or leave with him. She could drive their car back or be driven back. She was savvy enough to know what had happened and elected to be driven back. The butler then called a cab, fetched the coats of the departing guests and sent the guests home in the taxi, while a staff member followed in the guest's car. The staff member caught a ride back in the cab, which the butler then paid off. The butler, meanwhile, had cleared the two vacant covers and seats, and closed up the gaps left between the remaining guests.

An equally embarrassing event is the arrival of uninvited guests at a function, either trying to gate crash, or arriving coincidentally. A good way to resolve this situation in brief, would be as follows: The butler welcomes the uninvited guest(s) and ushers them into a separate room. If they have arrived without knowing there is an ongoing event, they can be told the situation and that their host is seeing his or her guests. The butler can offer them a drink before he lets the host know of their arrival. When he tells the host, he could suggest that, unless the host wants to see the uninvited visitor(s), he will relay his best wishes and apologies and fix an appointment for another visit. The butler relays the host's message, answers any questions, and asks if they would like a refill before he fetches their coats. After the refill, he brings their coats (if appropriate) and sees them out of the door. If they try to stay longer, the butler can apologize, saying that he really must attend to the guests at the event in progress. If the venue is not such as a private villa, but a public hotel, then the guests could be invited to enjoy any of the other facilities.

If the unexpected guests think that they have been invited when they haven't, or feel that they should have been, the butler again invites them into a side room and says something along the lines of: "I am sorry, a mistake has been made; there's a dinner party tonight, and I don't appear to have you on the guest list. I am very sorry about this." He then asks if they would like a drink before fetching their coats and promises to let the host know of their brief visit. If they insist on the host knowing straight away, the butler sees the host and continues with the steps outlined in the preceding paragraph.

In the event that a guest who has been staying at the hotel is asked to leave by the host, for whatever reason, then equally tactful handling is required. Take the case of the guest who had been making advances toward the hostess, even during the meal. The butler was called by the host after the meal, and instructed to tell the offending guest that he was no longer welcome. The butler went to the guest's room and found him hangdog about his behavior, which he realized had upset the host. The butler apologized about making his announcement, but made it anyway. The guest wanted to know why he was being asked to leave, but the butler sidestepped the question, preferring not to argue the case, as the host had not asked him to explain the reason why.

The butler was genuinely sorry for the guest's predicament, and said whatever he could to make him accept the host's decision. He offered to make the flight arrangements, which the guest accepted. As the flight was not until later that evening, he provided the guest with dinner in the guest's room, and had a cab arrive to pick him up afterwards.

The above examples provide an idea of the type of situations a butler may run into from time to time, and the flavor of the responses.

The Fly in the Ointment

There is one other sticky situation a butler may encounter in the course of working with guests (or other employees or suppliers) and which can be most upsetting if one does not recognize that the problem isn't with the butler but the other person. This is the guest who, perhaps as a result of some problem in his or her own life, is taking it out on the employees and everything else that moves and breathes.

The power enjoyed by the wealthy can be used either in the understanding that real richness in life comes from friendship and positive accomplishment, or by someone who has nothing constructive to offer. Whether some wealthy people are unable to find anything worthwhile to do with their own lives, or they consider they hold an absolute power over those servicing them, I have noticed a tendency for these *idle* rich to take on the characteristics of ill-willed people, even though they may not be truly evil. As the saying goes, "The devil finds work for idle hands." It seems those who have nothing to contribute to society, and therefore lack self-esteem, turn to strange games to amuse themselves.

The likes of Bertie Wooster in the "Jeeves" stories and the Prince of Wales as depicted in the BBC television series "Black Adder" characterize just such idle rich, with nothing worthwhile to do, but they are the harmless types. Miss Daisy in "Driving Miss Daisy" provides a mild example of the type of employer for whom time sits heavily and staff suffers as a result.

Sometimes, the games can be relatively harmless, such as a phobia about cleanliness. One employer suffered from this to the point where she would insist on personally cleaning the house from top to bottom, paying close attention to cleaning those places that had already been thoroughly cleaned by the maid. The result was an unhappy maid kept busy with useless motions while the furniture and fixtures gradually eroded.

But one cannot assume that those dysfunctional, idle rich are the kind of anti-social people one absolutely does not want to work for, the kind that considers others as competitors, even enemies to be thwarted. Some of my butler colleagues have been faced with such a mean-spirited person, yet dealing with unpleasant employers is not a subject that is covered in any butler textbooks or courses—employers are generally described as good-natured, if eccentric; and the butlers long-suffering, if tolerant, as in Jeeves and Wooster.

Only in the real world, "eccentric" is often a euphemism for irrationality that sometimes includes ill will towards anyone unfortunate enough to be in that person's vicinity. Being "long-suffering" in the presence of such a person is not a solution but a ticket to failing health, unhappiness and possibly an early demise. Butlers, in fact, are encouraged to bite the bullet and endure all sorts of insults—it's almost a trademark of the profession. While this may be a workable procedure when faced with the occasional unpleasant moment, it is exactly the wrong approach when confronted with a person of ill will who revels in being able to lash out constantly at or undermine someone who can't or is expected not to fight back.

It thus becomes important to spot these people by their actions and speech as soon as possible so one can be wise to their ways and not fall victim to their unfortunate games.

In focusing on the dark side of butling, I would like to emphasize that the great majority of guests are decent people for whom it is easy to extend oneself. Ill-willed people exist in all walks of life, however, and while they represent only a very small percentage of the populace, that's still a large number of people when considering six-billion souls on this planet.

One doesn't earn too many points for spotting Saddam Hussein as such a person of ill will. Neither is it hard to spot an employer who is always flying off the handle, firing employees, causing untold upset and making life miserable for one and all, as such a person of ill will. But what about those people who hide their real character? How does one spot a Richard Dahmler before one ends up on his lunch plate?

If one finds oneself servicing such a person, one needs to be able to recognize the sign—not endure while slowly having one's life sucked dry of vitality. Instead of thinking there is something wrong with oneself—a misconception these people invariably foist off on their "victims"—one can say to oneself, "Alright, looks like we have one of those mean people here; while maintaining my butler dignity and level of service, I need to expect insults, bad-mouthing of me to my face and behind my back, lies told to get me into trouble, and everything I am and do to be made less of." The simple fact is that nobody has known how to spot these people before, but once armed with the data about them, one can see them for what they are and thankfully, this simple knowledge alone prevents them from driving you down, it defuses the harm they do.

But what are the signs? Guests do not usually froth at the mouth and hold dripping butcher knives when they first walk through the hotel front door. But they do have telltale signs. Here are some from a private household situation where the lady of the house was a "meanie."

One day, I noticed that a housekeeper, who was in her sixties and had been with the family for a quarter of a century, was very ill: flushed, coughing, and weak. I told her to go home and rest, and alerted my employer to the fact. The employer responded by telling me that I was lucky to get sick pay, as they didn't normally allow it. Not being baited by this non-sequitur (illogical) response, I pointed out that the grandchildren would be arriving soon and that it might be risky for them to keep the ill housekeeper around. But the employer would have none of it until the thought occurred to her, "It's bad for ME," at which point she sent the housekeeper home immediately (while pointing out to her that she would not receive any sick pay).

The poor housekeeper returned two days later after visiting a local walk-in clinic. She had not recovered at all, but was unable to afford any more unpaid sick leave. She had pleurisy (walking pneumonia), a blood pressure of 190 and a temperature that had been measured at the clinic at 104-5 degrees. When the employer heard this, her only response was to assert that the housekeeper had only had the "sniffles" and "she always exaggerates her temperature." All said to me with a smile, of course, which I did not fall for. People smile when they are happy or glad to see another. Not this kind of person. Their smile has the distinct look of a snake sizing up its prey.

Then I began to notice that whenever the employer talked of the family, the conversation would invariably focus on deaths, illnesses, tragedies and break-ups. The employer would omit the successes and happy moments.

I once provided a meal for a member of the family who lived nearby. The relative phoned the next day to thank my employer for a wonderful meal. Later that day, my employer made no mention of that message at all, instead complaining that the dessert had been much too heavy, insisting it been made with whole wheat flour. Factually, the dessert had been made with white flour according to the recipe, and was light and delicious (even if I say so myself). Fortunately, the relative gave me the proper message when I saw her in person later in the week.

Another time, I was cautioned against taking an evening constitutional (walk) in the guarded community in which we lived, because "it was very dangerous," and "security is walking around with dogs." The person went on to say that a club member had been arrested and sent to jail the night before for walking around after dark. Being wise to the employer's games, and knowing that my many earlier walks had been completed without mishap, I decided to take my intended walk, enjoying the fresh air and calm night, admiring the stars in the sky and generally letting my thoughts wander. I chatted with a security guard (with no dog in sight) a short while later and confirmed that there had been no arrest or jailing of anyone.

Once, the employer emerged from the basement to accuse the housekeeper and butler of raising the thermostat down there. The employer had been the only person down there all morning and also often complained of the house being too cold. So one didn't have to be a Sherlock Holmes to determine who had turned up the heat (not that turning up the heat is a crime to be making much of a fuss over).

Another time, a maid was accused of burning a silk tie with the iron. The maid vehemently denied the charge to no avail. Another employee later consoled the maid by revealing to her that she had seen the employer earlier in the day, trying to iron that very same tie.

Looking at these examples, one might be inclined to shrug off these incidents as minor—they do not paint a picture of someone who goes ballistic at the slightest provocation and skins live cats for a hobby (the easy ones to spot). One is tempted to make excuses for such a person's behavior. It's hard after all, for anyone to believe that another could be so willfully mean. But research has uncovered that these mean-spirited people do in fact exist. The good news is that they have certain traits in common, which means you can spot them before they do you any real damage. American philosopher and humanitarian Mr. L. Ron Hubbard first pointed out the existence of such people and cataloged their traits. These warning signs are covered in detail in several of his works, but the easiest to review in this age of the Internet can be found at the following web site: *www.scientologyhandbook.org/sh11.htm*

Take a look at this web page and see if there is anyone at your work (or elsewhere) who fits this description. And then keep it mind when you find yourself suddenly feeling uncertain of yourself in connection with a particular guest, when you walk away from them consistently feeling you have done wrong or are not good enough. Odds are, you have a mean-spirited person to service. In a just world, they'd be locked up for the harm they cause others. But right now, he or she is a guest, and you are the person selected to service him or her. So do it with pride knowing that you can stand up to even them with a smile—because you see through them.

Sticky Staff Situations

Chapter Four includes some sticky situations a butler or head butler may encounter in the course of working with other employees or suppliers. As always, the purpose of each suggested handling is to smooth over situations and handle them as much as possible to be benefit of everyone involved.

As an example, when a car detailer accidentally buffed the paint off a black, $200,000 car, the guest concerned was furious. This detailer was a small-businessman who would go belly-up from the negative word-of-mouth that could be generated by this incident, as well as his lack of funds to pay for the damage caused. The butler involved had the insurance company cover the repainting costs; the detailer took care of the deductible, and the guest was given a discount on all future washes. That way everyone came out ahead. The detailer still had his business, his goodwill and his accounts; the guest had a new paint job, a detailer who would do anything to please him, and lower-priced washes; and the butler had a smoothed-over situation while avoiding the need to locate a new vendor, with all the trials and tribulations that entails.

There can also be problems with staff who are resentful, or lazy, or completely contrarian. A butler's concerns are primarily that other employees are performing their jobs well and working together as a team in doing so. Both of these goals can be achieved by instruction, example and good leadership. If a staff member remains defiantly negative or wholly shiftless despite the butler's best efforts, only then is it time to talk to Human Resources or their boss about replacing him or her.

The worst thing to do is nothing, or think that "Oh, it's just the way he is." Nobody has the right to serve spanners in the soup or walk around with an attitude the size of the Matterhorn on their shoulder. Nothing serves to reduce morale, business and job security faster than a sour puss on staff, so don't tolerate them. Help them do their job or help them out of the door.

Compassion and caring go a long way in developing loyalty from the staff; this can include taking an interest in their family life, as well as their problems on the job. Helping salvage a marriage is the kind of sticky situation that a butler may be required to address so that the head housekeeper isn't in the doldrums when she should be working happily.

Another point that could be considered a bit of a sticky wicket is the subject of breakage by employees. Always let the guest (and management) know (preferably after the item has been repaired if a simple enough task, so that no problem is created). However, if the item is hotel property and small and would not be missed (such as an inexpensive plate used by the staff) it is not worth informing management. For bigger-ticket items, the manager would, after an initial upset, feel happier to have been told so that he is not wondering what else has been broken without his knowledge, and so he can express his wishes concerning the repair of the item. Note: Very expensive items are often covered by insurance, and smaller items are usually of little or no concern to the management in the first place.

For example, an antique, crystal vase was delivered by the post office to a guest's home in many more pieces than it had left the hotel, even though it had been packaged properly. Naturally, the butler had insured the item for its full worth. Because everything had been taken care of, hard feelings were minimized.

When all is said and done, sticky situations add spice to life and are a learning experience as long as one has some measure of security in knowing how to deal with them.

The butler's relationship with employers, employees, guests and vendors can be a win-win proposition for all concerned, and hopefully the preceding chapters have provided enough tools to win even in the face of the direst circumstances. Most of the time, however, a butler's work is routine, without complication or high drama. The following chapters provide insight into the many mundane but satisfying actions that go into running the butler department in a hotel, spa, resort or private villa.

CHAPTER FOUR
THE BUTLER DEPARTMENT
And its Relationship to Other Departments

The following chapter deals with the day-to-day running of the butler department. When a butler department is first initiated, the usual question from other employees is 'How will butlers impact me," and "What will these butlers be doing that we don't already do?"

This chapter answers these questions. Butlers bring together some of the expertise of valets, concierges, housekeeping, room service, reservations and even management, add the traditional butler service standards, and apply these all to a select group of individuals who are willing to pay top rack rates for the convenience of having all these functions performed by the same individual(s). valets, concierges, housekeeping, room service, reservations and management still perform all their usual functions, even for these butler-service guests, to one degree or another.

Butlers will certainly be earning large tips working with such guests, a point of disgruntlement from those who might otherwise have received tips for work that butlers are now doing. But butlers would be wise to share their tip pool with those who make their jobs easier. And from the bigger picture, butlers will also be bringing greater solvency for the hotel as guests pay more for the service, repeat visit, and spread the word, bringing in new business—all of which is job security for all the staff.

Acceptance of a New Idea Does Not Just Happen

This potential undercurrent of resentment has to be addressed delicately by management and the new butlers when instituting a butler department. It's a Public Relations problem—a question of finding out what the actual thoughts of other employees are about the new department, how it will impact them, and then initiating a campaign to set fears to rest and bring about a spirit of cooperation between employees and the new butlers.

The new butlers can assist in this regard by dispelling any notion that they are somehow intrinsically superior to the other employees, and so refraining from any haughty, holier-than-thou, arrogance in their approach to other employees. The truth is that butlers depend completely on the other employees doing their jobs well, in order to provide Butler Service to guests. As public relations depends in large measure on good manners, the key ingredient called for is a basic liking and admiration for fellow employees—because each one is a jewel in his or her own right if one conceives this to be the case. "You get what you push" is the basic adage. If your view of fellow employees is that they are inferior, then you will be rewarded with inferior performance. You will also find no cooperation.

So if butlers make a point of sending out an introductory letter to all employees, such as the one detailed in *Appendix 4A*, if they do not assume that everyone knows who they are and is under strict orders to do their bidding, they will be accepted and supported by other employees. If butlers attend departmental meetings in their new uniforms to introduce themselves and the department, enthuse the attendees on what this means for the hotel and for them, and if the butlers answer any questions their fellow employees may have, and ask what they might need from the butlers in order for everyone to be able to work together smoothly, then all but the chronic sour-puss employees will be with the program.

When the butler contacts another employee in relation to something needed for a guest, then phrase the request as one, not a demand. Ask if the employee needs any help if there is a problem providing the service. Be on their side and they will be on yours. The butlers will soon isolate those few who are not service minded and who never deliver as needed nor respond to requests, who snap and snarl when requests are made, responding to none of the gentler arts. These can be asked, quite forthrightly, what issue they have with providing the guests with the needed service. Butlers can go to their seniors and write reports and generally increase the pressure until either the person changes or leaves. Everybody has difficulties from time to time, but nobody has a right to prevent another from doing his job. As the quintessential service providers, butlers cannot be reasonable or back down when faced with a teammate who has lost sight of which team he or she is on.

Finding Staff

Having said this, let's look at the first step in putting a butler department in place. A head butler is a vital position to fill in order to impose order on a butler department. Butlers may work well as a team, but they need leadership. So plan on finding or promoting a head butler when hiring butlers.

Finding employees these days is difficult enough without then blowing them away with inconsiderate demands or poor management. Such a department has low morale, low standards of work and a reputation that does not promote the vital cooperation from the other departments.

Head butlers and managers who have such problems can often be heard remarking on the difficulty in finding decent help, yet it never occurs to them that their problems are of their own making. Most people can be made into good staff with just a small amount of instruction and care. The head butler therefore can do much to set the tone of the department and ensure its smooth running for all concerned.

Perhaps the first question is, "How does one procure good-quality staff?" The definition of good quality often refers to someone who has experience and decent references. This definition falls short, as "experience" frequently entails procedures learned in a former location that you do not want used in your hotel; and "good references" can be fabricated (e.g. by a former employer who was also the butler's lover, as happened once. The truth was only discovered after the butler in question had been fired after causing thousands of dollars worth of damage in separate incidents, and leaving with items belonging to his employer and the guests).

My definition of a good staff member is one who may or may not have some formal training and/or experience, but who, above all, is willing and able to learn and willing to work as a team member. Time spent training such a staff member is amply rewarded in terms of initiative, honest work and caring by that staff member. No amount of supervision or coercion and searching for "good staff" will produce the kind of calm efficiency that results from a butler department forged in this manner.

How does one go about staffing a butler department, then, in liaison with HR?

The first place I would look is the hotel itself for those most service-minded among the existing employees. Promote those who want to become butlers. The staff will see a greater future for themselves and so remain loyal.

The second place I would check is your own resources—people you know in the industry who seem a good fit.

You can certainly check the top staff agencies around the country, or even abroad. You can advertise in quality national and regional newspapers and magazines, using a blind ad (post office or newspaper box). These will give you the experienced and pricey staff prospects with good references. You just have to check then whether they have become soured and bitter, or prima donnas, which would make it hard for them to work with the rest of the staff.

Hopefully, HR has a job description in the form of a proposed contract, which includes the following points:

1. duties;
2. wages paid weekly and reviewed annually; flexibility of schedule covering willingness and ability to work on their time off in exchange for time-off at a later date (time-off in-lieu or "TOIL"), as well as time and half pay (50% above normal);
3. chain of command, including whom they report to, and anyone they are responsible for supervising;
4. dress and hygiene codes;
5. possible body and room search in the event of a theft;
6. six weeks trial period;
7. one month's notice required if leaving;
8. vacations, allowed holidays, sick leave time and starting pay;
9. procedure to follow if ill or injured;
10. team member emphasis;
11. any board and lodging provided;
12. any health insurance and worker's compensation;
13. disciplinary procedures and an idea of what is to be disciplined;
14. such a contract can possibly include a one-year commitment to work, if much training on the job is required;
15. confidentiality agreement.

On the subject of wages, they should be higher than other non-managerial employees, with the understanding that the bulk of their remuneration will come from the tip pool.

HR will conduct interviews, but the head butler would do well to interview candidates before accepting them into your department. During the job interview, try to put the applicant at ease. These interviews can be intimidating, as you may recall from your own experience.

Have the applicant read the contract and answer any questions they may have. Meanwhile, take the time to observe the person's reactions to the contract and his or her surroundings. Is she negative and sour? Is he aggressive or angry? Does she ask loaded questions? These kinds of people do not make good team mates. Does the applicant have social graces and some idea of manners? Does his questioning display any understanding of the job? Remember, willingness and an open heart are the signs you want to see. Experience and know-how would be excellent bonuses, but are not the primary criteria. You could ask the applicant to demonstrate some aspect of his/her skill as part of the interview, but remember that the butler's functions are not so complex that they cannot be apprenticed on the job.

Decide which is the best candidate, bearing in mind attitude, skill, appearance, hygiene, and references, as well as any liabilities, such as dependents or troublesome familial ties.

In these days of rapid lay-offs in response to changing financial fortunes, it may seem unreal to insist on being over-staffed in the interests of providing excellent service to guests. Hotel owners, shareholders and management may notice a smaller payroll, but not as much as guests will notice any missing or inadequate service and decide to try any of your many competitors next time they travel. So if you hear rumblings of lay-offs and even the future of your own department looks in jeopardy, then just calmly gather up your carefully compiled statistics on increased rack rates, revenues, occupancy and customer satisfaction in the butler department and send them to whoever controls the purse strings, with the demand for more personnel, not less.

Supervising Staff

As the senior staff member, it is the head butler's responsibility to ensure all duties are carried out for the smooth running of the department. In a recently created and inadequately staffed and trained department, this may mean you do the work yourself while finding and training staff to take over the duties.

Having given a staff member a job to do and shown him how to do it, let him or her get on with it, ever mindful at first that you may have to jump in to complete the job properly. But until then, refrain from issuing streams of instructions. It is the staff member's job to issue instructions to himself or herself, and the more you usurp this responsibility, the less willing and competent he or she becomes. In my experience, departments run well where individual responsibility is exercised within the parameters of the person's skill and general staff duties.

Ideally, you would have enough competent and willing staff to accomplish all needed tasks. Your job would be the coordination of staff with each other in servicing the guests. Keep the staff briefed on daily requirements, special functions, guests, schedules, menus, and anything else that will help to make them into an intelligent, coordinated team. This can be accomplished by daily conferences with the heads of each department, and a weekly staff meeting to discuss progress, plans, suggestions and requests. Checklists should be made and marked off by each staff member, as they accomplish assigned tasks.

To avoid discord amongst the staff, discourage discussions of salaries and tips. Divide tips from guests between the staff according to an agreed upon apportionment that takes into consideration time spent on the job each week and seniority. Butlers would be wise to apportion some of the tip pool to those employees who make it possible for the butlers to do their own job—butler coordinators (those who handle phone requests from guests), room service, valet, concierge, et al. Housekeeping will continue to receive their own tips generally when guests depart.

Be consistent in praising and disciplining staff, thus avoiding favoritism. In large departments, avoid eating with other staff too often so as to maintain your presence and avoid over-familiarity.

Do not allow staff to complain about conditions, guests or employers unless their complaint is offered as part of a constructive suggestion to you alone.

Avoid allowing your own moods to color your demeanor while on the job—you want to appear accessible to the staff under your supervision.

In terms of address, it is normal to call the chef "Chef," the head housekeeper, "Ms. (Family name)" and the staff by either their first or family names, depending upon the custom in the hotel. You yourself would be called "Mr./Ms. (family name)." Proper forms of address help keep relationships on a professional footing. The guests are always called by the family name and any title by the staff, with the children referred to as "Master or Miss (family name)."

Obviously, if the guest demands otherwise, or the hotel convention is informal among employees, then one obliges. The danger with becoming informal is that familiarity generally breeds contempt. It is of interest to note that the introduction of a first-name basis in professional circles came on the backs of salespeople trying to ingratiate themselves with their prospects. It may not seem comfortable, friendly or "democratic" to call employees "Mr. X" or "Ms. Y." But consider this: they *are* professionals. Drop the professionalism, and familiarity creeps in, and there goes the whole professional relationship. The friendly thing to do is maintain that slight, invisible barrier.

Dismissing Staff

Once in a long while, it may be necessary for an employee to be dismissed. This is generally an HR job and an SOP no doubt exists for how to accomplish a dismissal in a society as vindictively litigious as today's.

From the head butler's perspective, unless a security aspect is involved, try to keep the person on the job until a replacement can be found, even if a temporary help. Remember, your main responsibility is to keep the department running as smoothly as possible.

If the person is being let go because of overstaffing, this requires a completely different resolution. The person is called in and the situation explained to him or her. (S)he is given proper notice, with severance pay and any back vacation pay. If living in, ensure (s)he is allowed adequate time to find alternate accommodation. And (s)he is always given a good reference, as well as any leads for employment.

If, on the other hand, (s)he is being dismissed for continued incompetence, dishonesty or unwillingness to work, (s)he is treated to the same rights, but given no reference and no help in finding alternate employment. It would be wise to make a recording of the dismissing interview, and (s)he would be required to sign for any monies given. Collect any keys, uniform and hotel property in his or her possession, as well as a list of any incomplete projects.

In the event that (s)he was violent, or had stolen property and you had verified this to be the case, you might call in the police and press criminal charges. In such instances, you would need to have another staff member of the same sex as the employee in the interview room with you as a witness. If living in, he or she would also escort the person to his or her quarters and see that they packed and left straight away (in a taxi to the nearest public transportation if needed), without fuss, violence or further theft.

The above is for reference only, as the hotel's SOP would be followed by HR. Where you feel the SOP could be improved by the introduction of any of the above, you may want to draw this section to the attention of HR.

Disciplining Staff

One thing that can severely undermine staff morale and happiness, is the wrong-doing of one which is known about by another who keeps it to himself; either through fear of retaliation, or a disagreement with "snitching," or because they have similar misdeeds of their own to hide.

It is important to encourage a system that allows staff to keep a clean breast of things. If they break something accidentally, they should let you know, no matter the cost. They won't be fired for it, and if the item is very expensive, insurance should cover the loss anyway.

If they notice someone else doing something wrong, whether breakage, goofing off on the job or petty theft, or anything detrimental to the hotel, its staff or guests, then they should let you know about it if the person himself doesn't. You would act as a clearinghouse for this kind of information by keeping files.

These files would not be used against the person, but rather to help him or her; if something serious is reported, or you notice a pattern, you could interview him and show him the information you are operating on. If the information were incorrect, you would acknowledge it as such, make a note in the file and leave it at that.

If it were correct, you would help the person spot any pattern emerging and ask for his suggestions (or provide some) as to what he could do to correct it. Most people are blind to their own failings, so it helps to have someone draw their attention to them. Write up the interview and have the person sign it.

In the event that enough verified incidents accumulate, and the person just will not change, then it is time to start issuing ultimatums—shape up or ship out. If you do have to fire, you have the record of the signed interviews and reports of wrongdoings, should the person turn around and try to sue. I mention the worst-case scenario, but most people are only too willing to correct their failings and appreciate being given the chance to do so. This system, adopted by agreement by all staff, will help keep them working well together as well as, interestingly enough, preempt staff resignations.

Again, existing hotel SOPs take precedence, but you can always suggest improvements in them according to the above.

The Organizing Chart for the Butler Department

The butler department has three positions within it: the head butler, the butlers/under butlers, and the butler coordinators.

The head butler's basic duties are to make sure that the butler department is adequately manned, with a workable roster so that sufficient butlers are on duty to provide exemplary service to the guests. He or she is responsible for the butlers each doing their job well, correcting them when they fall short, and stepping in himself to service the guests when required. See *Appendix 4B* for a sample job description.

The butlers work as a team to service guests in the butler style. They answer to the head butler. See *Appendix 4C* for a sample job description.

Also in the butler department are the "butler coordinators" who answer the telephone, taking requests from guests, relaying them to the appropriate department or butler and following up to make sure the requests were fulfilled. The butler coordinators also keep the paperwork, computerized records and master board (see below) updated. They do not need to be trained butlers, but they do need to be trained on the butler persona and phone etiquette, so they can represent the butler department properly when interacting with guests. See *Appendix 4D* for a sample job description.

Work Load

Butlers are best assigned to a specific section, covering several guests for their eight-hour shift. If the hotel can afford one butler per suite, so much the better, but with the exception of demanding guests who expect instant and constant service, these butlers will find themselves with not enough to do. So it works best with a ratio of one butler to four rooms for the first and second shifts. The night shift can drop to one butler for as many as 15 or 20 rooms, as generally the demands by guests will drop dramatically, and the night butler will be busy preparing for the following day's activities more than seeing to current requests for guests.

Obviously, a demanding (and deserving) or celebrity guest would be best assigned a single butler, or possibly even two, if he or she makes constant requests.

This can be a delicate point, as some guests may try to monopolize the butlers. If management is not of a mind to assign a single butler to a particular guest, then the butler may need to suggest gently that he will be happy to attend to the guest's most recent request, as soon as he has taken care of the requests of the other guests.

If the guest still does not cooperate, then the head butler can have a word, and if still no joy, then management can step in. Initially, the butler would try to fulfill all requests in a timely manner, and call for assistance from another butler on duty to keep the demanding guest happy, but where this guest is being thoroughly inconsiderate and thus impacting the other guests (and if he or she is not a guest that management is overly eager to service again), then one would start the above sequence of suggestions.

Communication within the Butler Department

Most problems with guests trace to a failed communication of one sort or another. This makes a workable and easy-to-use communication system a vital part of any butler department with regularly changing shifts and rapidly changing guest rosters and requests. The ability of a group to relay accurate information verbally has long been known to be faulty. As in the story of a request sent by front lines troops in the British army, "Send reinforcements, we are going to advance." By the time the request arrived at headquarters via various relay points, it had metamorphosed into "Send three-and-four pence, we are going to a dance." To clarify,

"Three and four pence" is a contraction of "three shillings and four pence," currency used in Britain.

I am indebted to hotel butler extraordinaire, Jeffrey Landesberg, for first bringing my attention to a communication system that forms the backbone of the system offered below.

Red Book

The department needs a large logbook for use as a central memo/message book for everybody in the department to note down general information, such as:

1) Things that need to be done.
   Example: On Tuesday, one butler notes that someone needs to call Mr. Hamilton on Friday about his daughter's arrival.

2) Record incidents or accomplishments.
   Example: John delivered six Fed Ex boxes to the Mrs. Zorch in the Palatial Suite. The paper work is stapled into the Red Book.

3) Notes of changes or things that effect the department.
   Example: The coffee machine has broken down and the call has been made to the engineers to fix it.

The Red Book is open to anyone to read, so do not write confidential items in it, such as "Mr. Jones is in Suite 5 with his girlfriend, not his wife. Be careful."

Pre-arrival Grid

Part of butler service includes calling on guests well before they arrive, so as to ensure their desires are known and everything arranged in advance. So each morning, a first-shift butler checks with reservations for the names of expected arrivals for the two weeks ahead. He or she enters these names on a wall-mounted erasable board upon which is drawn a grid showing:
- Pre-arrival interview done,
- Reservations made,
- Needed items in stock,
- Confirmation five days out that all reservations are still in place.

Once the person has arrived, relevant information is transferred to the Guest History/Profile by the butler coordinator and the name removed from the grid.

Guest History/Profile

Guest Profiles are the database the hotel has accumulated on the likes and dislikes and past experiences with each guest. They are a key element in being able to offer butler service that predicts and fulfills desires without the guest having to express those desires.

These profiles are built up by quietly observing what a guest says and does during each visit. Observe what items are used in the in-room bar, if there is one. Does he use the fireplace? What bubble bath does she prefer? Do they smoke and if so, which brand? Does she golf? Does he go horseback riding? Does he like Earl Grey, the Financial Times, butter or margarine? When is her birthday, etc.?

Each morning, the butler coordinator determines which guests are arriving that day and prints off a one-page summary of his or her Guest Profile. She places it on a small clipboard that is hung on the wall—one clipboard for each guest suite. The pre-arrival information is also included on this clipboard, providing the calendar, reservations etc. for each day of each guest's stay.

Butlers can then refresh themselves on the information for each guest on the day they are expected to arrive and refer to it during their stay. Equally important is that the butlers and butler coordinators note on the clipboard every time they observe another preference or item about that guest. After the guest leaves, the butler coordinators transfer the information to the computerized profiles of each guest.

Refer to *Appendix 4E* for the kind of points a Guest Profile should include.

The White Board

This, as its name suggests, is a wall-mounted, white, erasable board. It needs to be as large as the butler's pantry walls will allow and be accessible for butlers and butler coordinators to write on it.

The board is the mind of the butler department, telling everyone everything that needs to be done and when to service the guests, so that the department's resources can be allocated effectively.

Each butler and butler coordinator writes the latest information and developments as they occur. The board is the ongoing intelligence without which the department would rapidly descend into a frantic confusion of last-minute panic as guests make their displeasure known.

The board shows a grid, color-coded for easy recognition, providing the following kind of information:

- Suite number
- Guest's name
- Number in party
- Arrival date(s) and time(s)
- Departure date(s) and time(s)
- Method of arrival (so butlers can plan where/how to meet the guests)
- Arrival amenity—what type, when procured
- Any special needs
- Meals (especially noting the serving and clearing of an in-room meal—and whether clearing was prevented by a "Do Not Disturb" sign)
- Reservations (for meals)
- Activities (notes on tee times, etc.)
- Turndown, with amenities and paperwork delivered for the next day's weather, agenda and morning wake-up service.

Knowing, for instance, that Suite 23 is going for dinner at Zagreb's 6.00 pm, the first-shift butler can make the reservations, arrange transport and note both events on the White Board. The second-shift butler and housekeeping then know when they can refresh the room and deliver the turndown service.

"Driver's License"

When butlers are away from the butler's pantry, they often need access to the information on the White Board. The solution is to carry a mini White Board that they update at the beginning of their shift. It is also referred to as a "Driver's License."

The minimum information to keep on the Driver's License is the names of guests in each suite with check-in and check-out days and times noted. In addition, whatever other information is most useful, bearing in mind that the White Board changes by the minute and the Driver's Licenses are only updated three times a day. Information might be:

- Specials and soups of the day
- Convention information giving who is in house and where they are meeting
- Special events of the day, such as concerts
- Important telephone numbers

In an optimum scenario, the White Board and Driver's License would be combined into a networked system of wireless Palm Pilots or

BlackBerrys with cell phone capabilities, updated in real time by the butler coordinators who are given verbal or written updates by the butlers. This solution costs a few hundred dollars per butler on duty, but is so far superior in terms of keeping the butlers in touch and informed, that it is well worth the outlay. For instance, a butler is about to greet an arriving guest at the front entrance, and suddenly cannot remember how he likes to be referred to. With the Palm Pilot or BlackBerrys, all he has to do is key in the guest's profile. Or let's say the guest wants to know what he is scheduled to do on the fifth day of his visit. The butler does not have to guess, or excuse himself while he checks the White Board. He can either key in his palm pilot or call the butler coordinator and provide an almost instantaneous response.

Radios

Butlers can waste a lot of time looking for each other, and completely miss opportunities to provide excellent service if they cannot find each other or communicate instantaneously. This makes radios for each butler and the butler coordinator a very small investment and absolute necessity to create a real team. One channel would be for butler use within the department—other channels used for contacting other departments. While a specific butler was being contacted for something, other butlers would listen in and offer information or assistance as needed.

These radios need to be next-to-invisible and inaudible, so discrete earpieces and lapel microphones are a must. Rechargers and a couple of spare batteries should come with each radio: as soon as one battery dies, it should be recharged.

Radio etiquette is similar to CB procedure, along the following lines:

- When calling, identify who is calling whom. For example: "This is Suzie (or "the coordinator") to any available butler."
- Response should be: "This is John, come in."
- The information is exchanged succinctly, in a business-like fashion, and confirmed. by both sender and receiver. Radios are for short bursts of info. Use the telephone for long conversation.
- End the message by saying "Out."
- If a butler is busy, the butler needs to say on the radio: "John to coordinator, I will be with Mr. Jones for the next half hour."
- The coordinator and others will need to monitor the radio so they can respond as needed.
- A departmental shorthand and code will develop over the radio.
- No expletives, swearing or derogatory communications are acceptable.

Above all, butlers have to focus on dealing with the guests in front of them, and not suddenly introvert into their ear as a message comes through. Give guests your undivided attention, and at your earliest convenience after dealing with the guests, respond to the radio communication. One certainly does not communicate on the radio while servicing a guest. It should be understood by other butlers that a "no response" from one butler means he or she is unavailable, and another butler should step in to assist the caller.

Radios have their drawbacks though, as I found out when the limo I was riding in broke down in driving rain just after we had left the more-traveled main road. The radio could not reach anyone (so stranding us there for a while), not because of the rain, but as the butler/chauffeur detailed off to me somewhat irksomely, because the butlers had to share the same band as everyone else, and sometimes people accidentally hit buttons which made it impossible for others to talk or hear. Lesson learned: insist on a channel exclusive to butlers. Another issue is the bulk of the radios on the market, and their large antenna. No place to put them without them 1) being obvious and 2) hitching up one's jacket when bending down…as when with one's hands full of a loaded tray.

The Departmental Corkboard

This old standby is where communications concerning the department itself are posted. For instance:

- The schedule
- Important announcements
- Things that need to be read by the staff
- Policy changes
- Convention agendas
- "Thank you" letters from guests and managers
- Comment-card scores

Handing off Verbally

While as much information as possible needs to be written down, verbal hand offs between shifts are vital to providing a seamless servicing of guests. Information on what each butler is doing, what each guest is doing and plans to do—these all need to be communicated so that no balls are dropped.

Food Orders

Food orders are filled out either by the butlers in the presence of the guest or, where orders are made by telephone, by the butler coordinator. These food orders serve also as Time Orders. Ideally, these forms use carbonless copies with three sheets of different colors. One goes to the kitchen and the rest to the coordinator for a) follow up and b) for attaching to the guest's clipboard for butler reference and later input by the butler coordinator into the Guest's Profile.

Additionally, a notation is made in the Red Book that there is a food order for 9:00 am the next day, for instance, for Suite 15. Again, recording the data in the Red Book and on the White Board, as well as communicating the data verbally, is a double-check system, ensuring both butlers and butler coordinators are in on the loop and able to ensure timely and accurate delivery of the meal.

Coordinator Log

All calls in to the butler department are handled by the butler coordinator. He or she logs each call in a running log that includes

- The time of each call;
- Who it was from (name and suite number);
- What was requested;
- Who was contacted to handle the call and when—some the coordinator will handle herself, of course;
- This record permits follow up by another when the coordinator has gone, or to trace back errors if there is a snafu (and so reduce them);
- At the beginning of each day, the prior day's log sheets, Driver's Licenses and related paperwork (food order sheets, receipts) are collected, data extracted and input into computerized Guest Profiles by the butler coordinator, and then bundled together and filed for reference for the next ninety days.

Laundry and Repair Log

Laundry and dry cleaning slips are filed in a "current-guests" folder after being checked against the laundry to make sure that all items are actually included in the bag. If the guest placed the items in the bag and claims there are five pairs of socks and the butler only finds three, then he would need to query this with the guest at a convenient time, but before sending the laundry on to the laundry department. As items come back from the laundry, the butler checks off each item on the laundry slip to ensure all have been returned.

A log is also kept that shows the guest's name, suite number, date, time, who picked up and processed the laundry, and who delivered the cleaned items to the guest and when. Dry cleaning tickets are stapled onto these laundry and dry cleaning slips in the folder.

The same log is used to record shoe and clothing repairs. Repair tickets are stapled into the Laundry and Repair Log.

Once a guest leaves, their laundry and dry cleaning slips are transferred into the folder for that guest. The laundry department normally takes care of entering fees for all these services into the guest's portfolio.

The above communication lines and procedures may seem somewhat daunting, but once they have been set up and the butlers and coordinators drilled on their use, they become not just second nature, but vital to the smooth functioning of the department.

The Housekeeper and Cleaning

Housekeepers perform much work that often goes unnoticed. Sometimes they have to deal with thoughtless guests. Their work, however, is very important, and it helps to acknowledge and thank the housekeeping staff for work well done on a regular basis.

The butlers on duty should check rooms prior to the arrival of a guest and bring to the housekeeper's attention, in a low-key manner, anything that might have been missed—or fix it himself there and then if a minor point. In a crunch, the butler would roll up his sleeves to ready a room in time for a guest's imminent arrival.

It may be advisable for housekeepers and butlers to team up and deep clean one room a week or month on a rotational basis so that all rooms receive deep cleaning a minimum of once a year—preferably twice-yearly. Cleaning and maintenance checklists make the job much easier.

The housekeeper in private households traditionally helps the butler at functions, serving at the table for a small party, or taking and minding coats at large functions. In the absence of an under-butler, the housekeeper really functions as the butler's deputy. In a hotel environment, the above relationship can be encouraged, with appropriate training provided for the housekeepers, where the workload and employee complement suggest such a plan.

In many hotels and private villas, the furniture and household items are often of very fine quality, sometimes fragile antiques of great value. The housekeeper in this case needs to know proper care and cleaning procedures, and these are listed below, in brief (some suggestions being summarized from *The National Trust Manual of Housekeeping* by Sandwith and Stainton, Penguin Books). It would be up to the butler to bring these points to the housekeeper's attention where necessary.

Anything of extreme value, or in very bad shape, should be cleaned (and restored) by experts.

Furniture

Examine the item for any weakness before moving it and be sure to grasp it by its strongest point. Avoid spreading dust by flicking the duster; instead, gather the dust in the duster and then discard it. If using a hog's hairbrush to remove dust from crevices, though, flick the dust away rather than trying to scrub it off. Do not rub or wash gilded items or gesso (chalky base for paint); instead, use a pony tail hairbrush. Once a year, polish the furniture lightly with a soft brush (unless you notice the veneer is lifting). Place nylon screening on upholstery before vacuuming, so that the fibers are not pulled out. Use a piece of stiff card to protect fringes and mirror frames when cleaning around them.

The sun can fade furniture over time, so cover windows with an ultraviolet absorbing film or have sunscreens installed, which can be pulled half way down on a dull day, and fully down on a sunny day, or all the time in a little-used room that is full of antiques.

Floors

Protect floors from workmen by using coverings, providing plastic or cloth socks or booties, or at a minimum, by placing metal or coconut mats outside to clean mud off boots. If possible, ask that shoes be taken off on entry, as is the custom in many houses. Quickly remove any liquid or mud to prevent it spreading.

Limit cleaning to dusting with a vacuum cleaner (slowly float the head, don't scrub with it). Use nylon screening for fragile carpets. Always vacuum underneath a rush mat. Clean a polished wooden floor infrequently (using very little water or a cloth soaked in paraffin or vinegar, making sure to dry it immediately afterwards), and polish it using brushes that are kept clean and supple. Lift curtains and hangings clear of the cleaning. Marble floors should be dry-buffed. Put special padding under rugs that are placed on such highly polished floors, to prevent slipping.

Ceramics

In general, when cleaning items that are located high up, use a stepladder so as to avoid cleaning above shoulder height, which is tiring and increases the risk of damage occurring.

Examine items for any weaknesses, and use both hands to pick up one piece or section at a time. Dust flat areas with a duster and crannies with a hog's hairbrush. Wash with a very mild detergent only when necessary, and without immersing.

Metalwork

Use plastic gloves when cleaning with a solvent, otherwise handle with cotton gloves on. Use a separate brush and cloth to clean each type of metal. Then wax (copper, steel and brass) a small area at a time.

Gold

Clean only with water and buff with an impregnated cloth. Clean separately, and do not polish or dry with the same cloth as is used for silver items, or the gold may become silver plated.

Books

Remove old books from shelves by gripping their sides firmly and pulling them out gently; where possible, push them out from behind first. Support large books underneath and carry them vertically. Clear and dust one shelf and its contents at a time, starting at the top. Stack books only a few on top of each other, and carry them a few at a time between thumb and fingers. Vacuum heavy dust from them with a brush-ended vacuum attachment. Dust edges with a shaving brush. Only then open and dust inside the covers with the shaving brush. Keep and label any pieces that come off, for fixing by experts; also note and report any recent damage by pests. Replace books exactly as you found them.

As with furniture in general, keep the temperature constant and mild, and the humidity at RH (relative humidity) 50-65%. High humidity and heat, as well as wild temperature fluctuations, are the main enemies to avoid.

Hair and Clothes Brushes

Poke the hair out with a thin rod between the lines of bristles. Using cold water, rub hand soap and then shampoo into the bristle, then rinse. Place bristle down on a towel to dry. If the bristles wear down or fall out, a valuable brush can be re-bristled (try Clements in the Burlington Arcade, London, if you happen to live nearby).

Cleaning Cloths

I heartily recommend cloths by Terga that collect dirt electrostatically. They only require water, meaning harsh, smelly and toxic household chemicals can be dispensed with. The cloths come in sets of three, one designed for glass and similar surfaces, one for most other surfaces, and the third for floors and heavy stains. They cost about US $10 each but last two years if properly used. Cheap imitations of Targa cloth can be bought for a third of the price and work reasonably well, but not as well. For instance, they still leave lint on glassware and windows, which Targa cloths do not. As a final note, I do not own stock in Targa.

The Kitchen under the Chef

If you have ever worked with or under a chef, you will know how prima donna-ish they often can be. And if you have ever chef'd in a large kitchen for many people, you might understand why many chefs are like that. The chef is lord of his domain and usually works under great pressure to produce the right amount of food that is just right, at just the right time. As such, he deserves respect and the freedom to go about his business without interference. In a private household, it is a common courtesy for anyone entering the kitchen to knock first, and on entering, address the chef as "chef."

Guests sometimes ask for specific meals outside the chef's planned menus for the day. In a regular hotel, maybe the guest would be told by the waiter, after the chef had vented the day's frustrations in his face, "I am sorry, Sir, we are not able to satisfy your request." This is not, however, a standard response for a butler. If the guest asks for it, it is the chef's job, as the expert in his area, to solve the problem and the butler's job to present the required dish. If the chef vents, the butler calmly acknowledges understandingly and repeats his request and a demand for a solution. It is not the butler's job to trip up the chef, but to make his job as easy as possible by giving him advanced warning of the dietary needs or preferences of arriving guests, so he can order-in those items. As covered later, one of the key duties of the butler is to build up a data base of guest preferences and needs so everything is available for the guest without him or her having to ask for it. That's one of the expected benefits of staying at a hotel offering butler service.

Running an Efficient Kitchen

Sometimes butlers have mini-kitchens at their disposal from which they can cater to guests wanting breakfast, light lunches, teas or cocktail parties—with the bulk of the dishes being shipped in from the main kitchen. In such a case, kitchen protocol should be followed.

Safety is a primary consideration, as one has sharp, hot, cold, electrical and gas sources peppered throughout the environment, which in conjunction with stress and the rush to produce a meal on time can result in injuries. Apart from knowing their specific trade, an obvious concern, which is almost never mentioned, is that employees have to be reasonably happy with their own lives in order to be able to focus their attention fully on the job at hand.

The kitchen has to be free of encumbrances and piles of junk; everything should be stored in its rightful place. It should be spotless, including the areas that cannot be readily seen, such as extractor fan screens. Ideally, there would be two one-way doors—in and out, or at least a glass panel in a single door to prevent collisions. Glass should be kept out of the kitchen, except for any hors d'oeuvres dishes, etc. that are about to be used. Otherwise, glass and glasses are cleaned in the washing up area.

Glasses and knives are not left under water, out of sight, where someone might cut himself. Knives are kept very sharp, as the extra force needed to cut with a blunt knife often results in slips and cut fingers. Fully stocked first-aid boxes should be placed strategically, and two staff on each shift trained on first aid (so that one can tend to the other if needed). A good trick is to sprinkle some flour on hot items as a warning to others. Fire blankets and extinguishers should be placed strategically and operational. All the staff should be instructed on how to use them, and what to do in the event of a fire. There should be no running in the kitchen. All spills should be mopped dry immediately to prevent slipping.

Another matter of primary concern is hygiene. Flesh products should be cut on their own boards and the boards then disinfected. Contrary to established opinion, wooden boards are far more hygienic than the modern plastic versions, which harbor bacteria while the wooden ones are less hospitable to the wee beasties. Zappers can be installed for flies and a pest control company called in to spray and lay traps if needed. I once saw a rat scurrying up the wall of the food preparation area in a high-end English pub. My shock turned to disbelief when the chef just shrugged his shoulders and did nothing (he didn't have his job for long).

These kinds of precautions are vital to avoid food poisoning. To this end, pets (and children, for hygienic and safety reasons) should not be allowed in the kitchen. A hand basin should be positioned by the kitchen doors, with paper towels and a trash can, and used to wash hands by anyone newly entering the kitchen area.

If a staff member becomes ill with a communicable disease (from AIDS to the common cold), they should not be allowed to work in the kitchen. Quite apart from the fact that their own recovery will be hastened by rest and recuperation, the all-too-common expectation that staff work through illnesses often results in diseases being passed on instead of contained. Staff should be eligible for sick pay, and temporary staff can always be brought in. The only requirements for returning to duty are that these ill employees bring papers from a health practitioner confirming the existence of the illness and that it is no longer contagious; and that they sign an Illness/Injury Book on their return. This book is kept in the kitchen and details what times have been taken off and for what reason. The chef, housekeeper or butler countersigns the book for their recovered staff. The purpose of the book is to prevent false claims, keep track of sick leave and isolate chronically ill staff, for possible further assistance.

The refrigerator should be kept clean inside, outside and behind; each section should be labeled so that different users always return food to the right place. Older food should be moved to the front of its shelf; raw meats kept at the bottom in case of dripping fluids; smelly items wrapped; raw meat covered, but allowed an air hole at each end to prevent sweating. An opened box of bicarbonate of soda can be kept in the fridge to neutralize any smells. It is a good idea to keep a list on the fridge door, that everyone can add to when they use the last of an item, or when it is running low. Refrigerator temperatures should be kept close to freezing, so always shut the door as soon as possible.

As for the freezer, the same rules apply in general; one should label and date, and properly wrap everything before placing it in the freezer. Nothing should ever be refrozen once thawed out, most especially raw meats, as bacterial growth will occur.

Have all kitchen appliances, including the freezer and refrigerator, serviced at least once a year.

Lastly, there is the matter of cleaning up after a meal. Larger kitchens usually employ a dishwasher and (s)he should know how to handle the finer items such as crystal and china, as well as the proper tools needed for cleaning different types of pots and pans. Teflon, for example, doesn't respond well to a wire scourer, just as a heavily encrusted and burnt pot will not respond to a sponge. The sink taps in the dishwashing area should be fitted with rubber protective nozzles to prevent the most common form of glass breakage—hitting the rims on the taps while rinsing.

Glasses should be washed by hand in hot water and mild detergent. Place them upright on a towel and dry with a dry cloth. For wineglasses, hold the bowl with the cloth on the outside, bunch the other end of the cloth and turn it in the bowl. Hold the foot to dry the foot and stem. This will prevent undue stress separating the bowl of the glass from the stem, by holding the one while drying the other. Polish glasses with another, lint-free cloth. Glasses should be stored upright in a dust proof cupboard. Decanters can be hard to access, so the best way to dry them is by turning them upside down and pouring hot water over the outside.

Silver should be treated to the same washing regimen. When dried, silver is best stored in acid free tissue paper to prevent tarnishing (see later in this chapter for more information).

Crystal is similar to glass: clean by hand with warm (not hot) water with a mild soap added if needed. Vases and decanters can be cleaned on the inside with Sterodent, or by swirling with a solution of raw rice added to warm, soapy water; or bleach can be left inside for two hours. Lime deposits inside vases, bottles (and kettles) can be removed by rinsing them with vinegar-and-water solutions or fresh-squeezed lemon or lime.

Bone-handled cutlery should be wiped, not washed, to prevent hot water from shrinking the bone and neutralizing the glue that fastens the bone to the metal.

Dealing with Contractors, Vendors and Service Providers

Purchasing can be among the butler's duties, whether it is the stocking of dry goods (see *Appendix 4F* for a basic list of items to stock), selection of the best produce, the acquisition of appliances or the purchase of gifts for guests.

Most hotels and resorts have their own in-house suppliers of many items guests typically need. However, often a guest requires some item or service that the hotel does not offer. In this case, the butler needs to have a Rolodex of reliable professionals to call upon. *Appendix 4G* provides a list of likely professions. Aim for at least three sources in each profession, so that at short notice, you will not be confounded by one going out of business, being out of town, or being fully booked. Always select those that deliver the best quality, and only then, given a large choice, narrow the list down in terms of economy.

You may need to visit some of them, but others you can ask to send samples of their work, such as printers. The idea is that you actually eyeball some of their products, to confirm that the standard and quality of their product is adequate for guests of your hotel.

When ordering goods to be delivered, therefore, it is wise to insist on known and kept delivery dates, as well as a guarantee of immediate replacement for spoiled or broken deliveries. As covered earlier, have at least three suppliers short-listed, and ensure they know about the others on the list, to encourage competition.

Even when the best supplier has been found, continue to check for changes in other suppliers, or the arrival of new ones. Also, continue to check for new products, but whenever possible try them yourself or on the staff before introducing them to guests. When shopping, always consult the specialists for tips on their finest quality items and recommendations for the day.

Delivery

When an item is delivered, review the packaging slip and then the merchandise, cross-checking condition and quality, then weight, then price against the record of what was ordered according to the order-and-delivery-of-merchandise form (see *Appendix 4H*). You can give the driver a (non-alcoholic) drink while you check the delivery; handle any shortfall or poor quality with him/his office straight away; otherwise, give him a tip if appropriate and send him on his way. Warn suppliers when you encounter inefficiency or dishonesty (shortfalls, loaded bills or poor quality) and if they continue, find an alternate source and switch supplier.

On the subject of tips and gifts, deliverymen are sometimes tipped for large or long-distance deliveries that have involved quite some work on the driver's part. All deliverers and suppliers could be given small presents at the end of the year for Christmas.

If suppliers give the butler gifts, accept them on behalf of the hotel or the guest involved and pass them on to the Director of Lodging or the guest concerned. If the butler accepts them for himself, he will be obligated to the supplier and lose purchasing power as a result. The gifts, anyway, are a return for the hotel's or a guest's purchases, not the butler's, so they rightfully belong to the hotel or guest (although guests are just as likely to tell the butler to keep them—in which case, they should go into the butler tip pool).

Safety

It falls upon the butler to organize matters relating to the safety of those in the butler section of the hotel, as well as the integrity of the hotel itself. Chapter Ten deals with the butler as a bodyguard; while this section below is a good deal less dramatic, it is far more likely to be needed to save lives and property.

It is wise, where not already done, to insist that the appropriate department in the hotel bring in experts on security and fire to recommend the best equipment and systems and have them installed. Then set up and keep a log for the maintenance of these systems, as well as the drills done by staff in their use of them.

These automatic systems are valuable, but they alone will not accomplish the full job of security and protection; for that, you will need the co-operation of the staff and guests, which is best accomplished by instruction and then drilling. A roster could be drawn up, showing each employee's name and what their specific duties are in the event of a fire or, to take a leaf out of navy manuals, should they have to help repel boarders. The roster would need to be structured so that all functions were covered even though some staff might be off-duty or away on their day off.

For the fire drills, some would be assigned to fire fighting, some to evacuation, and some to salvage work. Someone spotting a fire would yell "Fire" repeatedly, stating its location. He would hit the alarm button, if not already going, and do what he could to extinguish the fire; as the first minute or two are crucial in bringing a fire under control. The first person to hear the cry would phone the fire brigade and then go about his assigned fire duties.

The evacuation people would ensure everyone was directed out of the building, and the fire fighters would help with extinguishing the fire (until the fire trucks arrived, or until it became too dangerous to continue). The salvage people would remove pre-determined valuables from areas they could still access without risk (as a note: during the first fire-fighting drill, use the real items gingerly, just to make sure there are no problems with removing them; in subsequent drilling, use substitute items).

Everyone else would muster away from the building for a roll call, and the evacuation people would be sent back to bring out anyone still in the building as long as this were still feasible (being careful not to try to rescue someone who was actually not there at all, but in town or somewhere similar).

The staff billed as fire fighters would have to be instructed on how to put out different types of fires; those billed as evacuators would have to be instructed on carrying unconscious or injured people, and on first aid.

The fire drills would be done for real at a time when all guests were out enjoying the day (you could light a fire in a bucket in an area where no smoke damage would be done), and the alarms would be hit (with word to the fire brigade beforehand that a drill was about to take place). You would want as much commotion and panic element generated as possible, to simulate a real situation. Smoke canisters could be purchased and set off. This may run contrary to fire drills recommended by others, but why run a drill that is completely unreal? In a real fire, people won't act as if they are walking into a church service. To be sure, panic is not the desired effect, but swift and effective action in the midst of great confusion (a burning hotel and endangered people and possessions are not an orderly affair by numbers) is what will win the day.

Windows and doors should be shut. The drill would be called at a set time at first and timed with a stopwatch to measure how long it takes to evacuate the building and bring the fire under control. The idea would be to have all the functions done as swiftly and calmly as possible.

These drills can be great fun, as well as marvelous team-builders, quite apart from their life-saving potential. Over time, it would be sensible to train each person in the butler department to perform each function, so that they can be of further use once they have accomplished their pre-assigned tasks. Instruction could include awareness by staff of what can cause a fire, so they can prevent them occurring in the first place. Lastly, ensure notices are posted in staff and guest areas, indicating where to go and what to do in the event of a fire.

A similar drill could be worked out for "repelling boarders," to borrow on old sea-faring concept. It would simply involve calling security and getting away if possible to a pre-selected safe point. Or cooperating with attackers in an effort to keep them calm until security and/or the police arrive. This drill could be extended for any staff interested and can include basic self-defense lessons, or possibly martial arts and small-arms training, should there ever be a need for such preparedness.

Ensure several people on staff are first-aid trained and work out some incentive to have them do the training if none volunteer (bonus, pay rise, time off).

Ensure there is an emergency generator for the hotel or the butler department area and that it is serviced and operational. Earthquakes, hurricanes, tornadoes, snowstorms or problems at the power company can all cause inconvenience through lack of power for basic activities.

Paperwork

Butlers are not exempt from paper shuffling, but these days, most of it can be done with a computer and printer. The centerpiece of a butler's paperwork is the "pantry book," so called because the butler's office used to be called the pantry and he would keep a book there with all his notes and information important to the position. Today, this book is more commonly referred to as the *"Butler's Book,"* and takes the form of computer files and records as covered earlier in this chapter.

A good butler and butler coordinator keeps a record of the likes and dislikes of his guests; he records all his suppliers and the people he calls on for services, whether internal or external; he notes anything of interest and importance in running the butler department, not just for his own benefit, but so that his successor can step into his shoes and continue the work without interruption for the guests.

Appendix 4J provides a self-explanatory list of the type of information kept in this book. As it needs to be kept updated and changed over the years, a computer really proves its worth to the modern butler.

Several computer programs could be utilized, including a calendar program, a data base program for filing lists of things, an accounting program for keeping track of expenses, and a word-processing program for writing letters and memos.

Some hard-copy files still have to be kept, including contracts, statements, letters and receipts received, warranties and instructions for the running of appliances. A working file for each major function or event put on is also very useful.

Keeping Accounts

This subject is really very easy, as long as the system set up simply shows money in and out, and you keep the records up-to-date on a daily or every-other-day basis. If you leave it much longer, that receipt you mislaid without realizing it will result in your books not balancing later in the week or month, and you will have no hope of remembering what expense could account for the missing money. Keep all invoices, dockets, petty cash vouchers, checkbook stubs, charge card receipts, etc. in date order, filed by week and month, and use these to cross check accounts. Then update, summarize and print out the account monthly.

When an invoice is received, check it against the order book and ensure the delivery was made, and the amounts and prices align with those of the bill as well as the original order. Phone the supplier immediately if there be any discrepancy. Never pay an invoice, etc., no matter how small, without cross checking records and knowing what you are paying for. If an invoice is received for something not in the order book, check with the other butlers if they may have placed the order, what the order was for exactly, and whether it was delivered. In the case of a service rendered, cross check for earlier such statements to ensure the bill is in the right ballpark.

Compile an annual report for management on expenditures, comparing them to earlier years, summarizing where the money went, giving the reason for any rise or fall, and making predictions of funds required in the year ahead. If the allowance is limited and not sufficient, then ask for an increase. One good statistic to keep track of on a daily basis, and include in the report, is the amount of money saved by reason of astute purchasing or financial management.

Appendix 4K suggests a simple form for keeping track of the ordering and taking delivery of merchandise and a format for the bills-paid ledger. Books can be used, but computers definitely have the edge now: with an accounting program, all financial records entered in are automatically added up, subtracted, divided and so on, as required. The work expended to set up the program is amply rewarded in time saved thereafter, while lessening the likelihood of errors in the accounting.

Appendix 4L provides a format for taking notes of phone calls. Several times I have been able to correct an erring contractor or delinquent supplier by reminding them of the exact original request.

Making an Inventory

The head butler should make an inventory of valuable items under his care if one has not been done already. This project can be quite extensive when done for the first time, but the subsequent entering of new purchases makes the annual update an easy proposition. The purpose of making and maintaining such an inventory is mainly for insurance, in case of theft, fire or breakage.

The inventory is best carried out with an assistant at a time when guests are away. The assistant adds an extra pair of eyes to spot what you might miss. If an inventory already exists, print a copy to work off; otherwise use a pad and pencil. Map out the wing or area of the hotel that falls under your responsibility as the head butler, assigning each room a number. Simply walk into a room and note the details of all items of value. Once that room is complete, move to the next. Use a digital camera to photograph important items, making a note of the room number and the date so it can be input into the computer later.

The following format includes the kind of information that you should record:

- Description of item (name; serial number, size, color, condition, pair or set)
- Place and date of purchase
- Original cost
- Replacement cost

Call in professional appraisers to value antiques and works of art. Once the inventory has been input into the computer, send copies with insurance update requests via the appropriate hotel executive to the insurance company. Guest and staff property of value should also be covered in the policy. An "All Risks" insurance policy would cover possessions when removed from the house.

Taking Care of Various Articles

Butlers are well known for their silver-cleaning skills. Not surprisingly, they still have to clean silver, so it helps to know how it is done these days—a lot easier, you'll be relieved to hear, than in the old days when they had to make their own polish and then use a lot of elbow grease to shine the silver. They produced a better shine for their pains in those days, though, managing to polish away the scratches on the surface, which modern silver polishes do not.

Silver—Cleaning, Storage and Purchase

Silver should be rinsed quickly of salt and other food residues to prevent tarnishing. It may then be washed in hot, soapy water, rinsed and quickly dried (with a motion, when handling cutlery, that goes from handle to tip) using a soft dry cloth. Once a year, use a bleach solution on the inside of silver coffeepots, rinsing and drying after the solution bubbles up.

If the silver has become slightly tarnished, you can immerse the item in silver dip while wearing plastic, rather than rubber, gloves. Use cotton buds to access recesses in elaborate pieces. Note: Do not use this dip on silver-plated items, or if you do, dip very quickly and infrequently to avoid eroding the plate. Then rinse thoroughly in cold running water, dry with a soft cloth, and leave in an airing cupboard to dry any recesses.

If the silver has become heavily tarnished, use a long-term polish, which comes in two forms. If a liquid, apply it with a cloth and brush it off with a "plate brush" when it has dried. If a paste, apply it with a moist sponge and then wash off with cold, running water. Repeat this process until no more black tarnish comes off on the cloth. However, you should avoid rubbing over hallmarks too much, as they can be erased. Then polish the silver with an impregnated cloth.

Silver that has been waxed or lacquered should of course not be polished. If salt corrosion has blemished the silver, immerse the article in a solution of one tablespoon of salt to a pint of water for five minutes; then wash in hot soapy water and polish with long-term silver polish or foaming silver polish. If no improvement after this treatment, take the item to a jeweler for repair.

Once you have the silver well cleaned and polished, it is easy to maintain the shine and preserve the silver items by dipping them from time to time in "Superonic-N" or a similar product, then drying and polishing them.

Silver is best stored in a couple of layers of acid-free tissue paper (available from artist-supply and other shops at reasonable cost) so as to shield it from the air, without being airtight. Most other materials, including the time-honored felt or baize, contain acids and sulfur, which eat into the silver. They can also smell horribly when damp and thus impregnate the silver. Keep the silver in a dry, well-ventilated, safe area, using silicon gel sachets to help combat damp. Cutlery should be wrapped individually and placed side by side, rather than piled up. Silver (as with all other) jewelry should be stored according to type of material, so as to prevent scratching or other interactions.

If you are buying silver or gold, it helps to know the difference between the various types available. For gold, the higher the carat, the higher the gold content of the metal. Twenty-two to twenty-four carat gold is the highest quality, working well for wedding rings, but otherwise being too soft for most uses.

Gold leaf is a very thin sheet of gold placed over some other material, such as silver gilt, which is silver with a thin layer of gold over it.

Parcel gilt is silver with a thin layer of gold over some of it.

Britannia silver is pure silver alloyed with 4% copper.

Sterling silver is pure silver alloyed with 7% copper.

Sheffield plate is copper with a thin silver cover.

Electric plate is similar, but with less silver.

German silver and *Britannia Metal* contain no silver at all.

Sterling silver usually has a hallmark stamped on it, giving information about its authenticity. These small square shapes usually follow a sequence denoting a) the sponsor's mark, b) sterling silver mark, c) the assay office and d) a letter in a certain script indicating the date the article was made.

Cigars

Quality cigars are still somewhat of a luxury item, and something that one should know how to deal with properly for the occasion a guest wishes to indulge. Often, high-end hotels will have cigar rooms and humidor banks for their guests.

In England, we have no restrictions on Cuban cigars and so have no problem enjoying their superior smoke. Dominican cigars are available in the United States, however, and are the next best in quality. Many Cubans these days, it seems, however, are not Cuban at all, and can result in a rough smoke. Only those matured (up to fifteen years), are recommended. They become milder with age, and are only put on the market after five years. Authentic Havanas must have the leaf and seal, "Vulta Abajo," on the box. Cigars in good condition will feel firm to the touch while yielding to slight pressure.

There are various brands, with differing strengths, as follows:

- Rafael Gonzalez - very mild
- Canary Island - mild
- Romeo - mild
- Upman - medium mild
- Punto/Punch - medium mild
- Rey del Mundo - medium mild
- Dunhill - medium
- Partagas - medium strong
- Ramon Allongs - medium strong
- Monte Cristo - strong
- Hoyo de Monterrey - spicy
- Bolivar - strong
- Cohiba - very strong, rich (and expensive)

The darkness of the cigar is also a rough guide to its strength and spiciness. Ascuro (the term for the darkest) is not generally available. The strongest and darkest available is Maduro. Colorado is medium in color and strength. Claro is the lightest. Green cigars have an immature leaf and are rather tasteless.

It is better to buy cigars in bundles for better retention of flavor; the individual tin- or cellophane-wrapped cigars available are really only bought for traveling.

The different sizes of cigar include length and diameter, which is measured in ring gauges. They range from the Margarita, a four-inch, 26-gauge cigar for the ladies, to the giant Havana, at nine and a quarter inches and 47-gauge (some shorter cigars can be as thick as 54-gauge).

So much for the Cubans. The size of cigars available in the United States is indicated by their name as follows, although these sizes have not been standardized and so vary between manufacturers.

- Petit Corona, 5-inches long, 42 ring gauge
- Robusto, 5-inches long, 50 ring gauge
- Corona, 5.5-inches long, 42 ring gauge
- Corona Gorda, 5.5-inches long 46 ring gauge

- Lonsdale, 6.5-inches long 42 ring gauge
- Pantalela, 7-inches long, 38 ring gauge
- Churchill, 7-inches long, 47 ring gauge
- Double Corona, 7.6-inches long 49 ring gauge

The proper storage of cigars is an important duty for a butler, who should have humidors (cedar-lined wooden humidifier boxes) available that keep the relative humidity and temperature at 70 degrees. The sponges in these boxes should be kept moistened with purified water once every one-to-two months, so that the cigars neither dry out nor gain mould spots. If green or white spots do appear, reduce the amount of water in the sponges and brush the spots off to avoid a bitter smoke.

When stored in a dry environment, cigars will dry and crack. If stored in an overly moist environment, the tobacco releases tobacco mites, which occur naturally in the tobacco and create pin-sized holes in the cigar. Both conditions render the cigar un-smokable, so do not offer such to guests. When stored correctly as above, cigars will last indefinitely. If no humidors are available, then keep the cigars wrapped in cedros (a thin cedar lining) to sweeten and moisten the leaf. Or at the very least, use a plastic bag with a moist towel inside, making sure not to allow the cigar and towel to touch.

Offering and Lighting a Cigar

Yes, there is as much ritual and technique to this as the peace-pipe ceremony, and about as much enjoyment, too. The first requirement is that you know the cigar types and strengths being offered. Women have smoked pipes and cigars decades and centuries before women's lib, so do not feel timid about offering ladies a cigar. You might want to discourage the use of holders, as they deny the taste of the leaf on the lips.

Offer the person the humidor to select the desired cigar—a process the guest will most likely savor as he turns the cigars, feeling and smelling them before deciding. If not already present on the table, offer a cigar cutter and butane lighter (or a cedros or other spill the guest can light with a match and then use to light the cigar). Only if no other resource is available (hard to imagine, as a butane lighter should be one of a butler's standard possessions), should one use a match to light a cigar, and only once the initial flare has subsided and the chemicals, such as sulfur, have dissipated.

Off with his Head

The goal in cutting a cigar is to create an ample opening through which to smoke, without damaging the cigar's construction. The best type of cutter for the job is the guillotine cutter.

When using a *single-bladed guillotine*, the blade should be placed gently against the edge of the cigar, and then the blade moved through the cigar swiftly, otherwise the cigar will be pinched, damaging and often ruining the wrapper. Ensure the compartment sheathing the blade is kept free of loose tobacco to avoid jamming and compromising its effectiveness.

Double-bladed guillotines are the better option, as the cigar is cut simultaneously on both sides, giving a smooth, clean cut without the risk of pinching the cigar. Again, the best method is to bring the blades into contact gently with both sides of the cigar, and then cut with a swift motion.

On most cigars, cut about one-sixteenth of an inch from the cigar's head (end). Or look for the cigar's shoulder—where the cap of the cigar straightens out—and cut there.

Lighting the Cigar

The cigar should be rolled just above the yellow portion of the flame until there is a glowing ring around its circumference. Only then should the smoker inhale with a long, slow, even draw. If the cigar starts to burn down one side, put it down with the burning side underneath, until the end starts to burn evenly. Properly smoked, the end of the cigar will be ash, not a red-burning ember. Only if an inexperienced guest seems to be struggling might one quietly offer advice on how to enjoy the smoke—following the above procedures and taking long, slow draws, not puffing on the cigar furiously for fear it may go out.

Once the cigar has warmed enough to melt the glue, remove the brand name label if preferred. As a note, the paper rings on cigars were left on while smoking only to prevent the staining of the white gloves that smokers used to wear in days gone by.

If the cigar goes out, re-ignite and blow out before inhaling so as to avoid a charcoal flavor. If the cigar is to be finished later (that day), guillotine the head and blow any remaining smoke through the cigar, again to avoid the charcoal flavor that comes with re-lighting an extinguished cigar.

Flowers

You may have gardeners to look after the garden, and florists to bring arrangements every week, but you may also be called upon to re-arrange an existing arrangement, create some bouquets or vases from the flowers in the garden, or order appropriate arrangements for different rooms. In this case, you really should have some understanding of the basics of flower arranging. It would also help to know how to care for cut flowers, so that the arrangements in the rooms look fresher longer.

Arrangements are not restricted to flowers in a crystal vase. They can include flowers, wood, stones, fruit, vegetables, water, figurines, pottery, and so on.

Arrangements should fit the character of the table, room, furniture, or a meal being presented, in terms of texture, size, color, theme and purpose. Formal dinners, for instance, would probably have precious or fine flowers to match the china, silver and crystal in use. For the dining table, arrangements should be positioned in such a way, and be of such a size to allow guests to see each other easily without having to peer over or through the flowers.

There is a certain sequence to putting together an arrangement. The first step is to decide on the character of the piece, whether it is to be simple, such as a single rose in a small vase, or a resplendent and regal display. The size should be decided next, as well as the coloring and the outline (i.e., all around or to one side of the base). Availability of flowers and bases or containers may offer some constraints that you have to work within. Having an idea in mind, you can then start the arrangement.

Unless you're using a vase with a neck that holds the flowers in place, you will need to use either a green foam base that the flowers can be stuck into, or construct such a base out of wire meshing that is twice the height and width of the container (and which you crumple into the container so that some strands protrude slightly over the rim).

Establish the desired outline, using tall, fine pointed material on the outside or center of the design. Then place the dominant flowers with larger, heavier, textured blooms or dominant colors to provide visual weight and create the focal point of interest. Fillers are then placed, such as spray material or green or gray leaves, to bind the whole arrangement together visually.

Step back and see if the tall, outline flowers lead the eye down to the dominant pieces at the base of the main stems where they converge. Is the arrangement well balanced? This can be corrected by either drawing a line down the middle, with the materials on both sides being symmetrical; or by giving both sides visual weight with a long, light colored item on one side, balanced by a shorter, darker item on the other side.

Is the scale of the arrangement correct in relation to the table or the rest of the room; are the flowers scaled to the vase or base, and to each other? Does the piece have rhythm, a feeling of motion obtained by curving lines, graduating sizes, shapes and colors, especially those leading to or from the center? Do the colors complement each other, and are textures used to advantage? Have the lighter or brighter colors been used at the focal point of interest? Warm colors (red, yellow, orange) give gay, striking effects. Blues-pinks, mauves, blue, purple and gray give soothing and delicate effects.

This is only a thumbnail sketch on putting together pleasing arrangements. You will improve the more you work on them and study the arrangements of others in magazines or real life. There will always be arrangements by the professionals that break all the tenets I have given and which look absolutely stunning.

If picking your own flowers, it is best done before they are fully mature. Pick them during the night or early morning, placing them in a container with water in it. When back inside, strip off the lower leaves, re-cut the stem ends while still under water and leave them in deep water in a dark room until you are ready to arrange them.

If they are woody-stemmed, split the stem ends before putting them in water. Leaves and sprays of greenery (though not hairy leaves) should be submerged in water for several hours. If a flower bleeds much sap, hold the stem to a flame to cauterize it.

When picking wild flowers, place them in plastic or wet newspaper for transport home. If you receive hard-stemmed flowers by mail or courier, cut their stems and place them in warm water. Even cut roses, out of water and thoroughly wilted, can be revived by being submerged in warm water for one or more hours. In working with flowers, it is best to lay them on a damp cloth while working, and handle them as little as possible.

The best way to keep flowers once they are on display, is to top them up with warm water to which you have added two teaspoons of sugar per pint. A charcoal tablet placed in the container will prevent rotting of the stems.

The Bar and Cellar

The bar is the butler's domain in the private household, but not so in hotel suites. However, the butler should check to see that the en-suite bars are properly stocked, most especially with the specific preferred drinks of the current or soon-to-arrive guests. At least the butler no longer has to brew the beer for the staff (the most plentiful, cheapest and pure drink available in earlier centuries)! *Appendix 4M* gives a sample list of what to stock in a bar that butlers are manning for a special occasion, as well as quantities required for a party of a hundred guests. Ice would have to be brought in for such a large party, but for average demand, an ice machine would suffice, preferably one that allowed the ice at the bottom to melt and drain away, and which was fed purified water.

Various books exist that detail the different types of glasses used for different types of alcoholic drinks, as well as the composition of various cocktails; these books are best purchased and kept in the bar for reference purposes.

When someone wants a refill or another of the same at the bar, provide it in a clean glass. Transport the drink on a salver and present it to the right (or left, if left-handed) of the person.

As for the wine cellar, it needs to be kept at a constant temperature of around 13° centigrade or 55° Fahrenheit, away from sunlight and motion or vibrations in order for the wine to stay well and mature. Temperatures can be as low as 45°F or as high as 70°F, but the important factor is that the temperature remains constant. I have drunk a superb thirty-five year old Lafitte Rothschild that was properly kept, and also a three-year old Pinot Noir that had been subjected to much temperature change and was only good for the sink. Bottles are laid on their sides so the corks stay moist, thereby maintaining their shape and keeping out the air.

As the butler, it is often up to you to choose or suggest the wines that will best match the food being presented at a meal. The old working maxims such as fish taking white wines and meat requiring red wines are too simplistic. It is best to know the various characteristics any wine has, and to practice combining these tastes with a meal in the same way that one plans any other part of the menu to form a pleasing whole.

For instance, it is better to match the degree of sweetness of the wine to the sweetness of the food. The same applies to the acidity of the food and wine. Flavor is another consideration: a strong, full-tasting wine is best matched with a tangy or rich tasting food, while a delicate wine works best with a mildly-flavored food. Mismatching on any of these points will result in the taste of either the food or the wine being lost.

Wine can be used, on the other hand, to offset some aspect of the food. A fatty dish can appear less so when served with a tangy, acidic wine, while a fizzy wine will work well in lightening a dish that is essentially heavy (such as a pudding). Sweet wines contrast well with salty or smoked foods.

Many books exist that describe the different types of wines available, and often the labels on the bottles give enough information for you to judge for yourself. In the end, though, you need to be able to confirm whether a wine is right for the meal or course before it is served.

Acidity is important, because too much will make the drinker pucker, and too little will make a flat wine that has no pizzazz. Sweet wines sometimes have this problem, so look for ones with higher acidic ratings.

Tannin in full-bodied red wines that are being drunk before they have properly matured also creates a puckering effect and leaves a furry feeling in the mouth. It is best to drink reds at the times indicated by various guides, but one can deliberately use a wine that is high in tannin to counteract fatty foods.

The amount of alcohol in wine (varies from 7% to 15%) will give a wine a heavy or light character, called its "body." Heavy wine is matched with strongly flavored foods and lighter, lower alcohol wines are preferred with delicately flavored foods.

Wines also have flavors of their own, often of different types of fruit. Young wines tend to be the fruitiest, and are best drunk alone. If combined with lightly flavored foods, they may well overpower them.

Drinks before meals, called aperitifs, are best when dry, sparkling, or tangy (champagnes, wines, or fortified wines) because they stimulate the appetite. Avoid cocktails which, being full of alcohol, will prevent proper appreciation of lighter wines during the meal.

If serving more than one wine at a meal, it is best to move from lighter, younger, drier or white wines to heavier, older, sweeter or red ones.

To best appreciate the flavors of each wine, full-bodied reds should be served at room temperature, newer reds slightly cooler; Beaujolais, roses and dry whites should be served cool; sweet whites slightly chilled; sparkling wines and champagnes well chilled. Of course, if a guest wants the red served chilled, then that's obviously the best way to serve it in that instance. Red wines benefit from being exposed to the air before being served (for several hours or even a whole day if young, an hour or less if more mature) as oxygen helps develop the bouquet and taste. For this reason, decanting wines and serving them from decanters can be a smart custom. The best way to quickly cool a bottle is to place it in iced water for twenty minutes or more, and turn it upside down if not fully submerged.

There are various bottle openers on the market that are easy enough to master. The only bottles that require care in uncorking are old ones with corks that have decomposed, and champagne bottles. Cork extractors can be used to fish out cork in the bottle if a quick flick of the bottle fails to dislodge the cork together with a small amount of wine. The best opener for old corks that won't budge but just crumble used to be the pneumatic type; a needle is inserted through the cork and air pumped into the bottle that forces the cork up and out. Reports exist, however, that the pump can also explode the bottle, so a better approach is to use a regular cork screw and aim the tip at an angle against the inside of the bottle's neck.

For champagne, the trick is <u>not</u> to shake the bottle before or while opening; to hold the bottle at a slight angle; and to place a cloth over the cork to hold it still while slowly turning the bottle. Done properly, there will only be a slight "sigh" as the cork is released, and no wastage of champagne.

Some wines may need to be decanted, especially if they are old and sediment has accumulated, or if the cork falls into the bottle on opening and cannot otherwise be extracted. In this case, you "decant" using a candle or other light source to illuminate the contents of the bottle as you gingerly pour the wine through muslin or a coffee filter into a decanter, and stop before any of the sediment migrates into the neck of the bottle. It is wise if, in removing bottles from the cellar, they are kept horizontal and moved delicately, so that the sediment is not stirred. The best tool for this job is a wine basket that holds the bottle steady at an angle close to 45°. In this way, the sediment is encouraged to settle and remain at the bottom.

Having opened a bottle of wine, it is the unhappy duty of the butler to sample it and confirm it is still in good condition. If the wine itself smells of cork, then toss it. If it tastes overly acidic or unpleasant, toss it. If it is fizzing (secondary fermentation), toss it. If it is opaque, toss it. Otherwise, savor the taste!

Incidentally, after looking at the color and clarity of the wine and swirling it around in the glass to release its bouquet, the best way to determine the quality of the wine is to inhale the bouquet through mouth and nose at the same time; and then taking a sip, move it around in the mouth while identifying its taste and strength. Look for strength of tannin (in red wines), acidity, sweetness, body, how long the taste lingers in the mouth and with what levels of complexity (different flavors that manifest), and the overall balance of the taste. It should then be possible to sensibly match wines to menu.

In pouring the wine, half fill the glasses so the diners can savor the bouquet. You may want to show them the label and state the wine they are drinking, if doing so does not interrupt their conversations.

A way to prevent drips after pouring, is to bring the bottle to a horizontal position and give it a quick twist while raising the neck above the horizontal.

As a side note about purchasing crystal wine decanters: to ensure a decanter is of good quality, check that the stopper is airtight and has the same number etched on it as on the decanter itself.

Driving and Cars

Generally, hotel butlers will not drive guests for insurance and other reasons. But where the butler is called upon to drive or care for dream cars, whether Bentleys and Rolls Royces or Ferraris and Lamborghini's, he should resist the temptation to go cruising, pop wheelies and do zero to sixty in three seconds and sixty to zero in twenty yards. If you want to keep your job, then a better operating basis would be to treat that car as you would your own. Not as an object of extreme veneration, but an object to be driven responsibly. An advanced driving course, including skid control, as well as a basic book on how cars work, will do wonders to improve competence behind the wheel. Then when you do inevitably put the car through its paces, you'll do it sensibly.

The essence of good chauffeuring is a smooth and safe ride. That means gradual application of accelerator and brake, and slow, long cornering. Perhaps they still do the full-wine-glass test in London, in which drivers only pass when none of the wine spills while driving through the city. If you can do this, you'll have arrived as a chauffeur.

Looking after cars usually means supervising the chauffeurs, or checking for obvious points oneself (such as tire pressure, fluid levels etc.); making sure the cars are kept cleaned, and are serviced on schedule or when needed. The key really is regular visual inspection of the cars, and maintaining easily consulted records. But this is a duty more likely to be assigned to the valets than the butlers in a hotel.

Chauffeuring often requires picking up unknown guests and visitors from an airport, railway station or other public place. If you have time, have a picture e-mailed or faxed to you by the person's secretary so you can recognize them. Ask for a description of their luggage and the number of any cell phone they may be carrying. If you cannot obtain a picture, then you may resort to holding up a neatly printed card showing the person's name, or some other key word they will recognize if security is an issue. Have a porter to hand if luggage is more than you can comfortably manage.

As soon as you have made contact, arrange for the luggage to be secured and escort the person, plus luggage, to the vehicle, which should be at the closest possible location to the meeting point. In some heavily trafficked locations, parking an unattended vehicle is not permitted. This would be the time to have an assistant standing in the wings with the vehicle, and call him or her in as soon as you make contact with the person being picked up. Even better is escorting the guest to the vehicle immediately, while another employee secures the luggage and returns in a second vehicle. The object of the exercise, of course, is a positive, speedy and secure pick-up and delivery to the intended destination.

The Greening of Butlers

Traditionally, butlers have been thrifty: they personally came from poorer families and, on the employer's estate, wished to properly utilize scarce resources and painstakingly homemade products. There is no reason this prudent attitude should not extend to the greater environment of which we are all a part today. Butlers can reduce waste, recycle, employ alternatives to heavy use of synthetic pesticides, energy conservation and so on.

This is something a butler would do behind the scenes and without bothering the guests. Most guests do appreciate conservation efforts as long as they are instituted gradually and without any drop in service or standards.

The drive to be environmentally frugal should not be confused with enforcing low standards of living on guests. This is particularly true where a butler comes from poorer circumstances. Where the butler may have thought Greyhound, he must now think private jet. Where he thought Motel 6, he must now think George Cinque or The Four Seasons. "Only the best will do," and "Money is not an object," is the approach he should now take to servicing guests. This expectation of the best is entirely consistent with environmental responsibility in most situations.

Butler's Etiquette

For butlers, there are several time-honored procedures that still have their place in today's world.

Answering the Door

The butler customarily answers the door and phone, and there are certain points to keep in mind when doing so.

In answering the door for a guest, appearing at a door a guest is opening, or entering a guest suite, it is advisable to check your appearance in the mirror first.

For security purposes, when opening a door for a guest whose doorbell has just been rung while the butler happens to be in the guest's suite, it is better to verify who the caller is before opening the door.

If the person outside is expected according to the guest, then they are let in with a smile that says "Welcome" as the butler gestures into the suite. The butler takes the person's coat if necessary, offers them the bathroom facilities to freshen up if they have just completed a long trip, and then escorts them into the room where the guest is, gesturing the way and preceding them so as to open any doors and standing aside while the visitor walks through the portals. The butler would then announce, "Mr./Mrs. ____," giving the name of the arriving visitor. The butler then stands discretely by to see if the guest and his visitor would like a drink or any service. If not, he withdraws discretely.

If the person is not expected, but is a friend or family and usually welcome to the suite, then they are also let in.

If the guest has not stated whether he or she wants to see whoever is at the door, your task becomes trickier, especially if family or friends are outside. You could say something along the lines of, "Just a moment, Sir/Madam, let me see if Mr./s.____ is in." If the guest *does* want to see the visitor, you only have a guest possibly miffed at being left outside while you checked.

If the guest does *not* wish to see that person, you have to persuade the visitor to leave without upsetting him or her. Try something like, "I am afraid Mr./s.____ is not available, but I will certainly tell him you called; may I relay a message to him, Sir/Madam?" If the person still insists, you would have to be firm, perhaps saying, "I am unable to allow anyone in—I am very sorry indeed. Might I suggest that an appointment be made?"

Is this just paranoia on the butler's or guest's part? It may be, but there is a good case for the rich or famous to be alert to the ploys of the criminal or fanatical elements in society—as they sometimes are targets. A person in the public eye or very busy at work also tires of intrusions and so resorts to strict policies on people dropping in, to protect his or her privacy. Someone living in New York City can appreciate these precautions. Someone living in San Luis Obispo, where the crime rate is low, might not go to such lengths.

Answering the Telephone

Answering the phone is simpler, though it follows much the same lines. Depending upon the guest's position in society, he may want caution used for security purposes. A neutral, "Hello, who is speaking, please?" answer to the phone, repeated politely if required, allows you to know who is calling without confirming that a celebrity or dignitary is indeed staying at the suite.

In a more open situation, a cheery and forthright, "Good morning, this is Suite 123, Jeeves the butler speaking, may I help you?" can be followed up with, "Let me see if ____ is available." And if not, "May I take a message? I will certainly tell him you called." Record the caller's phone number and any message. Never give out information on the guest's whereabouts or plans, or any phone numbers or addresses over the phone, unless you are certain that the person at the other end is who he says he is and should know that information.

As a courtesy, if you deal regularly with a person over the phone — such as the personal assistant of a regular guest — but never see him/her, an exchange of photographs would improve communications and rapport.

Daily Duties/Graces

There are some duties that are regular as clockwork when performed. In the morning, the butler wing/floor must be opened, daily papers rounded up, the breakfast buffet set up as well as the morning (tea) trays with newspapers and flowers, departures and arrivals prepared for — the list can be quite varied, depending upon the needs of the guests and should be made into an SOP so the night-duty butler and the early morning butlers can service all guests smoothly.

The same goes for the end of the day. Rooms have to be tidied, amenities placed in rooms, flowers refreshed, curtains drawn, beds turned down, lights turned on, and even a choice of two sets of clothing laid out for the following day for the known activities. The next chapter covers these daily duties in the caring for guests. *Appendix 4N* explores the typical "Day in the Life" of a butler, which actions become the typical daily graces of the modern hotel butler. These will also be described in more detail in the next chapter.

Some General Pointers Concerning Personal Etiquette and Professionalism

Butlers should always consult and use experts where they lack know-how or skill.

A butler carries items on a small silver tray or platter, preferably with white gloves on, and walks at a sedate or stately pace. On the other hand, fast-moving guests won't appreciate a butler executing his duties at a pace that would appeal to a turtle. Each guest has different needs, so move accordingly, but with as much dignity as the situation will bear.

There are various rules concerning deportment and bearing that apply in any situation, however; such as one doesn't slouch, sit around smoking all day or carry on conversations as if negotiating at a fish market. But if one grasp the essence of a butler, one will have no trouble in moving around in the appropriate manner. Whatever "motion model" one decides upon, it will probably include varying degrees of dignity and decorum, smooth and well placed motions that efficiently achieve the results desired without attracting undue attention.

A note of caution: one's attention needs to be on servicing guests, not on how one's own body is and should be moving, so the time to get all this sorted out is during training and then fine-tuning during the first days on the job.

Naturally, a butler is always impeccably dressed as suits the occasion, and in a low-key manner. Personal hygiene is a given, with hair and nails trimmed and clean, teeth brushed, body washed and neutral in smell—meaning no odors at one end of the scale, or strong after-shaves or perfumes at the other end of the scale. The purpose is to be there without attracting attention.

While one's behavior is expected to be highly professional when at work, there may be a temptation to let one's (well-groomed) hair down unduly while off duty. Nobody expects to see a butler walking stiffly through a shopping mall in full regalia, bowing to passers by and doffing his hat to the ladies as he does some window-shopping. Nobody expects to see him downing a pint at a local bar and taking the bar tender to task for failing to clean under his fingernails. But just as off-color is a butler who dons cut-off jeans and a dirty T-shirt, and walks around the grounds scratching his belly while ash falls from the ciggie butt hanging from the corner of his mouth. If a butler really feels compelled during his time off to do wheelies through town in a guest's or hotel car, irritating local law-enforcement officials, or other actions designed to bring disrepute upon himself and by extension, the hotel, then he should consider another

72

career. If being yourself on your time off is a middle-of-the-road affair, then you will be fine.

With a clearer idea of ground zero for a butler and of his general duties, let's review how he would deal with the entire reason for his position: looking after guests.

CHAPTER FIVE
LOOKING AFTER GUESTS

The concept is simple: treat guests as the most important people in the world. Doing so will see you through any difficulty. If this is the general idea, what are the specific actions a hotel butler takes to service his or her guests?

They start well before the guests arrive—in fact, as soon as the guest's reservation is known. Guests are generally a source of unending requests once on property, so whatever can be arranged before their arrival will reduce much of the stress in dealing with "I need this now!" requests.

The first thing the morning butler does on his way to work each day is drop in at reservations or the front desk to pick up the list of confirmed arrivals for the next two weeks. Those new to the list are contacted by telephone that afternoon during down time and interviewed to determine their needs. The butler also looks for any cancelled reservations and takes actions to alert hotel venues impacted by the cancellation. Before calling, it would be smart to find out from the reservations personnel which bookings they may have made already for a guest. Sample pre-arrival interview questions are provided in *Appendix 5A*. The person's preferred butler should make the call if the guest is a repeat visitor, and the butler would not ask questions for which he already knows the answers, or state anything that the guest already knows.

Included at the beginning of the questions is the escape valve to exit the call if timing is not convenient. Some guests will be happy to chat with their favorite butler about a trip they are looking forward to. Others will be too busy to talk, or just not into talking at all. So the butler's antenna has to be out and in high-reception mode. Generally, unless the guest wants to chat, these interviews should be in the 5-10 minute range, or two minutes for a quick data dump by the guest who is an old hand and very busy.

There is one caveat concerning these calls. It may be that the Mr. has scheduled a weekend getaway with his girlfriend (not that uncommon), about which his wife knows nothing. To avoid giving the game away (whether or not you approve of his lifestyle, it is not for you to tell the Mrs. that her husband is a cad), it is best to call gentlemen at their office and ladies at home at a time when they are likely to be alone; and when you do call, if the spouse answers, talk about his or her last stay, and future visits, until you can tell from the conversation that the spouse knows of the partner's trip and may even be coming, too—at which time you can ask the pre-arrival questions. It is unfortunate that one has to be disingenuous, but when you understand that a butler smoothes over situations rather than creating them, it may make the lack of candor on your part more palatable.

The butler may need to explain to the guest that some venues have busy periods or are fully booked at certain times, and work with the guest to fine-tune his or her desired schedule so that the guest's bookings will be feasible. It is this issue of ensuring the guest's desired agenda is made possible—securing the best seating, best tee time, best masseuse etc.— that is the reason for contacting guests at least two weeks before their arrival.

In order to avoid having to go back and forth between the guest and the venue, it is advisable to ask for a second option or choice, in case the desired time is not available.

Lastly, the butler needs to know what questions to ask the guest with regard to each reservation. Each venue will need to know certain things, such as dining outlets need to know the number in a party, smoking or non-smoking preferences; a spa needs to know what kind of massage and for how long, preferred gender of the masseuse, and whether in-room or in the spa. An equestrian center needs to know experience level, height and weight of each rider. Etc.

During the interview, the butler notes the guest's answers on the question sheet and after the interview, writes out a neat report summarizing the information. A sample report form is provided in *Appendix 5B*.

All reservation requests are arranged by the coordinator and logged in the coordinator's log, or by the butler. As each is confirmed, the confirmation is recorded along with the name of who confirmed it in the facility where the reservation is being made. Everyone at the property needs to understand that when a butler or butler coordinator calls with a request, it is for a VIP who needs to be accommodated.

The butler or coordinator than makes a list of things to purchase or do to provide the guest with the items requested in the interview or indicated by the Guest Profile, and orders any items not in stock.

All this information is then input by the coordinator into the computer, including the occupancy database to show which suite is now taken for those days, and is filed in the guest's (computerized) folder.

Between three and five days before arrival, the butler coordinator confirms all the appointments are still in place and that all the items needed are in stock and earmarked. She notes this in the Guest's Profile. The department is now ready for the guest.

The end result of this evolution is twofold:

a) The creation of an agenda for each guest that can be posted on the White Board for easy reference. The agenda should cover every day of the guest's stay with all reservations noted so they can be checked off as the stay progresses.

b) The acquisition of all items not in stock that are needed to service the guest on his or her arrival.

As covered in the last chapter, it is important that hotel personnel support the butlers in making these reservations. Butlers would do well to thank and find some way of rewarding those who do, and either improving the performance of or reporting on the transgressions of those who do not.

If butlers meet any resistance or poor service, they should immediately ask the associate's superior for assistance and once the reservation has been finalized, note the name of the person who was unwilling to provide ready service and see him or her. He can tell the person that he can't afford to spend ten minutes on the phone every time he needs to make a reservation. And then ask (something along the lines of) "What do we need to do to sort things out so we can work together smoothly and not get up each others' noses?" If no joy with the person, the butler can let the employee's superior know and find ways to work around that person until they change their attitude.

Customizing

And so we come to the day before the guest arrives. The second or graveyard shift butler or butler coordinator prepares all the paperwork for each guest as follows:

- Personalized letterhead, envelope and business card showing the person's name on hotel stationary.
- A welcome letter introducing the guests by name to the butler service (*Appendix 5C*).

- A goodnight card that includes the following day's weather and calendar, as well as suggestions should the weather forecast conflict with the planned activities (*Appendix 5D*).
- A summary of the guest's calendar for the visit (a smart version for the guest room, and a copy for the White Board).
- A wake-up service request card (*Appendix 5E*).
- Guest information is posted on the White Board and added to each butler's Driver's License.
- The daily agenda is added to the White Board and Driver's Licenses for all to be aware of arrival times, reservations etc.

Day of Arrival

The guest's suite is vacated by prior occupants and serviced by housekeeping during the morning or early afternoon (we assume 100% occupancy as the norm). The butler teams up with housekeeping using an inspection checklist (*Appendix 5F* provides a sample based on the AAA standard). They always start on one side of the entry door to each room and work their way around in the same direction until they arrive at the other side of the door. In this way, they systematically cover each room. They look for cleanliness and housekeeping issues and that all engineering items are up to par (HVAC working and set at the guest's desired temperature, fireplace, all electronic media and electrical appliances, painting, windows, doors, curtains, etc. in 100% order).

Any shortfalls are corrected on an immediate basis, including airing the room if stale or permeated by some foreign smell (including housekeeping-type smells).

The butler then places the following in the room:
- The special amenity
- The personalized stationary and business card, welcome letter, and the calendar for the guest's entire stay on the desk
- Flowers and fruits
- Personal items the guest may have in storage that are used to create a home-away-from-home

He also
- Ensures any cultural facets or personal preferences are properly addressed, as noted in the Guest Profile or in the general knowledge of that culture's requirements. This could be anything from replacing certain types of pillows to rearranging the items in the room, as in Feng Shui, or exchanging paintings on the wall that might offend
- Puts on appropriate music on the CD player
- Turns on lights and sets them correctly
- Ensures the alarm clock is not set, but the radio is properly tuned to a pleasant station and at a low-to-medium volume.

- Ensures keys/entry cards are working
- Guest agenda is in the room along with any tickets, vouchers or other things needed for the stay

With regard to the amenity—or welcoming gift—this is most often food and drink meant to serve as refreshment after a long journey. This basic concept is extended in the butler service department according to the hotel policy, which should take into account the budget, the "value" to the hotel of the guest in terms of business or public relations, as well as, of course, the guest's likes, and lastly, what the guest has already been given by way of amenity on earlier visits. Essentially, these amenities, which include a larger one for the arrival and special birthday or anniversary celebrations, and smaller ones each night with turndown service, are not charged to the guest and should be factored into the cost of the room and be of some substance.

Amenities for arriving butler service guests may include tickets, vouchers, clothing, champagne or wine, and anything that the guest is known to like strongly. Flowers are also included as they brighten up suites. They are refreshed each day by the butlers in the mornings and during turndown, removing wilted flowers, adding water as needed, for as long as they can be made to look good, then removed. If just a few remain in good condition, they can be placed in a smaller vase and rearranged.

Appendix 5F-1 provides a typical checklist used in the private household when preparing rooms for guests.

Welcoming the Guest

We finally come to the moment the guest arrives. In most hospitality venues, this usually involves checking in and finding one's own way around. Not so with butler service, which, following the doorman's personalized attention, seeks to set the tone for the guest's stay from the moment he or she walks through the front door.

The chauffeur or head doorman will radio through that Guest A is arriving. The first butler who can break free from servicing other guests responds, giving his ETA in the lobby, and proceeds there rapidly with his (small) tray, upon which is placed the registration card and room key(s), and small glasses of the guest's favorite beverage.

The head doorman (or valet) shows the guest(s) to the lobby and seats them, indicating their butler will be with them in a matter of moments. Their luggage is taken directly via the service elevators to the butler wing, where the first butler who is free places it in the guest's suite (this is why the butlers need to include the valets, doormen and others in the tip-pool handouts).

If the butlers cannot make it down straight away, one of them radios the doorman with the earliest time they can make it down. The doorman offers the guests a complimentary drink at the bar and ushers over the bar attendant to service the guests.

As soon as a butler arrives, he follows patter along the lines of:

1. "Mr. And Mrs. _____, my name is ____, I am one of the butlers at (hotel name). On behalf of (owner/management), welcome (or welcome back) to (hotel name).
2. (If they are drinking because the butler was delayed) I am sorry to have kept you.
3. Your suite is ready; your luggage is being taken there as we speak. If you're ready, I can take you upstairs.
4. The butler offers to carry guest drinks on the platter he brought down.
5. As he escorts the guests to their suite, he explains features and amenities. As they ride the elevator, he gives the guests their keys with an explanation on use. He can ask the guests how their trip from _____ went, but otherwise, does not chatter incessantly to them, just answering their questions briefly and to the point.

Alternatively, the guest suite is not quite ready (because of late-checkout or early guest arrival) and there are no other suites to put them in. In this case, the butler tells the guests that their suite will be ready as soon as possible, letting them know when, if he is fairly certain of the fact. He escorts them to the butler level Club Room or equivalent and invites them to enjoy the amenities available until their suite is available.

The butler can ask the guests if there is anything he can do or get for them, and also takes the opportunity to brief them on their calendar, the expected weather, events that will be occurring during their visit that may fit their profile. He can also ask for a cell phone number so he can call them if they decide to leave the Club Room.

For first-timers, the butler can offer to take the guests on a brief tour of the resort and orient them to the various activities.

Assuming the suite is ready, the butler escorts the guests to their room. If they are first timers, he shows them any Club Room (or the equivalent), explaining the hours of any services offered there, such as complementary breakfast, lunch, tea, or cocktails.

When in the guest's suite, the butler explains and demonstrates to the guest(s) those elements of the suite and the services available, which are not obvious to the guest. The guest does not need to be told, "This is the bedroom," as it should be obvious. But he will want to know how to operate the fireplace or numerical safe, etc., and will *not* want to read through directions or struggle to figure out how to use the Jacuzzi, room temperature controls, etc.

Some form of the procedure outlined in *Appendix 5G* should be followed in full for guests visiting for the first time. Returning guests are only briefed on those elements that will be new to them.

First of all, however, make sure the guests are ready and willing to do the tour. Maybe they need to freshen up, have a drink, even sleep. If so, see to their needs and do the tour at a later time when they are interested. Otherwise, deal with their queries and difficulties as they arise. It is better to follow a regular routine and patter so nothing is left out

With the tour of suite and/or hotel completed and guests settled in, butlers can focus on seeing to guest needs on an as-requested basis. In unpacking clothes, the butler may notice some clothing needs to be ironed, cleaned or mended. Shoes may need cleaning. The butler should deal with these points without distracting the guests. Or if the guests would not be disturbed, he can indicate that he would be happy to see to the needed items, once he had assessed what items needed to be cared for. It is a good idea for butler service guests who arrive in their own non-chauffeured vehicles, that the valets gas, clean and service the guests' cars, and then have them garaged if space is available. The butler could confirm this had been done.

Typical Butler Services

Let's look now at the typical services butlers provide each day, other than dealing with arriving guests. *Appendix 5H* gives the major points of the morning wake-up service, a splendid way to start off the day for the guests. The one key difference between the traditional wake-up in a private household and a hospitality setting is that one would not let oneself into a hotel guest's room in the event that there is no response to the knock on the door. The effect of a gentle wake-up is spoiled somewhat if one has to anyway call the guest to wake them and only then enter the room. But such is the nature of our litigious society that one cannot risk walking into a guest's bedroom uninvited.

This wake-up service is not the same as breakfast en suite, a common confusion for those who have not heard of a wake-up service before. A guest may choose to be woken up with a cup of tea, enjoy a bath and dress leisurely, and then enjoy breakfast (see *Appendix 5J*) served in the suite before heading out for the day. Another point to clarify between these two services is that the butlers prepare the morning wake-up service, whereas the kitchen and room services prepare breakfast, and all other meals served en suite.

It is obviously a change for room service to bring meals to the butler service section and then not deliver them to the guests. This can be a point of friction initially, as room service wonders why it has to do the grunt work of schlepping the food to the butler services area, and then not have its palms greased for the effort. This is why it is important for butlers to pass on to room service and others, a portion of the tips they receive.

Lunch and dinner may similarly be served en suite. *Appendix 5K* provides a pretty basic version, where the first part of the meal is served and the butler then withdraws discretely, leaving the guests to enjoy a private meal, the butler only returning to clear away the meal.

Obviously, guests staying in suites with separate and sufficiently large dining rooms can be provided with a formal lunch or dinner using synchronized serving or butler service, as described in Chapter 9, *The Orchestration of Fine Eating Experiences*, in which the butler(s) are in attendance throughout the meal. Such an event may well require extra butlers being brought in to continue service for the other guests.

Guests may place food orders by telephone to the butler coordinator, or directly to the butler when he happens to be in their suite with the guests. In either case, *Appendix 5L* provides the kind of questions to ask and points to follow in taking orders.

The last major evolution of the day is turndown while the guests are out to dinner. It is at this time that housekeeping tidies and cleans the rooms, empties trashcans, draws the curtains, switches on lights and turns down the bed. The butler can follow to refresh the flowers, place the calendar for the following day and the wake-up service card and breakfast order hanger with that evening's amenities. The butler can also lay out the appropriate clothes for the following morning if requested, as well as bath robe and slippers on the bench at the bottom of the bed.

It is a good idea to develop a list of possible amenities such as those listed earlier, and on a fourteen-day rotation, so that guests are exposed continually to the creativity of the hotel butlers. The list might include any of the following, and certainly many other variations that address each guest's personal likes, cultural background, the specialties of the region in which the hotel is located, or anything the guest may have expressed interest in while at the hotel.

- House–branded Belgian chocolate/truffles;
- Chocolate dunked fruit, with the guest's name written in chocolate on the plate;
- Figurines and other items made of chocolate or other edible items;
- Half bottles of champagne or wine;
- Milk or home-made hot chocolate and cookies;
- Pieces of art in various media;
- House brand clothing and accessories, especially related to sports or spa;
- Orchids or other exotic flowers.

Shopping

Scattered throughout the day may come requests that require the purchasing of an item. Guests ask for all sorts of shopping items, whether mundane or fancy gifts for other guests. A butler would naturally take care of this "chore," as long as the request is not to buy something that is illegal, such as recreational drugs or contraband. In some hotels, a runner from the transportation department is the person who actually heads out to make the purchase, pick up the tickets, etc. Often the item requested is already in stock in the butler's pantry, and equally often, the item is available in any of the on-site boutiques, pro shops, etc.

In which case, the butler drops in on the shop and signs for the item the guest has requested. Managers of each of the resort shops need to know that the butlers are authorized to sign for items at these shops with a guest's name and the butlers name and his/her employee number, so the shop can trace whom to charge and who picked it up.

The butler should deliver the item to the guest and note the details of the shopping in the Red Book. If possible, a copy of the receipt should be placed in the Red Book.

1. For items that are not available on the property, such as prescriptions, cameras etc., call the store ahead of time to ascertain that the item is available. If not available, then have them order it if it will arrive on time.
2. If not available from them, find another source.
3. If absolutely not possible from any source, then the best substitute should be offered to the guest and their agreement obtained, and on the price, before placing the order.
4. If the store accepts charges, then the item may be picked up and charged back to the property and guest.
5. Post the charge to the folio right away.

6. If the store does not accept charges to the property, then something along the lines of a paid-out from the front desk will have to be made to the person doing the shopping.
7. When the shopper returns, he or she returns the change and receipt to the front desk. Here, too, all records of the shopping mission should be part of the coordinator's log and Red Book

Note: Butlers should have a petty cash fund of a pre-determined amount. If a guest requests a large ticket item, the price must be discussed with the guest before purchase, as well as the Director of Lodging for assistance with resources if necessary. Large-ticket items (over $200) are generally reimbursed through a check request if the butler uses his or her credit card.

Having a complete list of basic items in stock in the butler's pantry (see checklist) will prevent much running around and save the day when stores are closed. It should stock a selection of aspirin, Tylenol, band-aids and first aid-type items, condoms, sewing kits, eye glass repair kits, batteries, housekeeping supplies, etc. Think of providing a fully stocked house. These items should be inventoried on a regular basis, and charged to the butler department as operating expenses.

Equally smart, of course, as having a fully stocked butler's pantry, is to review the guest's history for past requests at the time of the pre-arrival interview. It is much easier to purchase/bring together the guest's needs prior to arrival, than to run around once the guest is on the property.

Showing Interest

Acknowledging a deed with a "thank you," or noticing somebody and remarking on how colorful they look, etc. (everybody has something one can admire about them) all go a long way to perking others up and improving their opinion of the person who made the comments. For this reason, the follow-up of guest activities, meaning enquiring how they went, and then doing something to set right any upset, are included in the standard activities of butlers in hotels.

Appendix 5M provides a checklist of steps to take that, if practiced until second nature, will bring about a heightened appreciation by guests of the level of service being offered to them.

Finally, there is the process of smoothing the guest's departure from the hotel. *Appendix 5N* gives a checklist of suggested actions.

The relationship a butler develops with guests represents a good part of their value to the hotel as well as to the guest (and the butler!), and so the guest's departure should not act as a disruption of that relationship. In other words, butlers would do well to stay in touch from time to time with guests, not so as to bug them, but within the willingness of the guest to be contacted—a point the butler should have a good sense for after servicing them closely.

The trick is to find things to communicate that assist the guest. For instance, alerting him to the next event at the hotel that corresponds to his interests, and suggesting he arrives for that, or sending her replacements of consumables she acquired at the hotel—such as some spa item she will have run out of. Or a copy of the latest book by the tennis coach he came to train with, or a heads-up about a fashion show she may want to participate in.

Some More Pointers

Bowing

There is the question of bowing, a formality that has existed for centuries as a way of showing respect and recognition. It's a handy way for the butler to demonstrate that he recognizes the guest and is at their service. It is not a servile action but a statement of intent, in a way. A neck bow often suffices, but one can bend at and to the waist—in the same way that a conductor often acknowledges his audience's applause—on more formal occasions, or when confronted with important personages. It is expected, certainly, when meeting with royalty. Practice bowing in front of a mirror until you can do it without feeling self-conscious or stiff.

Tips

The subject of tips can be awkward unless guests know what is expected. Tips were given as early as the Sixteenth Century in England. After two hundred years, the system had become so abused by staff expecting "vails" for the slightest action on their part (such as opening the door) that just going to dinner was liable to set a guest back by the equivalent of several hundred dollars at today's rates.

A society was even formed by the gentry to counter-attack, and although it had little direct impact, the Victorian era that followed put a damper on the excessive demands for tips. The word "tip" is the modern term for vail, but has its origins over a century ago in the clubs of London, where the gentlemen servants would hang a notice just past the entrance with the letters "TIPS." These letters stood for "To Insure Prompt Service." When the employees heard the "ka'ching" of money being dropped into the box by the sign, they would quickly materialize and service the newly arrived guest.

While acknowledging that tips are an important part of the scheme of things in the hospitality industry, this is not the kind of environment we want to encourage when servicing guests. Whether or not he or she is a big tipper, each guest is given 110% by the butlers. The butler's main concern is the comfort of the guest, which a concern on his part for remuneration does little to enhance. A low-key tradition of tipping discretely on departure has therefore evolved in the private household. This has the same effect as the proper attitude on the part of a hotel butler — namely, if you chase the tips, they will evade you. If you chase the principle of superlative service with a discrete smile, then the tips will chase you.

Visitors' Book

Some hotels and private villas have a Visitors' Book. It is normally signed by a guest on the evening prior to departure, on the morning of their departure after breakfast, or just as they are on their way out. They can add any comments on their stay. The butler usually presents it with a: "Would you care to sign the Visitors' Book?" The book can be viewed on a fine table in the hallway and is best bound in leather with vellum sheets and a top quality ballpoint beside it.

If a special event has brought certain guests together, a separate page could be titled and dated. If any guests miss signing, pencil in their name and ask them to sign it next time they come to the hotel.

CHAPTER SIX
VALET—THE GENTLEMAN'S GENTLEMAN
(or: The Lady's Lady!)

When Beau Brummel spoke of the gentleman's gentleman, he referred to the male servant who looked after the personal affairs of an employer. The valet usually took care of his master's clothing; helped with his personal appearance, including matters of hygiene and dressing; he sometimes even cooked and served the meals. The difference between a butler and a valet is that the valet principally looks after one male employer—traveling with him and seeing to all the organizing that traveling involves. The character Jeeves is really a valet for Wooster. As already mentioned, the modern term for the female equivalent is "personal assistant."

Valets have their origins in the middle ages, when they groomed the master's horses. By the Sixteenth Century, the idea of grooming the master himself had become de rigueur and the gentleman usher, responsible for the goings-on upstairs, came into being. After the English Civil War, ushers were no longer drawn from the ranks of the young gentry and were replaced by the sons of artisans and shopkeepers. So the valet (and lady's maid) emerged. Valets became too specialized a position as households were rationalized in the Nineteenth Century and so had their functions covered by the more versatile (and thus cheaper-to-hire) butler, and became a rarity. Where these men catered to wealthy bachelors, they found their duties expanded into factotums: men hired to do almost anything. While there are few single-hatted valets in the world today, butlers still double as valets when called for and certainly some of the duties of the valet are now offered as services by butlers in hotels.

The valet has to have the same kind of personality as the butler, and, being that much closer to his employer, doubly discrete, as valets were warned:

"As the valet is much about his master's person, and has the opportunity of hearing his off-at-hand opinions on many subjects, he should endeavor to have as short a memory as possible, and, above all, keep his master's council." [3]

There are a few areas of expertise peculiar to a valet and valuable to any hotel guest that are worth detailing.

Packing and Unpacking a Suitcase

Rare is the traveler who does not arrive with a suitcase or six. Stale from the journey to the hotel, the last thing any guest wants to do is unpack while the hotel's attractions beckon. Fresh from a wonderful time at the hotel, the last thing a guest wants to bother with is packing bags. These perspectives leave a wonderful opening for butlers to offer a desirable service. Of course, some females—especially American—do not want a male butler poking around in their undies and they will decline the offer. Knowing this likely response, it might be better for a female butler to offer to unpack an American lady's suitcases—especially if her Guest Profile shows she declined the unpacking offer by a male butler during an earlier visit.

So, how does one pack and unpack?

We used to have large trunks to travel to and from boarding school, as I thought it, so that we could throw clothes in and still have enough room for the illicit things that schoolboys seem to enjoy. It was not until I started to fly commercially that space became a premium, and I was obliged to master the finer art of folding clothes neatly.

But did you know it is possible to fold shirts and suits into suitcases, travel half way round the world, and unpack those same clothes without need for a single stroke of an iron to make them presentable? The secret lies principally in the use of acid-free tissue paper to pad shoulders, sleeves, and also place in the fold of clothing where it has to be folded to comply with the contours of the suitcase. You, of course, have to refrain from stuffing the suitcase so full that the whole family has to be brought in to stand on the lid while you attempt to ratchet the locks into place.

First of all, I would recommend using the large, hard, Samsonite-type suitcase with two separate compartments. If not lined, then line the suitcase with a layer of tissue paper. Then lay trousers (pants) in the bottom of the case, with the trouser legs protruding over the edge.

Do up the middle jacket button, fold the arms parallel with the jacket seams; stuff crumpled tissue paper into each shoulder. Place the jacket in the suitcase with the bottom sticking out of the suitcase. Fold the sleeves of each shirt to the back of the shirt, initially parallel with the shoulders, and then fold again down toward the bottom of the shirt, so that the sleeves lie parallel with the shirt seams. Then fold up the bottom of the shirt and sleeves just above the cuffs; fold once more so as to bring the cuffs to the back of the collar, and place in suitcase. Use tissue paper to separate different materials.

Once jacket and shirts have been placed in the suitcase, fold the trouser bottoms and bottom of the jackets back into the case, over the shirts. Close that compartment and pack everything else into the other compartment of the case.

For someone who is regularly on the go at a moment's notice, it is worth having a suitcase packed permanently with enough clothing for one or two days away. The items would have to be aired and allowed to hang free once a week.

On arrival, if there be any wrinkles, they can be erased with the use of a steamer. Another possibility is to turn the hot water on in the shower or bath so as to heavily steam up the bathroom, and then hang the clothes up for a maximum of two minutes.

If you are unpacking for another person, then leave possibly embarrassing items, such as prophylactics and false teeth, in the sponge bag, while laying out the other items in the bathroom.

Lastly, when packing, check absolutely every nook and cranny, every drawer and walk-in recess, under every item of furniture and even behind and under sofa cushions in search of any guest possession that might have gone astray.

Preparing for the Following Day

Helping the employer dress is an integral part of the valet's business, but a hotel butler might want to draw the line at assisting his Lordship when in the nude. Laying out two choices of clothing for the next day, however, does fall within what might be considered acceptable duties. This is best done either at night, as part of turndown, or after bringing up the morning-tea tray.

The most convenient way to lay out the clothes is as follows: place the suit jacket on the back of a chair (or use a dumb valet if available) with the trousers laid out over the chair seat with belts/braces attached. Place the shirt on top of the trousers, folded, with cufflinks and any collar studs already in place. Place the shoes to the side and front of the chair, with a shoehorn on top, and socks folded on top (in the royal fold, which is to say with the shin part folded down over the foot part). Place a choice of three ties and any pin, on a table in front of a mirror. Place undergarments on the chair seat, in front of the shirt.

Obviously, a lady may well have different items of clothing, and it might work better to let her make the choice of what to wear in the morning, unless she specifies her wishes beforehand.

Clothes

Clothes should be put away in drawers and walk-in closets/dressing rooms, hung in some semblance of order for easy retrieval and donning. Subdivide by business, casual, evening and sports wear. Subdivide again by type of clothes (i.e. jackets, trousers). Then categorize by color. An alternative is to group a jacket with two or three trousers and their belts, and ties that match, for ease of selection.

Ensure all the shirts and jackets face the same way. Then you can inspect all the clothes and any in need of cleaning or mending can be turned the other way. Mark on a laundry sheet, in the laundry book and Red Book those items you remove for repair or cleaning. Mark them off when they are returned and you have verified that the needed work was completed satisfactorily.

Wooden hangers are the best, and for the ladies, shaped and padded ones. Racks or shelves should be used for storing shoes. Special belt and tie racks exist, some of which are even motorized so that the press of a button allows the ties to be individually presented for consideration, should a guest be known to travel with a large selection of such accessories. Otherwise, ties can be rolled around four fingers, starting at the narrow end of the tie, and stored in drawers.

Care of Clothes after They Have Been Worn

Once the wardrobe has been organized, then the major part of your work becomes caring for the clothing after it has been worn. To this end, here are some tips, some of which may seem obvious, but they bear detailing.

First of all, keep cleaning to a minimum. When a garment is beginning to show dirt or smell is the time to clean it, not when it has been worn briefly. Too much cleaning wears out clothing.

Trousers (pants)

Empty all pockets, brush thoroughly, check for and fix any missing buttons, broken zippers or general wear and tear. Check for and erase any stains with a dry-cleaning solution if possible, or send to the cleaners. Let the trousers air and hang overnight, and if needed, place in a trouser press or iron them.

Jackets/Coats

Empty all pockets, check for and fix any missing buttons or wear and tear (i.e., rip in vent/pockets, lining gone, collar riding high). Brush thoroughly, including pocket linings. Check for stains and remove, or send to cleaners. Check for odors and air longer, or send to cleaners. Use a steamer on minor wrinkles that hanging does not remove. Polish the brass buttons on a blazer (unless they are lacquered).

In the case of Barbours (quality rain gear of old), just wipe them down with a damp cloth. At the end of the season, wipe them off, liquefy a tin of dressing wax in boiling water and rub in all over the jacket, especially the crevices. A hair dryer can be used to reliquefy the wax if the coating needs to be smoothed out.

When brushing clothes (or suede shoes), use a firm flick of the wrist against the nap, and then with it for a smooth finish.

Shirts

Remove any collar stiffeners, cuff links, studs, etc., check for missing buttons and then send to the cleaners. Only use starch if your guest insists, and then only on cotton collars and cuffs, as starch stops the pores of the material from breathing and cracks collars. Collars and cuffs can be replaced with white ones if worn down, although some quality shirts come with spares that can be substituted. Cotton and silk shirts should be cleaned by hand with care.

Ties

Check for and clean stains, dry cleaning only if you have to, as silk dry-cleans poorly. Iron the backs of the ties lightly, using a damp cloth.

Shoes

Change shoes daily for variety and evenness of wear. Put trees in them as soon as they are removed (so the warm shoes are pliable enough to be pushed back into shape without cracking the leather), and let them air. If muddy, let the mud dry before cleaning.

If very muddy, place the shoes under cool, running water and clean them with a knife and nailbrush. Stuff with newspaper and let them dry for a day by an open window or at room temperature somewhere away from a heat source, so that the leather does not crack. After twelve hours, replace the newspaper. When dry, insert the shoetrees and apply cream to condition the leather. When the cream has dried, apply polish, including on the instep of the sole and tongue, and let the shoes stand a while before polishing with a brush using a light motion, and buffing with a chamois duster.

For that extra shine, combine (parade) gloss with water or spittle, and work into the toes and heels with a rag, using light, circular motions with your finger. Use a cotton bud to apply a metal polish to any metal attachments.

Occasionally apply saddle soap into a lather with a sponge in order to keep the leather supple. Also on occasion, apply waterproofing to outdoor shoes. It is advisable to alternate wax with cream polishes, as wax protects the leather while cream softens it. If lacking the correct color of polish, use neutral to at least create a shine.

Keep Wellington/rubber boots out of sunshine, which deteriorates them; hang waders upside down.

Sweaters

Fold sweater carefully in the same way jackets are folded into a suitcase. Clean only if needed, following instructions.

Belts

Roll or hang up like ties; use a transparent polish on occasion.

Hats

Brush hats with a bristle brush. Felt and velvet hats can be rejuvenated by brushing them while holding them in the steam of a kettle. Store them individually, rather than one inside the other.

Various (underwear, pajamas)

Launder daily. A clean, pressed handkerchief can be placed in the jacket pocket daily, although this is rarely done these days.

Cleaning

As a valet, one sometimes has to wash or iron clothes—even in hotels, where an item may be needed in a rush and the laundry employees are backed up or have gone home for the night. Understanding the signs and symbols used on the labels of clothes is therefore imperative. Maybe you learned this the hard way as a student when your favorite sweater shrank three sizes after being put through a hot wash. You can't really afford to repeat that error with a $2,000 sweater made by monks in the

Italian Alps, who only have enough wool to make one hundred such sweaters a year.

Apart from the self-explanatory temperature signs, you will see triangles, which refer to bleaching. A "Cl" within a triangle means that chlorine bleach may be used. A triangle on its own means that the article may be bleached. Obviously, a triangle with a cross through it means that bleach may not be used. A square with a circle in it means that the garment may be machine-washed. An iron shape with one, two or three dots within it means that piece of clothing may be ironed cool, medium or hot.

Delicate or stringy items such as stockings, bras and other fine items won't have labels counseling you to place them in a netting bag with a draw string to protect them, but you'd be well advised to if you don't want a ball of hopelessly entangled and most-probably damaged clothing to emerge from the washer. These items are often best washed by hand, anyway.

Know before you Iron!

As for ironing, the good news is that the less one does, the better it is for clothing. Often, creases fall out of heavier garments, such as suits, during hanging. If not, a steamer can be used, or a dampened brush stroked first against and then with the nap will smooth out wrinkles.

General tips include brushing off any hair, fluff or other foreign substances before ironing, using a dampened and lint-free cloth between the iron and garment, to avoid any shininess (or use a steam iron if you have to, but it does create a slight sheen). Iron in the direction of the nap of the cloth, follow the contours of the garments and always move toward the cuffs. Iron linings first, and avoid ironing against the outer garment in such a way as to leave an outline there of the lining. Always check the base of the iron to ensure it is clean before using it.

Sometimes guests request starch in their shirts. Spray-on works, but the better option is powdered starch. You'll need to follow the directions on the box, but take heart—you are following in a fine tradition that has resulted in perhaps more perfectly starched shirts being worn by satisfied owners than MacDonald's can boast of the volume of their questionable edibles having been consumed by satisfied diners.

If the original crease is hard to locate in trousers or pants, simply line up the seams on both legs and then iron each leg, starting with the front seams.

I acquired the following useful list of ironing temperatures somewhere during my travels:

Silk/Chiffon:	Unless very creased, low or cool; material can be dampened
Satin:	Low or cool
Nylon:	Low or cool
Polyester:	Medium, steam
Crepe, wool, polyester:	Medium high with cloth, steam
Wool (flannel, wool blend):	Damp cloth, hot iron, steam
Mohair (inside out):	Warm
Cotton:	High, steam
Fine cotton (lawn/muslin/gauze):	Medium
Lace Cotton/Nylon/Polyester:	Damp or dry cloth/med or cool iron
Linen:	Press on inside if necessary high, steam, cloth
Denim:	High, damp cloth or steam
Micro-fiber:	Low or medium without cloth, hot with damp cloth
Leather/suede:	Hang; do not press
Linings — acetate, nylon, taffeta:	Medium or cool
Appliqué:	Iron on inside, damp cloth, hot iron

There are certain tools that make the job of looking after clothes easier, and these are listed in *Appendix 6*.

Another traditional area of butler expertise is the orchestration of fine eating experiences. Most people in the hospitality industry are no strangers to F&B and serving at table, and so might feel they have that SOP down cold. And so they do, but the refinements that butlers have brought to the table over the centuries might be well worth considering with a view to adapting them to the hotel environment. So read on!

CHAPTER SEVEN
THE ORCHESTRATION OF FINE EATING EXPERIENCES

Traditionally, a butler is in his element at formal dinners. By the choice of drinks, decor, table settings, silver, crystal, and even entertainment, the butler seeks to create an elegant and refined ambiance that complements the food presented and provides the makings of a highly pleasing evening. During the meal, the butler adds an almost invisible service that foresees and satisfies each individual need just before it arises; that cares for and comforts each guest in a low-key manner.

A butler is like a true musician on stage who so knows his instrument and the piece being played, that he communicates the message directly, without the distraction of misplayed or mistimed notes, to an enthralled audience.

Whether providing a wake-up tea in the morning or a full banquet, the butler concentrates on the quality of the presentation for the enjoyment of his guest or employer.

There are various types of service, and it is perhaps helpful to differentiate them:

Silver Service—Employed at better restaurants and hotel dining rooms, guests are served from a tray by a waiter using a spoon and fork. The food is served and dishes are cleared from the left.

Banquet Service—Swift, smooth, silver service for many guests.

Ballet of Service/Synchronized Service—Serving and clearing by multiple butlers/footmen or waiters, each serving one or two guests in perfect synchronization.

Buffet Service—Guests help themselves from a selection of hot and cold foods at a buffet table. The chef is sometimes present to carve roasts and assist guests with hot dishes. Waiters may also be in attendance.

Plate Service—Most common in restaurants, where the entire course is put on the plate by a chef and served by a waiter.

Butler Service—Employed in homes staffed by butlers. Guests help themselves from a tray proffered from the left by the butler, and one or more under-butlers or waiters if service needs to be speeded up. With two dozen or more guests, the butler supervises. Soup, gateaux, melon and hot drinks are not "self-serve" for the guests. Drinks are served from the right.

Russian Service—The term used in America for what is essentially Butler Service.

French Service—A combination of Butler/Russian Service and Plate Service, wherein the butler uses a tray to convey a plate of food to each guest, rather than the guest serving himself or herself.

Gourmet Service—Served from a trolley at the table (e.g. flambé) in finer restaurants and hotel dining rooms.

Service en Famille—Meat served by a waiter and vegetables placed in tureens on the table.

Hospital Service—Where a guest passes out at a meal, two waiters may carry the unfortunate person out, using the chair as a stretcher, so that recovery may not interrupt the meal. The cover (the place setting) is removed (unless the person will be able to return) and the neighbors are asked to move closer together. Of course, if for any medical reason the person should not be moved, hospital service would not be employed.

Meals to Remember

Let's start at the beginning of the day and move through the presentation of each possible meal.

First of all, you iron the newspaper and take the morning tray, as discussed in Chapter Five. *Appendix 7A* gives the list of items that might be needed for a breakfast tray. While most people would be happy with a mug of hot coffee in bed from a loving spouse, the butler pays close attention to the quality of the presentation, making sure that the drink is exactly as the guest prefers, comes with the required additives, such as cream, and is accompanied by the newspaper and a flower. And all delivered smoothly so as to gently waken the person to a new day.

Breakfast

As mentioned in Chapter Five, meals are prepared in the kitchen and brought to the butler floor/wing by room services for serving by the butler, whose attention to detail and absolute care for the every need of the person eating the breakfast makes the meal special.

It is customary, after the butler has poured the second cup of coffee, to approach the guest and ask for any instructions for the day or days ahead, which the butler then notes on a small pad.

Appendix 7B gives an idea of the scope of food and drink offered at a breakfast served in a Guest Lounge or similar, as well as the cutlery and china required. Breakfast is served buffet style (or plated - i.e. food placed on the plate by the chef if only a few guests), with the butler in attendance, clearing dishes, pouring drinks, making fresh toast and tea.

Attention to detail includes observing when a guest leaves the table temporarily, and either keeping his food hot in the kitchen until his return, or providing him with fresh items such as toast and coffee on his return.

Luncheon

Luncheon is similar to the dinner presentation that follows below, or the breakfast buffet, and so receives no individual write-up.

English Afternoon Tea

This social occasion is as much a part of England as its green fields, and as much a ritual as a Japanese Tea Ceremony. While English tea houses around the country do a fine job of creating an afternoon tea for their clientele, nothing comes close to the experience of an afternoon tea delivered by a British butler in the sanctity of the drawing room of some fine house — or for that matter, in the Guest Lounge or even the grounds of the hotel. This is a special service that butlers can offer guests, especially the ladies, and can be combined with some presentation, such as a fashion, arts, craft or hobby show. For ladies, it is a genteel social occasion that could well be revived, not just for hotel guests, but as a service to the ladies of the local community.

There can be as many as eight courses, all bound together by the ever-present cup of hot tea, optimally a different tea for each course. *Appendix 7C* lists the suggested items needed for a full English afternoon tea.

To prepare the room, chairs are placed around one table for small numbers, or several smaller tables when many people are present. If possible, guests have small side tables available by their chairs to place their teacups and plates.

The butler has the tea, cups and extra plates on a sideboard. He takes a salver around to the ladies with the teapot, strainer and its base, hot water pot and milk. Sugar, honey, sweetener and lemon slices are on the table. Just as there are two opposing camps disputing whether one should let a red wine breathe before serving it, so there are two camps disputing whether one pours the milk or the tea into the cup first. Some swear there is a difference in taste. Certainly, if one pour the tea first, one can then regulate how much milk to dispense. But some say that if one pour the milk in first, the milk will be better distributed, the cup will not crack, or the scalded milk will bring out the flavor of the tea. Whichever sequence one prefer, it is best to check with each guest, "Milk, madam?" and pour the milk if that be her preference.

The butler pours the tea unless there are four or less guests, in which case any lady acting as a host can pour the tea brought to her by the butler. The pot of hot water is available in case guests find the tea brewed too strong.

The butler then brings in the food, which is served either butler style, with the guest helping herself with a pair of tongs from the platter proffered by the butler; or the butler places the food on the table, on triple-tiered trays with doilies.

The butler brings in the next course when some have stopped eating the food available, and he only clears away the food when no other guests avail themselves of any particular platter.

The butler changes plates between courses where plates have become dirty. He boils a large kettle of water in the kitchen for each course, which he uses to make regular fresh pots of tea. If a guest has allowed the tea in her cup to turn lukewarm, the butler will provide a clean cup and remove the old one.

How does one properly brew tea?

1)   By using the finest quality teas, in bulk, not bags.

2)   By running the water for a minute or two in order to aerate it before filling the kettle (water that has been sitting un-aerated in the pipes tastes dead)

3)   By bringing the water to a rolling boil.

4)   By immediately pouring the water into the teapot, because boiling water loses oxygen and any tea made with over-boiled water will also taste flat. Timing becomes so critical that one should bring the teapot to the kettle and pour in the water as soon as it reaches a rolling boil.

5) By using bottled spring water in preference to any tap water that is full of minerals or toxic chemicals.

6) By heating the teapot with hot water that is then discarded before placing the tealeaves and boiling water in the pot.

7) By using one teaspoon of tea per person, with one teaspoon for the pot. For a pot that holds more than four cups, the ratio should be lessened.

8) By letting the tea sit for 3 minutes before stirring once and then pouring in the case of small-leaved teas such as Assam; 4-5 minutes for medium-sized leaves such as Ceylon/Orange Pekoe; and 5-6 minutes for large-leaved teas such as Oolong or Earl Grey.

9) Once tea has been poured from the pot for all guests, the butler pours any remaining tea into a second heated pot so it does not stew (become bitter) in the leaves of the original pot. This second pot is covered with a tea cozy (a pot-shaped warming blanket) and used for any refills (removing the cozy first!).

After tea has been served, sandwiches are brought in. The chef cuts them into bite-sized finger shapes, de-crusted and thinly buttered. They contain a variety of savory fillings, from crab to gentleman's relish, paté to cucumber.

The plates are then changed and hot crumpets served, dripping with butter. Next come toasted muffins with currants and at least two types of jam.

When the guests have had their fill, single-bite pastries are provided. And when the guests are no longer sampling those, coffee and chocolate éclairs are brought in. Tartlets follow, and then cakes (Madeira, cherry, fruit).

When the guests have done these courses justice, scones are provided with fresh clotted cream and jam.

And just as the guests think they can manage no more, the grand finale is served: fresh strawberries and cream.

Given today's health-conscious, low fat, low-sugar dietary inclinations, such teas are a rare experience indeed. But for an occasional splurge, set inside on a cold winter's day, or in the garden on a balmy summer's day, it takes the cake (so to speak).

After a tea like this, a good three to four hours should elapse before dinner is served (of note is that teas were instituted to quench the thirst and quell the hunger experienced by the gentry while waiting for dinner, which was served only at 8.00 p.m.).

Dinner

Where dinner is informal, the checklist given in *Appendix 7D* will help set up for the occasion—or indeed, for a luncheon or any informal meal. A formal dinner party or banquet is an entirely different proposition, requiring a good deal more work and resources. For this reason, the butler exists to take on as much of the planning and execution as possible.

The first step is to establish with the guest who is the host, certain material facts, such as:

- When and where (s)he wants the event to take place;
- What guests are to be invited by whom;
- What food and wine is to be served;
- Should bar or cigars be made available:
- Are any presents or favors to be given;
- Any special theme desired;
- Seating arrangements;
- Type of service to be provided;
- The nature of the budget.

The more you iron out at the first meeting, the less your need to disturb the guest subsequently and the easier will be your task. The first part of *Appendix 7G* provides a list of possible points to work out at such a meeting, as well as the checklist for the entire event, from planning to thank you cards.

If you are overseeing the invitations, then you can use the Printer Checklist (*Appendix 8B*).

It may be that you need a list of potential guests (the "B" list) who can be contacted and invited in the event that some of the original guests cannot make it. Some of the people on this list should be old friends of the family or family members, who will not feel snubbed if they are brought in at the last minute to fill in for any cancellations.

Contact guests or their staff to confirm travel arrangements, any needed facilities at the hotel, special diets, or forms of address.

Then see the chef and order any needed food, such as Kosher, non-fat, non-wheat, vegetarian or vegan meals or items. If any of the recipes are new or tricky, arrange for the chef to conduct a trial tasting for the guest, which you and the chef also sit in on, making recommendations for improvement as needed.

Bearing in mind the number of guests and the proposed menu, check the bar and wine cellar; select the wines for each course and make sure you have enough in stock.

The host may like the idea of sitting at each table during different courses, in which case, you will need to select one person from each table willing to play musical chairs. He or she would be introduced to the host, and then move to the table that the host had just vacated, allowing the host a chair at a new table. For each move, a photographer could be on hand to photograph the host with his guests, and the butler would see to the smooth transfer of plates and glasses, obviously using waiters to assist.

In this case, a photographer would have to be hired (*Appendix 8M*) and instructed on the routine, as well as two waiters drilled on their roles.

Use a magnetic seating plan to show each guest if there are only a few of them. If there are no more than two dozen guests, then arrange for a seating plan to be printed and handed to each guest before they enter the dining room.

If there are more than two dozen guests, arrange for the seating plan to be printed, as well as a table plan showing where each table is located; and an index, listing each guest in alphabetical order and indicating at which table and seat he or she is assigned.

These plans would be handed to guests and can be augmented by a large representation of the table plan, seating arrangements at each table and the index, and displayed on a board near the dining room entrance.

Finally, in the event this guest has thrown such a formal dinner before, consult the Guest Profile and remind any hostess of what she was wearing, including jewelry, the last time she entertained the expected guests, so that she can plan accordingly.

Setting the Table

On a day-to-day basis, it is wise to keep an eye out for damaged or soiled tableware, linens and furniture and have them repaired or cleaned, so that sets are complete and you do not have any unpleasant surprises when you need them.

On the night before the event, have the dining room cleaned, especially any chandeliers, and have any dud bulbs replaced at the same time.

Then, on the morning of the dinner, use the checklist of items needed for a dinner (*Appendix 7F*) to bring all the items for the table into the room, with 25% extra to be kept in the sideboard as spares.

Then count the number of chairs for the number of guests, and position each chair two feet out from the table, at the location of each cover (place setting). Doing so anchors where each place is to be set, while allowing you access to the table to lay it.

Lay a felt under-cloth on the table, and then the tablecloth on top of that, allowing a six-inch overhang. The tablecloth can then be given a final, light ironing if needed.

Don a pair of white gloves (to prevent fingerprints) and set the table in the following sequence: centerpiece, china, flowers, candlesticks, and figurines. It is a good idea to use recent acquisitions or heirlooms to act as a talking point at the meal. Strive for a different setting with each dinner, looking for themes to tie the table setting together.

The word "cover" used to refer to the cloth that was placed over a place setting in medieval times, to signify that the place had been set and was verified as void of poison or other booby traps. Now it refers to the place setting as a whole. Lay a sample cover, therefore, for the staff to emulate, using the largest plate to establish how far apart to set the cutlery.

The cutlery should be brought to the table on a silver salver with a cloth placed on top of it to prevent scratching and noise. Lay the first-course cutlery furthest from the plate, and the last course cutlery nearest the plate. All cutlery should be measured at a thumbnail distance from the edge of the table, so that a straight line is formed along the length of the table by the ends of the handles.

If the seats are too close together to allow all of the cutlery to be laid, then place some before the meal (usually three deep) and the rest halfway through the meal.

The middle of the side-plate should be placed level with the tip of the largest fork. The salad plate is placed above the setting unless there is no side-plate. Ashtrays and silver matchboxes are placed in front of smokers when they begin to smoke (or after the host announces that guests may smoke, usually after all the eating and speeches are done). Mustard and cruets (bottles for vinegar and oil) are placed in front of each setting or shared between two.

Place cards and menu cards are positioned in front of each setting, with names and titles checked for accuracy in spelling.

Glasses are placed diagonally from the right of the largest knife in the sequence in which they will be used. Napkins are folded simply so as to minimize hand contact by those setting the table.

The above is merely a suggested and classic layout for the cover. There are many other formats, equally aesthetic and/or functional.

It is then a good idea to air the room, verifying that the ventilation (or air-conditioning or heating) will be adequate for the number of guests over the expected time period. Also check lighting levels.

The butler uses a sideboard to the side of the room as a base or relay point from which to provide items quickly for diners. As well as nuts and chocolates for each guest, and extra cutlery, napkins, etc., he keeps cigars, cigarettes, ashtrays, coffee cups, saucers and spoons, sugar, sweetener and finger bowls there.

Then ensure the cream and butter dishes are ready in the refrigerator, the coffee is set up, the bar fully stocked, and all the wine is available at the right temperature, decanted if necessary.

Late Afternoon and the Reception

Now is a good time to take a shower, change and double check everything you have already done to pick up anything missed or not fully done. Ensure the rooms in the public eye are spotless and serviced (i.e. flowers on display, rest rooms). Ensure the valets have arrived and that they know what to do, where to park.

Call the staff together and ensure they are all there, looking clean and sharp. Brief them on the ground rules, the schedule of events and give each a copy of the menu ingredients (*Appendix 7E*) so that they can answer guest's questions as to ingredients when taking the food around.

If possible, have the serving staff sample each dish so they can describe it if called upon to do so by a guest. Have the staff eat so they will last the night without eating half the guests' food. If some of the staff are temporary, take them on a tour of key areas, so they know where they will be working and where to direct guests for rest rooms, exits, etc.

Have all staff locate for themselves the coatroom, rest rooms, seats in the reception rooms, bar, ashtrays, table/seating plan. Ensure, meanwhile, that all functions are covered and everyone knows what to do.

The ground rules set the pace for how waiters go about their duties when working for a butler at a private dinner. These would need to be covered for any staff or temporary staff not used to the requirements, which are as follows:

Service is at a casual but dignified tempo. Waiters are minimal in number and always in the background so as to obtrude as little as possible. Complete silence is observed, which means only two plates are cleared at a time to a station outside the dining room to avoid clashing of china. If cutlery or a napkin is dropped, it is swiftly and silently replaced.

Complete silence extends also to the staff. The American habit of chatting to diners is a complete error in butler service. I once tried to enjoy a four-course meal in a four-star-hotel restaurant and was interrupted no less than fifteen times by five different employees wondering how I was, how the meal was, if I needed anything. The fact that I was engaged in conversation each time I was interrupted with these questions escaped each one of these waiters, maitre D's and busboys. They all had their policy: make friends with the guests, talk to them at least three times each meal. Whoever made this rule never sat on the receiving end. He or she also tried to replace intelligence and observation with rote procedures.

The basic violation is that a waiter should be interested in the guest, meaning he or she observes the guest. Is he happy, does she look like she needs anything or is about to need anything? The waiter then acts invisibly to provide that item or service. Ideally, the guest would not even notice the item arriving. In all this, the flow of attention is outward from the waiter to the guest.

In the American way, however, often the attention is inward upon the waiter. "Look at me, I am here doing my bit, 'How are you doing?' did you notice me?" The guest's attention is yanked off what he or she is doing and onto the waiter. The waiter becomes the focus of attention. Most people do not eat out to applaud or notice the waiter, but to enjoy the food and company. It is the skill with which the waiter ensures the guest enjoys his or her meal without distraction that makes a meal memorable and enjoyable.

Centuries of this service in Europe have resulted in this invisible service as the ideal, and that is why butlers continue the tradition. This one point will be the hardest to drill into temporary staff who have some experience in waiting, but it is probably the most vital to communicate.

Each waiter is expected to be able to answer questions, however, as to the menu and its ingredients, and to swiftly, without fuss, obtain an alternate meal from the chef and present it to a guest who does not care for the offered dish.

When you have drilled the staff on this idea of being invisible, clarify the sequence of service.

In America, the female guest of honor seated to the right of the host at the head of the table is the first to be served, and then guests in counter-clockwise order, finishing with the host. If two butlers, the second would start with the guest of honor to the hostess' right and continue counter clockwise. Or some would start with the hostess.

Butlers in Europe tend to follow the traditional serving of the guest of honor and then proceeding in a clockwise direction past the host. Others still will serve the host first, then the guest of honor to his right, and then reverse tracks in a clockwise direction. If two butlers, the second generally starts with the guest of honor to the hostess' left at the foot of the table, and continues clockwise.

The anticlockwise theory is based on the fact that you come in from the left side naturally as you walk around, thus obviating the need to walk past the person and swing in on their left side, which is required in the clockwise direction. The differences above were pried apart by protocol consultant, Mr. John Robertson, after much heated discussion with butlers around the world. Follow the sequence your employer or hosting guest prefers, and if no strong opinion on his or her part, that is used in the country you are serving; or if no strong protocol exists, which you find to be the most workable.

If someone is eating an alternate meal, serve him/her in sequence. If a guest does not want to eat a dish and does not wish for an alternative, then move on to the next guest but leave the cover set up in case the guest changes his or her mind.

If a guest continues talking and does not notice the salver, say in a low voice (this is about the only occasion one would interrupt or speak to a guest, on the basis that not to do so will delay service for the other guests and allow the food to cool), "Excuse me, Sir/Madam," and if they do not divine why you have interrupted them, "Would you like to help yourself?"

With many guests, a butler taking a salver round on his own would have cold food on the plates before he had finished the rounds. In this case, he enlists the help of waiters. If there are many small tables, then one person could be assigned to each table.

If there is one large table, then either the table is divided into sections between waiters or the whole table is managed by the butler, followed by three waiters. Each carries a different dish: for instance, the butler would go first, carrying the meat, the second in line would carry the sauces and gravies, the third would offer the vegetables, and the fourth would present the starches.

If a guest is eating slowly and will finish more than a few minutes after the rest of the guests, alert the host, who will decide whether to delay the clearing of the plates. If guests use their fingers, immediately present a finger bowl from the sideboard, with rose petals or a lemon slice in warm water.

If a guest is extremely happy with a dish, you might ask for the chef to write down the recipe, place it in an envelope and give it to you for relay to the guest when she leaves at the end of the evening.

Dealing with certain Problems

Should a guest spill food or drink on his or her clothes, a cloth dampened with cold water is usually effective if applied immediately. Do not attempt to clean any item if unsure how to treat it. If the clothes are unusable due to the spill, give the guest a change of clothing and have the dirty garment sent for dry-cleaning accompanied by a note stating what was spilled.

Do not pour into one glass over another and never touch napkins in use. Do not pour wine or serve food when doing so will cut the eye line between two guests in conversation. Wait for them to finish if they are almost done (without prompting them to finish sooner by hovering over them) or serve the guest from the other side. Do not educate a guest making a mistake, such as using the wrong spoon, but make up for any shortfalls, such as replacing the wrongly used utensil without fanfare when it is time for it to be used.

If a guest is being greedy and apologizes, put him at ease with such as, "The chef will be delighted, Sir," or "It's good to see someone with a hearty appetite."

This may seem like a lot of information to impart to temporary waiters, but it only takes five minutes for an alert crowd.

Before the guests arrive is the time to see to the final points of organization. Ensure that the chauffeur and valet room is set up with entertainment, food and drink. Check with the chef on his progress. Have some staff meanwhile wash the fruits for the meal by dipping them in iced water and allowing to drip-dry on a towel. Remove the cheeses and butter (one for each guest) from the refrigerator to warm to room temperature by the time they will be needed, and open the red wines so they can breathe. Young and tart wines can and should be aired for a couple of hours to mellow. Old wines should be aired for just a few minutes to lose any unpleasant odors from being cooped up for years or decades.

Let the host and hostess know that everything is ready and the chef on schedule. Alert them to any items of interest concerning the food, drinks and guests. Satisfy any last minute wishes they may have.

As the guests start to arrive, open the door and welcome each one. Take any invitation card they may have brought with them (without checking it!), Take their coats and hand them to the housekeeper, who hangs them up and may give tickets back to you. If so, give the gentleman the tickets. Then announce the guests to the host, who will be standing nearby.

After speaking briefly to the guests, the host would direct them into the reception room, where a waiter takes orders for drinks/aperitifs and serves them, while another circulates with hot canapés. Cold canapés are brought out by another waiter and kept in circulation until there are either no more takers or dinner is announced.

As the guests are entering the reception room, and before they give their drinks order, they can be given the seating, table plan and index, as well as being shown the location of the table and seating chart near the dining room door. In this fashion, they can determine their seating location early on and confusion will be minimized when dinner is announced.

If there are only a few guests, the butler would circulate once all the guests had arrived, and show each guest the magnetic seating plan. He would tell them any information of interest about their neighbor(s) (in the event that they do not know them) and where they will sit in relation to the entrance.

For a large gathering where "musical chairs" will be occurring, the butler circulates, speaking to those guests at each table who will be changing places with the host or hostess, securing their cooperation and letting them know after which course they will be changing.

In the event that a guest has not arrived, telephone them and liaise with the chef and host for a possible delay. Or if the guest is unable to come and no immediate and willing replacement from the "B" list can arrive in time, clear the guest's cover and seat and close the gap between the seats.

If the guest will be arriving very late, move his name card to the bottom of the table, and let the host and new and former neighbors know.

Coordinate the chef's needs with the host's wishes concerning the start of the meal. There are some dishes, such as soufflés, which cannot be delayed, so the chef's needs sometimes take precedent over the host's. Check with the host and then a likely guest (such as a Bishop) whether grace will be said.

When the chef is ready, and with the host's blessing, announce clearly, with adequate volume, (bearing in mind the hubbub of guests talking and the size of the room): "Ladies and gentlemen, dinner is served." For a lesser number of guests, say twelve, a more appropriate announcement would be, "Ladies and gentlemen, when you have enjoyed your drinks, dinner is served."

The difference being that you do not want the start of the meal delayed too long, and you have more control over a dozen people being slow about moving into the dining room, so you can be a bit less "pushy" at the outset. But with one hundred guests, you want to give them as little leeway as possible for delay.

Two waiters can open the doors into the dining room and stand there with trays to take aperitif glasses. In the event that a glass is still full, they can ask, "May I take your drink in for you, Sir/Madam?"

A minute later, if there is no motion in some groups, ask individuals in those groups to proceed to the dining room. For any die-hards, you can say something like, "The host and hostess are seated and have requested your presence; would you please move through *now*?"

Have waiters standing by to help seat the female guests or VIPs by pulling out and then pushing in their chairs, perhaps asking, "Are you comfortable, Ma'am?"

Serving the Meal

The serving now begins. Start by pouring the water, offering fizzy or still, and remove any table numbers at the same time.

If a grace is called for, stand behind the host and announce, "Ladies and gentlemen, pray silence for (guest), who will be saying grace." If several religions are present, a non-denominational grace you could suggest is, "For food and good fellowship, we give thanks."

Bring in the first course and then pour the wine for that course. Keep the chef briefed on progress, so that he or she knows how long before the next course needs to be ready.

Clear the plates when everyone has finished, or the few stragglers are almost complete. If musical chairs are to occur, ensure the photographer has taken a picture of the host (and/or hostess) at his table, give the host a nod, and then alert the guest at the next table to the impending move. Waiters stand by to remove and replace napkins and transfer glasses as soon as the host and guest stand up, and switch before they sit down at their new seats. This sequence is repeated after each course, at each table.

Next, serve the main course and pour the wine for that course.

If a guest arrives late, take his or her coat, ask if he or she would like to use the rest room to freshen up, and ask if they would like an aperitif, offering to bring it to the table. Show him or her the menu, explain what he/she has missed and persuade if possible to have all courses anyway. Tell him about his neighbors, show him to his seat and introduce the neighbors. Alert the chef, fetch the guest's aperitif, and smoothly plate-serve his courses without rushing, until he has caught up with the other guests. Where possible, you slow down the serving and clearing of the other guests' courses, by such devices as topping up the drinks, clearing one plate at a time.

Top up wines and water and, before offering second helpings, ensure you have about half of what was taken in the first round, so that you don't run out on the second round before everyone has been offered more. The better wording for seconds is, "Can I tempt you with some _____," rather than "Would you like some more _____?", which can suggest the guest is being greedy.

Unless cheese and celery follow, clear away the condiments and bread with the main course plates, and remove crumbs from the tablecloth.

If cheese is being served, place butter, margarine, celery, grapes, radishes and four or five types of crackers and breads on the table. Then take around the cheese board with eight or ten cheeses. If you cannot recognize or remember each cheese, then affix small labels to the backs of each, so that you can answer any questions as to name, origin and description. Cut the amount of specific cheese(s) they ask for, placing them with the knife on a plate that an assistant carries on a salver.

Have a fresh cheese board brought to you if any of the cheeses are running low, and have the first one replenished in the event that the second one also runs low. Then top up their wines, or offer port. If someone asks for more cheese, bring it to him or her and then offer all other guests the board.

When done, clear everything away and crumb down.

Serve the pudding and clear the dishes. Then serve the fruit as follows: place a doily and finger bowl onto a side plate and place on top of a pudding plate, which has a fork on the left, spoon to the right and knife across the top. Place this set in front of the guest; if he or she does not place the side plate and finger bowl above the setting, then do so yourself. Then offer the fruit bowls. As with the cheese, if a guest asks for more fruit, offer it to that guest and then all the others. Once again, clear everything away.

Then put out the petit fours (bite-sized cakes, pastries and chocolates) and nuts. This calls for another procession: the first waiter puts down side plates for the petit fours and asks if the guests would like coffee, offering tea if not. The second waiter, who is listening for the answer, puts down either a coffee or teacup, saucer and spoon, or none at all. The butler follows, pouring the coffee for those with coffee cups, but first checking whether decaffeinated is required. If so, the third waiter provides it. The fourth waiter follows with the cream, milk, sugar and sweeteners. By the time the first two waiters have put down the cups and side plates, they immediately bring around the tea, milk, sugar and sweeteners for those taking tea.

The port is then served by the butler, who recognizes that its consumption is no less a ritual than the English afternoon tea, and treats it with appropriate decorum, not to mention reverence. He has earlier secured the cork from the bottle around the decanter by means of a silver chain, and placed the dusty bottle on the sideboard, with extra decanters as needed. He then places the decanter in front of the host, and removes the stopper with a flourish, placing it by the decanter. As the first decanter is about to dry up on its rounds, the butler replaces it with a fresh decanter.

By tradition, the host pours the port for the guest of honor to his right, then fills his own glass and slides the decanter to the left with the right hand. The decanter thereafter continues in a clockwise direction, always being slid with the right hand. This custom originated in the days when all knights were right-handed and had to be restrained from using their swords to skewer their fellow diners by requiring that they keep their right hands gainfully employed in the passing of the port. Port decanters, unlike others, have a smooth base to permit sliding across table surfaces without scratching. If not, the butler would ensure some felt or other buffer were placed under the decanter to facilitate sliding without scratching.

Should the butler notice the decanter unmoving, he gently whispers to that person, "You have the port, Sir." Any guests who pass on the port without partaking are asked if they would prefer a liqueur or other drink, and it is brought if so.

The port is customarily for the men who stay at the table after the ladies retire to the (with)drawing room; but if the ladies are still at the table when the port is served, they are also offered other drinks as required.

If a toast is to be proposed, or a loyal toast (the loyal toast in the United Kingdom is made to the Queen and in America to the President), or a speech to be given, position yourself behind the intended speaker. Rap the table sharply twice for quiet, and announce, "Ladies and gentlemen, please may I have your kind attention," or, "Pray silence for your host/Mr./Mrs./title____, who would like to say a few words."

Pull out his or her chair, stand behind him during the speech, and help seat him or her afterwards. At this point, the host may announce, "You may smoke if you wish." In this case, quickly place ashtrays by known smokers and those who light up.

Offer cigars in a humidor, leaving an ashtray with any who take cigars, as well as lighter and cigar cutter. Offer refills of tea, coffee, and liqueurs; ensure the port is making the rounds, or pour it yourself. Ashtrays are replaced when they have extinguished stubs in them. Placing a clean ashtray over the dirty one to prevent ash flying over the guests, remove them both from the table, return the clean one to the same spot and move the dirty one behind your back—three deft movements.

When the dining room is finally empty, have the waiters clear, clean, polish and stow everything (dealing with the glasses last). Have them replenish the condiments but empty the salt containers, if they are made of silver, to prevent tarnishing and corrosion. While clean up is proceeding quietly, keep an eye on the guests, topping up their drinks and generally seeing to their needs.

Even after the last guest leaves, the project is not over: note in the Guest's Profile who attended, food and drinks served, how they were liked, gifts given or received, clothes and jewelry worn by the hostess and special diets required by different guests.

Follow-up for the dinner includes sending any letters of thanks needed, as well as any photos of the musical chairs, with a compliment slip from the host and hostess.

If all this seems like a performance to you, you are right. It's also a lot of work, but therein lies the difference between a meal and an occasion to remember. Select whatever works out of the above chapter for your own dinners. Whatever extra effort you put in will not go unnoticed or unappreciated by your guests.

CHAPTER EIGHT
OTHER SOCIAL OCCASIONS

There are naturally a good many alternatives to dinner for a social occasion or function, any one of which a guest may request, especially if the hotel management realizes that these represent added value and a revenue stream when organized by the butler at top rates for his time spent. Where the demand for these special events increases, the number of butlers on the payroll will need to increase. The less complicated events take an hour or two to organize and as many again to execute. Others, such as the Christmas celebration, need to be worked half a year in advance.

Obviously, the idea is that the hotel offers to organize and host these events to increase service offerings, revenue stream throughout the hotel, and occupancy rates. Occasionally, a guest will want the butler to organize off-property events in the local area, a request that the hotel would be smart to fulfill, given that there will be spillover to the hotel in terms of business, as well as income for the work done by the butler, and one very satisfied and loyal guest. For this reason, checklists are provided also for services rendered by other providers. Additionally, there may be a time when the hotel's resources are not able to cope with the demand, in which case outside caterers or valets might be needed, for instance.

This chapter covers the broad outlines of organizing such occasions, but relies mainly on checklists in the appendices to give the exact actions required. The checklists include steps that you may want to omit, and on the other hand, may also omit some actions that you consider necessary. However, they do provide a sequence of actions which, when followed intelligently, allow you to organize and produce a function smoothly when requested to do so by guests.

The first step is always to determine exactly what type of function is wanted, its venue and time, who will be invited and how, and a host of other questions, which can be found in *Appendix 8A*. It is important to thrash out as many details as possible at this time, so that correct planning can occur. Is the planned event in keeping with the message or occasion? Is it too ambitious for the existing resources? You will want to do justice to the event, and with that in mind, it may be better to produce a more modest but professional celebration than attempt a complex one that flops.

Having completed the checklist in *Appendix 8A* and established exactly what is wanted, you then select the required checklists referred to in this chapter, and mark against each target who will get it done, and by what time. As each step is completed, mark it "Done" with the date, so that you can keep track of the progress and see clearly where you may need to wade in and sort out any blocks delaying a step from timely completion.

As soon as the guest list is decided upon, and any celebrities on the list are confirmed as being available that day, you will want the printing checklist (*Appendix 8B*) completed, so that invitations can go out. Ideally, invitations should be sent out at least six weeks ahead of the planned event. Otherwise the rest of the guests are likely to have their engagement calendars booked up already.

It could be that the planned event is as simple as a dinner at a restaurant; in which case an "investment tip" may have to be made if the restaurant is heavily booked and/or hard to book. Find out the going rate and present cash in an envelope to the restaurant manager, asking him if a table is available. It will be, if your actions are discreet enough. If your guest is unknown at that establishment, you could give the manager a small photograph with your guest's name on it, so that the manager and headwaiter can recognize and greet your guest by name.

Next, organize with the manager the procedure you would like followed for the dinner party. If this is a restaurant that any of your guests like, and visit on a regular basis, it is a good idea to give occasional sweeteners to the manager throughout the year. *Appendix 8C* gives the checklist for arranging a dinner party at a restaurant.

If the guest wishes to hold a function at another location, or the hotel's resources are booked, then another venue may well be required. *Appendix 8D* gives the steps to accomplish this.

Possibly the function is too large to be held inside the hotel. If the weather is generally fine, a marquee could be rented. *Appendix 8E* gives the necessary steps for renting one and hosting a function in it. Sometimes it is possible for the marquee to remain on the premises an extra day, in which case you could propose to the guest that a local charity or club might be grateful for the opportunity to utilize it that day. If the guest and management agree, contact the charity or club and brief them on the dos and don'ts. You would have a legal agreement drawn up that cleared the hotel of any liability for any phase of their activity.

If the guest's event does require a marquee, you might need to bring in a caterer to provide the food, in which case *Appendix 8F* would be valuable in hiring one. If possible, assign your own staff to oversee and act as liaisons for each catering function. Otherwise, act as a liaison yourself, troubleshooting when required to ensure the event is serviced smoothly. One of your staff could act as a gopher to assist you.

If a caterer is not to be called in, then you will be using your own staff to handle food and beverages. You may need to call in additional temporary staff for the function. *Appendix 8G* delineates the actions you could take to bring in staff from an agency.

Appendix 8H can be used to hire any additional uniforms that may be needed.

If an event is being organized away from hotel premises, or existing hotel resources are otherwise engaged, it may become necessary to hire an additional valet service just for this event, *Appendix 8J* provides the steps for the smooth hiring and supervision of a valet service.

At larger functions, especially outdoor ones, security may well be an issue, so *Appendix 8K* provides a simple checklist for hiring a security firm that will provide the service you require.

Some form of entertainment is invariably required at functions, and so *Appendix 8L* shows you how to organize it.

Some other services may be necessary, and these are listed in *Appendix 8M*.

There are several events or functions which can require quite some organization to pull off professionally, such as a champagne reception (*Appendix 8N*) and a dinner that is broken off in the middle to attend the theater, opera or some similar event (*Appendix 8P*, used in conjunction with *Appendices 9E, F* and *G*).

For outdoor events, barbecues are covered in *Appendices 8Q* and *8R*. Picnics and similar events are covered in *Appendix 8S*.

The checklist on *Appendix 8T* organizes a special event: Christmas, the English way.

Lastly, Appendix 8U provides a checklist for hiring a limousine service.

For events not covered here, I strongly advise you to make up your own checklists—from experience, I have found they provide a fixed point of certainty in what may seem like a sea of confusing motions. They also allow forward and orderly progress to occur that can guarantee your goal of a successful and pleasurable occasion is reached.

Next, let us look at a concept that is completely new at this time of writing: the spa butler. This is not the same tawdry concept as "bath butler," "fireplace butler, "technology butler," "baby butler," "dog butler," "ski butler," and "beach butler" which some marketing whiz with no understanding of what he was marketing persuaded hotels to do a few years back. The spa butler is a real butler who has additional training in spa methodology.

Why? Read on!

CHAPTER NINE
THE SPA BUTLER

Many high-end hotels and resorts offer spa services and are looking for a way to excel even further and so differentiate themselves in the minds of their guests. The same could be said of the butler service offered by many such institutions. Both programs add value and prestige, but is there a way to improve these service offerings? The short answer is, "Yes!"

Spa service has one key flaw: it ends the moment a guest leaves the spa to return to his or her suite. The way to make a guest's experience a complete one, and offer a total immersion in the "get away from it all" relaxation and rejuvenation, is to make the butler service an extension of the spa experience, wherein spa-trained butlers provide their usual high-end service in the hotel, but with the added knowledge and techniques that enable the spa environment to continue in the guest's own suite.

A guest, for instance, may well undergo a catharsis or detoxification as a result of his or her spa experience—knowing how to deal with this with understanding and empathy can create quite an impact on guests. Moments of drama aside, when a butler knows and understands the spa program of a guest, he can converse about the guest's experiences with good reality, should the guest so desire, and can also take actions to enhance that program—such as adding a complEmentary (not complImentary!) bath salt to the bath, rather than one that conflicts with the spa program.

The spa butler is really the architect of the ultimate spa hospitality experience, designing and arranging the entire spa guest experience. The spa still delivers the spa services, but the butler acts as the main point of contact before, during and after the guest's stay. Because he understands and knows what the guest is going through, and the basic spa methodologies, he can be there for the guests and extend the entire stay into a smooth experience for them. That's the simplicity of the program.

Translated into the real world, this program means the butler asks and cares about the guest's goal in coming to the spa; he cares about the guest's room, ensuring that the space reflects the guest's needs and wants. The butler supports the guest by being a sounding board and conversing with understanding and empathy. He introduces the guest to the people, places and services he or she will be experiencing at the spa, answering all questions and resolving all concerns. He smoothes the preparations for each spa experience and helps the guest through the ramifications of each spa treatment, asking the right questions.

The spa butler understands the mechanism of each spa treatment in order to give accurate and convincing explanations of treatments to the guest. The application of hot or cold therapy to the body may seem odd or even silly to the guest without an understanding of the expected physiological effects and benefits. Earning the guest's confidence and compliance with intelligent answers to his/her questions is an important part of the spa butler service.

The purpose of this chapter, therefore, is to provide a basic idea of the spa butler program. It cannot substitute for the training needed to actually deliver the program properly.

Types of Guests

There are at least four categories of spa guests. Identifying them is key to serving them successfully.

"Fluff and Buff" guests are delighted with the ultimate in pampering. They are investing time, energy and money in the expectation they will be treated as kings and queens. They are enjoying a mini vacation from the stresses and strains of everyday life.

"ROI" guests are looking for a return on their investment. They are spa savvy, meaning that they have been to spas before and have preconceived notions about what a great spa experience is and should be. They expect their spa experience to deliver on the health enhancement and therapeutic expectations they have formulated.

"Solution seeker" guests want a spa experience to alleviate pain and discomfort from their ongoing medical conditions, such as multiple sclerosis, osteo-arthritis, etc. and are hoping to find relief and answers that will alleviate some of their suffering.

"Transformer" guests are committed to transforming their own worlds, understanding they play an integral and vital role in optimizing their health and well being. They trust the spa to have highly specialized facilitators who honor the holistic nature of man.

By knowing and understanding each guest's goal and being there for them in their pursuit of that goal, the butler forms a unique relationship with guests and so brings about the ultimate spa hospitality experience.

Preparing for Arrival

The spa-trained butler conducting the usual hotel pre-arrival interview asks a few additional questions of a guest arriving for a spa service. As the spa guest's first encounter with the hotel begins with this spa butler, not a spa therapist, the butler's communication skills and knowledge therefore set the stage. As mentioned earlier, good communication skills are vital for a butler; they are even more so for spa guests, the butler being there for them, rather than having his or her attention half on something else while talking with guests.

Why is this true? Because when talking about someone's spa expectations, one is talking about something personal to them and even asking them to introvert momentarily to ask about themselves. This differs from the normal conversations one has with guests, which are generally directed towards the guest's environment, not their person or issues. And because the first step in caring for another and showing it, is giving them all one's attention as one speaks with them.

Appendix 9A, Spa Guest Pre-Arrival Interview provides the kind of additional questions a butler would ask of a future spa guest. Obviously, questions vary according to the services being offered at the hotel's spa.

Guest Arrival

On the day of the guest's arrival, the butler prepares the room with housekeeping using the standard room-inspection checklist and SOPs, laying out the amenity, and so on. For the spa guest, the standards are slightly more exacting, requiring additional inspection points and actions to prepare the room by the butler.

Checklist 9B, Spa Guest Room Arrival Checklist provides an idea of the points to check.

Some of the terms and items on the checklist need explanation:

Smudging is a Native American practice of burning sage and/or cedar to eliminate odors and so purify a space. In this case, the idea is not just to eliminate unpleasant smells, but also synthetically derived fragrances that are sometimes employed inside guest rooms, rented vehicles, public conference rooms and the like.

117

Aroma mists are made of a few drops of natural/essential oils (such as of flowers) shaken into purified or spring water and then sprayed as a fresh mist.

Beeswax or *soy candles* are used because they do not give off carcinogens, like those candles made from petroleum products.

The need to mitigate sharp corners and to close toilet seats is part of the *Feng Shui* method of creating spaces that are relaxing and comforting. Feng Shui is a way of laying out a guest suite and incorporating certain elements within it, while avoiding other elements, so as to bring about a relaxed environment that is conducive to creativity and serenity. This art of room design focuses on optimizing the flows of energy within the guest suite.

To understand this idea, which may seem somewhat ethereal to the Western mind, let us take a gross example of Feng Shui not being applied. Imagine opening a door onto a room in which the cracked back of a large bookcase stares one immediately in the face. Negotiating this, one may be disconcerted to find torn and mismatched curtains half drawn, throwing heavy shadows across the purple walls and peeling ceiling paint. Immediately past the bookcase is a faded leather armchair that smells like a cat has been camping out on it for a week. Need I go on?

Obviously, no high-end hotel would offer such a suite, but by the same token, few go the extra distance by incorporating Feng Shui principles so as to cause a definite impression on the guest beyond that produced by the usual amenities and fixtures expected by the demanding modern guest. Such Feng Shui refinements may not be desired by the average guest, but when it comes to spa guests, many are aware of and do respond to and appreciate the kind of design that Feng Shui provides.

This concept of allowing flows to flow is much like the eye-line designers try to achieve in two dimensional paintings, pictures and artwork for such as magazines and brochures. Feng Shui artists do the same in the design of three-dimensional rooms. The eye line is the line that a viewer is directed to follow with his or her eyes, when looking at a picture. The idea is to lead the eye into the picture from the most important element smoothly to the next and so on.

In Feng Shui, the idea is not just the guests' eye line, but also their comfort while living within the confines of a suite—does it set them at their ease or irritate them?

How is this philosophy realized in practice? Here are some basic elements:

1. Place some water feature in the entrance to the suite, such as a small fountain, fish tank, or a bowl filled with water and colorful stones at the bottom.

2. If a mirror is located directly across from the entrance door, remove it.

3. If the suite has high ceilings, use chandeliers or ceiling fans, or wall borders at the guest's head level. Also ensure there is plenty of light.

4. The view from a guest suite needs to be pristine and aesthetic.

5. Place furniture diagonally in front of corners, or place a decorative light fixture or urn in the corner to round out the space. If the furniture has harsh edges, arm blankets and fabric treatments can help to camouflage these angles.

Returning to the checklist items that may need explanation: the footwear in question is that required to walk from bathroom to bedroom, as well as from suite to spa and back.

The point about the ceiling is that housekeepers rarely look up at it, as it is out of their normal cleaning zone. The butler needs to look for anything unsightly that a guest's attention can hang up on—cracks or stains in the ceiling, cobwebs in the chandelier.

Guest Arrival Tour

All arriving guests are taken on the basic tour of their suite and the butler wing by the butler, as covered in Chapter Five. When guests are ready for the extended arrival tour that will introduce them to the spa facility, the butler also does the honors. This tour requires knowledge of spas, their philosophies and methodologies. The following guideline provides basic points for the butler to cover during the spa portion of a property tour and should help the spa butler give an informative tour to any guest, while also respecting the privacy of the guests already in the spa.

The butler should know which routes provide a safe (from inclement weather, chance encounters with possibly obnoxious guests, or behind-the-scenes work at the hotel), aesthetic and distraction-free path from the guest's suite to the spa. Before taking the guest to the spa along this route, the butler calls the spa associate who will be overseeing the guest's spa services, and lets him or her know the guest will be arriving in so many minutes. As a note, the butler doing the tour needs to be of the same gender as the guest, as they will both be walking into gender-dedicated locker rooms.

During the walk to the spa, which should be at a relaxed pace, the butler can provide information about the spa that will help expand the guest's understanding of the spa experience, philosophy, or the highlights of the spa itself. Again, this is not a hard-sell communication, but points of interest lightly made to engage the guest and put him or her in the mood.

When the butler and guest reach the reception area, the spa associate is there to greet the guest and to be introduced. Moving on to the locker room, the butler formally introduces the spa locker-room associate, who should assign a locker to the guest and equip it with the correctly sized robe, slippers etc. that the guest will require during his or her stay.

The butler continues the tour of the facility, showing the steam room, sauna, whirlpool, deluge shower, cold plunge etc., pointing out the health-enhancement benefits and general safety concerns of each. The butler describes the therapeutic benefits of the products and amenities available in the spa and lets the guest know that they are all provided for the convenience of the guest.

Spas invariably provide lounges for guests to relax in before and in some cases after their services. In some instances, these lounges serve as pre-staging areas where guests wait for their spa service. The butler likewise describes the benefits of any complimentary spa beverages and natural snacks—such as lemon water, herbal teas and fresh fruit—that may be available in each lounge.

The butler then takes the guest on a tour of each of the (unoccupied) treatment areas, allowing a peek at what is in store for them and providing them with a sense of familiarity prior to the actual experience of their spa treatment. In addition, the guest is introduced to the other areas of the spa, such as gym, spaces where fitness classes are held, the pool, and any spa café, salon or retail boutique.

The tour is best ended in the reception area with a formal introduction to the spa director.

The following points can be made to guests being toured around a spa:

The benefits of the spa "wet areas" such as sauna, steam room, whirlpool, cold plunge, Swiss shower etc. include:
- Increased relaxation
- Improved circulation

- Increased body temperature to promote tissue-cleansing and detoxification

First-time spa guests entering a steam room or sauna should remain no more than ten minutes in them and should drink room-temperature water afterwards. Guests who have been exercising should be encouraged to cool down and bring their pulse down for at least fifteen minutes before entering a steam room or a sauna.

A cool shower is an excellent way to finish a hot-steam experience and should be encouraged. Guests leaving a heated space should allow their bodies about fifteen minutes to adjust temperature in a warm-temperature space before entering an air-conditioned space, and vice versa.

The end product of this tour is a guest who knows where to go, how to get there, what is available, what to expect, what to do, and finally, who is enthused about participating.

In-Suite Spa Services

Once the guest has started his or her spa services, it is up to the butler to anticipate and respond to whatever the guest may throw at him or her in the way of conversation, problems or crises. It is given that the usual butler aplomb will be applied, and to this we add an extra dash of empathy, as discussed earlier.

Spa butlers need to be aware, therefore, of how spa guests are reacting to their spa treatments. Some key indicators a spa butler should look for are:
- Emotional tone changing
- Rapid eyelid fluttering
- A shift from shallow to deep breaths
- Being spaced-out as opposed to being aware of the environment
- Twitching
- A shift in energy flow, such as from much motion to lethargy
- Change in skin temperature or color.

These are signs of a physiological shift occurring in the guest and may require action by the butler to help settle the guest where the guest is experiencing discomfort. Generally, the body is a self-regulating mechanism that will bring about optimal functioning when provided an environment of support to do so, and this is all that is required of the butler.

Additionally,

- Dehydration in its full form results from the body losing too much water during exercise, being in the sun, after alcohol consumption or after excessive time spent in a heat treatment. When this occurs, the guest should be made to rest quietly and should be offered water.
- Fainting is the brain's way of obtaining more blood by forcing the body into a horizontal position. If this occurs, have the guest lie down, elevate his/her legs and place a cool, wet towel under the neck.

In the event that either of the above should occur, inform management immediately. Note that the hotel's first aid training guidelines take precedence over this information where they conflict; and any butler is smart to engage in first aid training.

Often, the butler can act without seeking permission or agreement, because he can see what is happening to the guest and knows what to do. An offer of a drink of refreshing water, for instance, to a guest who is obviously somewhat dehydrated, doesn't require words or permission.

In dealing with such occasions, however, the butler maintains an attitude of respectful curiosity, conducting himself (or herself) professionally in a way that never compromises a guest's dignity or privacy. The spa guest is highly impressionable to the suggestions of the spa butler. He, therefore, has an ethical obligation to maintain integrity, tell the truth, and create and uphold an environment of trust and confidentiality so as bring about a safe space for the guest that allows him or her to focus on fixing his or her world.

In addition, specific therapies relating to baths, showers and other spa program elements, are facilitated by the butler in a guest's suite.

General Guidelines for Drawing a Therapeutic Bath

The butler can utilize *Appendix 9C, Bath Choices Questionnaire* to find out when and where a guest may want a bath, or can ask for the information verbally. He prepares the bath and then instructs the guest in various elements as needed, per the below. He should exit the bathroom and bedroom area and remain available elsewhere in the suite, or return after ten minutes.

Preparation

1. Add the appropriate ingredients when the tub is half full.

2. If the tub is equipped with therapeutic jets, fill the tub to one-inch above the highest water jet.

3. Keep in mind when determining the level of the water, that an "oversized" guest will raise the water level more than the average.

4. Turn on the jets to achieve uniform consistency in water temperature, distribute the ingredients, as well as prevent any cold water from hitting the guest when the jets are first turned on.

5. Adjust the water temperature if needed until 99°F is reached — do not exceed 102°.

6. Prepare cold compresses or an ice pack and a cool glass of water and place them by the tub and in reach of the guest, should he or she feel too hot during the treatment.

7. Place a towel, bathrobe, and slippers by the tub.

Treatment

1. Instruct the guest to enter the tub, find a comfortable position and remain there for about ten minutes for the hydrotherapy to take effect.

2. Encourage the guest to:
- adjust water jets and/or pressure according to his or her spa-program requirements
- use the compress or ice pack, or apply cool water from the hand shower on their upper chest area before exiting the tub, if he or she feels too hot.

3. After hydrotherapy, the guest will be very relaxed and often sleepy. The butler needs to be on hand (out of the bathroom but in the suite) to ensure the guest exits the tub safely. He should then invite the guest to relax in a chair for approximately twenty minutes with a fresh glass of water while the body temperature returns to normal.

Appendix 9D, Hydrotherapy Treatments lists out some of the conditions guests may want to resolve, and the regimens the butler can apply to them as an extension of their spa program.

Appendix 9E, Spa Treatment Shower Instructions provides the regimen for therapeutic showers. If the guest shower does not have temperatures marked, then the butler needs to use a thermometer to establish which settings approximate which temperatures and find a way of marking these or alerting the guest to these before he or she takes a shower.

While the spa butler services can be expanded, the above provide the basic concepts and allow for an adjudication of whether or not any hotel, resort or villa with regular butler service and a spa, or with no butler service as yet, wishes to upgrade to spa butler service for its guests.

From the safety of the spa experience, let's look at the somewhat unsettling idea of the need for security.

CHAPTER TEN
SECURITY AND THE ODD JOB FACTOR

To any litigation-happy readers, I give formal notice to ignore the information in this chapter. Contact the police for all the information you need. When you inevitably mess up, you can take it out on them.

Since the days of the Assassins in Persia a thousand years ago, the wealthy and important in society have been the target of violence against them for political, financial or other reasons, such as religious zealotry. The modern version of this phenomenon can be found in psychiatric "successes" such as Mark Chapman (who killed John Lennon outside his apartment), Charles Manson (who killed actress Sharon Tate in her home) and Osama Bin Laden (who went completely rabid under the influence of psychiatrist Ayman al-Zawahiri).

This threat of random violence then provides another avenue for butlers to offer service to guests, acting as a second line of defense for Hotel Security. I am sure butlers through the ages have jumped to the defense of their lords and ladies wherever required and possible. Their weapons would have been whatever came to hand—possibly the silver tray they carried, itself a heavy and formidable weapon. This concept of a butler/bodyguard is not entirely new: "Oddjob" of James Bond fame seems to have played this role to some degree.

Any person willing to learn the skills and assume the responsibilities that being a bodyguard entails, will be able to provide this extra service to his employer and hotel guests. There are various ways to protect self and others. Prevention and deterrence are the best ways. But given an intruder situation, how does one best respond?

As a first step, one would simply try talking to the person and escorting him/her off the premises. The next level would include various degrees of martial arts. And only as a last resort would a firearm be produced or used.

There may be a romantic or macho image to carrying a gun, but in truth, it is a nuisance to have a hard and heavy lump rubbing against one's chest. I can almost guarantee it will never be used, but it has to be carried anyway, according to the old umbrella principle.

In the event I would have to use a gun, the grim reality of the destruction those bullets would wreak leaves no room for posing and creating an image. It's sweaty business ducking behind cover, being deafened by the blasts and scared out of ones wits by the near misses. Let's not even consider the hits.

As a bodyguard, one is obliged to physically interpose one's own body between the person one is protecting and any assailant, so that one can take the bullets. If that is not an appealing thought, then read no further.

If you are still with me, fine. I won't comment on what kind of perverse streak we share, other than to say that possible consolation lies in the fact that most people have rotten aim when it comes to shoot-outs. The average exchange of fire lasts just a few seconds and the average number of shots fired by each person is three, with usually none of them connecting. Obviously, if some trigger-happy criminal is discharging an Uzi from point blank range, chances of a hit are high. But most homicides do not follow that pattern.

To become a bodyguard, you have to obtain a firearm legally, train on its use at a firing range, and then obtain further training from a bodyguard trainer. The firing range can probably connect you with such a person or school.

Different states and countries have different laws concerning the carrying of a concealed weapon. There are still some places, such as Alaska, where one can walk around town with a gun in a holster, like in the old frontier days. Obviously, as a bodyguard butler, your weapon would have to be concealed. So you have to ascertain the laws concerning the carrying of concealed weapons on private property, in public areas, and so on.

Different states also have different laws concerning the owning of a gun. In some states, permits are required and tests have to be passed.

Where body guarding is a formal part of the job description, one becomes a paid or working gun and therefore may well need to have insurance and be licensed.

The employer would cover the insurance, and it would have to include death or injury by accident or design to guests or intruders. You might injure a maniac who was peppering the decor and guests with lead and some jury somewhere could be counted upon to award him damages.

One may also need to obtain a security license (much like a business license) for about $200, and an armed security license for about $100. The local police would be a good starting point for finding out about the various requirements covered above.

My own preference for weaponry is a 38 Magnum revolver, as they are lighter and more compact, easier to care for, easier to operate, and more economical than semi-automatics. They chamber five shots, two more than the average three per incident.

Let's look, then, at the actions you would take in the event of a hostile and/or armed intruder coming onto the grounds or into the butler wing of the hotel.

The first step is to call security while you coral the guest(s) with a view to taking them off the property if that can be done without exposing them to the intruder. Otherwise, take them to a safe area and position yourself between them and the attacker.

With your back to walls at all times, and from a position of cover, talk to the intruder to establish intentions and any other information. Keep him talking, because that allows security and the police more time to arrive, as well as increasing the possibility of defusing the situation. If not armed, or if you can persuade him to throw down any weapons, have him kneel and then lie face down, legs and arms spread-eagled, palms up.

When the police arrive, they may have you do the same until they can establish for themselves who the white hats and the black hats are in the situation.

Like military plans that fall apart on the battlefield, your intruder may not obligingly follow your plan. Maybe he will jump out from behind a potted palm, while you have your hands full of that soufflé the chef spent hours sweating over, and demand that everyone aerate their armpits while he punctuates his words with staccato bursts from his semi. In this case, you are on your own, but I would start off by gently putting down the chef's soufflé and then doing as bidden. I know the chef would definitely be in a killing mood if the soufflé collapsed!

If you do end up in a shoot-out, then make sure your field of fire is clear (i.e. that anyone you are trying to protect is not located between you and the intruder, or behind the intruder you are shooting at), and aim before you pop off any shots. If possible, do the old "Israeli dodge," which involves quickly peeking round a corner to locate the intruder, ducking back and then from a different level, coming out from behind the same or a different corner, aiming and firing.

The question of when to shoot needs to be clarified. I once read that a would-be burglar in New York broke his leg when the roof of a building he was about to break into collapsed under him. He successfully sued his intended victims, the owners of the building. That kind of logic seems to highlight the complete inanity of the modern U.S. justice system, where technicalities and abstruse precedents take priority over common sense. For this reason, you need to know when you are legally in the clear to shoot another human being.

The basic idea is that you only shoot in self-defense, where not doing so would reasonably result in injury to yourself or another.

This means that you should only shoot if the intruder has any sort of weapon that you can see, and is either advancing on you, or otherwise about to use it.

If he is advancing on you without a weapon, and an extreme disparity in strength exists, warn him that you will shoot. If he ignores your warnings and you fear for your or another's safety, then you may shoot.

In any event, shooting is only a last resort to defend yourself or another from personal injury. It cannot be used to protect possessions or to stop someone who is fleeing.

Your view is to immobilize your adversary as swiftly as possible; he is behaving psychotically and can be regarded, if somewhat callously, as a sort of "weapons system" that has to be "neutralized." So if you have already tried the reasoning approach and he is still in attack mode, then it is time to overwhelm him hard and fast. Bullets do just this, but only if you direct them to the right spot.

You always aim for the chest, shooting two bullets as fast as possible.

If he still does not go down, then he is probably wearing body armor and you have to go for the headshot.

Do not try to wing the assailant by shooting for his limbs like actors do in movies. Your adrenaline will be flying all over the place, as will your aim and the assailant's, too. In this kind of situation, you have to aim for the biggest target that offers the best chance of a hit, and one which will also be effective in stopping an attack. A shot in the arm or leg will probably do little to stop a maniacal attacker.

You do not shoot to kill; you shoot only to end his attack. As soon as the attack is ended, you have no right to use the gun any further.

The above gives an idea of the worst-case scenario—actually having to use a weapon in defense. I have given only a thumbnail sketch of the response you might initiate.

I mentioned earlier that the best form of body guarding is deterrence and prevention. These two subjects account for ninety-nine percent of a bodyguard's activities. Obviously, this is something that security at the hotel handles and not something the body-guard-trained butler would focus on.

If there *is* a real or known threat of attack to a high-profile guest, then the guest will probably bring in his own goons or management would be advised to call in an armed security service.

CHAPTER ELEVEN
NOTES FOR THE BEGINNING BUTLER

The Tools of the Trade for the Twenty-first Century Butler

The primitive tools of an Eleventh Century bouteiller would not stand today's butler in good stead. A damp cellar, poorly made bottles and jugs with wax or other tops, and metal or clay goblets, may have been high-tech and de rigueur in a long-since collapsed castle. But today's demands include instant communication, the orchestration of events over great distances involving many people and much materiel, and lives packed with an extraordinary variety of activity.

As such, a butler is well advised to become "office literate," able to operate a computer, printer, fax machine, cell phone and copier machine. An electronic Personal Digital Assistant is also recommended. The functionality of PDAs increases in leaps and bounds, currently offering wireless Internet access, telephony as well as networked computerized capability. What else should the butler have in his armory?

A digital camera is handy for taking photographs of inventoried items, a guest's (or his children's) exploits, or damage to some item.

A butler needs an office where he can keep all his tools and equipment. He should have access to a large safe to secure valuables.

He should have a supply of packaging and mailing items, as well as gift-wrap accessories.

An iron and ironing board are required equipment, especially if he is also being the valet, and perhaps even an industrial steamer.

A hygrometer and thermometer are needed if the hotel is furnished with antiques that need just the right temperature and humidity.

He should carry with him his PDA, radio or cell phone, keys, bottle opener, cigar cutter/lighter combo, credit and phone cards, coins and bills and paper handkerchiefs. These can be discretely secreted about his jacket without turning him into the Michelin man, so that he can service most of the immediate needs of his guests.

Formal day-to-day wear includes a black single-breasted jacket and waistcoat, gray pinstriped trousers (pants), white shirt and gray or black tie. Otherwise, gray trousers and blazer with a shirt and tie or cravat, or whatever the employer prefers or provides. Informal evening attire might include a variation of gray tie and waistcoat. On formal occasions, an evening suit or tails are worn, but with a white bow tie or white waistcoat to distinguish him from the normal wear of the guests. In hot climates, the butler can dispense with the jacket during the day. In really hot climates where the butlers have to work outside air conditioned spaces during a good part of the day, then an entirely new wardrobe would be more appropriate, with shorts and short-sleeved shirts — perhaps with cravats and long socks.

If being a toastmaster, the usual dress would be crimson tails with a white waistcoat, and evening-suit trousers.

For the ladies, a female equivalent would do, with make-up, perfume and jewelry that are low-key: if she draws more eyes than the lady guests at dinner, she will not be winning any brownie points or accomplishing her mission!

If also being a bodyguard, he would probably require a handgun and/or mace spray.

Appendix 11A provides a fuller checklist of items a butler needs.

Where to Start once You Arrive on Duty

Without a set plan of action, starting on a new job can be quite a harrowing experience. Your new employer and the employees in the butler department and the rest of the hotel may cut you some slack for jobs undone or poorly done at the outset, but usually not for too long. The tendency of the new appointee to waltz in and change everything is sometimes over-riding and can create upset. Old staff sometimes resent new bosses, feeling threatened or unacknowledged.

The first steps in a new position involve finding out what the existing procedures are. Becoming acquainted with the other employees and fellow butlers, and the constantly changing roster of guests, what each requires of you and what each likes and does not like. And then working hard to satisfy those demands which fall within the legitimate duties of your position. *Appendix 11B* provides a checklist to assist you in making all the right moves in a new position.

As you continue to focus on improving your performance, your employers and colleagues will be increasingly pleased and rely on you more and more. After a while, you will be worth your weight in gold to them.

Your value may increase even further if you can perform the duties delineated in the next chapter, on the occasion a guest decides to host a formal party or an occasion with speeches.

CHAPTER TWELVE
THE BUTLER AS A TOASTMASTER

What is a toastmaster? What does he (or she) do? A toastmaster's basic duties are the introduction of speakers to an audience and the proposing of toasts.

What is a toast? It is a stated wish for success or good health for a person who is named, and then the symbolic downing of alcohol by the whole gathering, to show agreement with that wish.

A master of ceremonies usually just introduces speakers or performers. He does not propose toasts. If a guest would like the extra authority, grandeur and spectacle of a formal figure, usually clad in red tails and eveningwear, to both introduce the speakers and propose (some of the) toasts, then a toastmaster would be called for. This is where the hotel butler can add to his value by assuming the duty.

Given that a hotel butler may be asked to act as a toastmaster, there are a few standard actions that should be undertaken to organize the event. The first is to establish with the guest the time and occasion around which the event is being structured, and to liaise with the banqueting and events manager for availability, so he can propose the best venue for the occasion.

Normally the guest has a personal assistant or secretary organizing the guests and any speaker list and contacting them all in good time. If not, the butler/toastmaster may have to contact speaker(s) who are experts on the subject and secure their agreement to speak on that date. He may have to liaise with the guest to establish a schedule with exact times for each speaker, leaving the best or key speaker until last. He allows time for a short introduction by the toastmaster before each speaker, and if a lengthy schedule, for a break in the middle.

He may have to make travel, accommodation and meal arrangements for the speakers and agree with them on fees. If so, he will need to instruct them on the subject of the conference, the subject of their speech, and the time allotted to them. They will need to know the venue, the exact time they will speak, who the other speakers are and the composition of the audience. In turn, the speaker needs to send the butler/toastmaster some biographical material for their introduction as a speaker.

The butler/toastmaster arranges for hosts and hostesses to look after the speaker(s) while they are in town. He sees the chefs to arrange the menu and decor for the event, and uses the checklist in *Appendix 10A* as a starting point to organize any other functions that have to be covered, such as valet service.

In most cases, the event will take place within the butler's own facility, so most of the following questions will be known already. Whether on or off site, the butler/toastmaster needs to inspect the room or space in which the event will actually take place. Is the ventilation, heating and cooling system adequate? How are the acoustics? Too much echo, or are sounds swallowed up? Do kitchen, street or other noises such as airplanes intrude into the room? Are the microphone and speaker system of top quality, by actual test? Is the building properly licensed, of sturdy construction and with adequate fire safeguards and so forth? Is parking space adequate, etc.

The butler/toastmaster then needs to compile a list of guests, with correct pronunciations of their names established, and some brief information on each for introduction purposes if needed. Debrett's book on etiquette and Letitia Baldrige's book on manners both contain the more common forms of address for dignitaries, and these should be part of any butler's library. Have table and seating plans drawn up and place cards made, so that you and the guests know where they will sit.

Making Toasts

If the butler/toastmaster is expected to propose a toast for the occasion, prepare some toasts suitable for the occasion and audience.

He should be alert for the use of words that may have an (embarrassing) meaning other than the one intended, and be sure to verify that the context of any piece he may have extracted a quotation from, is also in keeping with the intended message and audience.

When toasting, he should do so, and not say anything else. Toasts are usually offered while standing, even though the practice of standing up for a toast was no longer mandatory after both Charles II and William IV of England bashed their heads on the beams of navy vessels while attempting to stand for a toast. Even though low ceilings are rarely a problem these days, I suspect a toastmaster who proposed a toast while seated would receive little sympathy from his audience; so the butler/toastmaster would be better standing.

Keeping the Occasion on Track

The butler/toastmaster ensures the guest speakers and those at the speaker's table meet each other before the event. He gives each speaker a list of the key guests attending and answers any questions a speaker may have about the audience or event.

Security checks are often a requirement these days and should be made as guests enter an established foyer area. The toastmaster then introduces each guest to the host(s). If the guest hands the butler/toastmaster an invitation card, he accepts it and brings it to his side without inspecting it. If he does not know the guest and/or partner, he asks their name and introduces them in a clear voice. An alternative is for each person to be introduced by announcing their name to the room as a whole.

The toastmaster is responsible for the smooth running of the event, in close contact with the host, organizer and headwaiter. If formal toasts are to be made, the earliest would be after the main course; the sommeliers should ensure that each guest has something to drink (not necessarily wine) before the toast is offered.

A loyal toast is usually proposed after the last course. Informal toasts, of course, can be made during the meal, either by the host or any of his guests. The butler/toastmaster should already know the name and title of any speakers, or those proposing toasts. If, however, he is unsure, he picks a time when that person is not eating and asks, "I understand you will be saying a few words, and I'll have the pleasure of introducing you. How do you prefer to be introduced?" Fix a time for the person's speech/toast if needed, preferably after dessert when the waiters are not distracting the guests.

The butler/toastmaster should stand behind the person who is going to propose a toast, raps sharply on the table twice and says, for example: "Excuse me, ladies and gentlemen, may I please have your attention, Mr. _____ would like to take wine with Mr. _____." Or "Your host, Mr.___, would like to say a few words." Or "Pray silence for...."

When introducing the speakers, the butler/toastmaster introduces himself first to the guests, and then introduces each speaker to the rest of the audience. The best approach is a light touch with some humor; a chance for some showmanship that adds sparkle to the event. The idea is to please everyone and offend nobody while smoothing the way for the speaker and making him or her feel at ease. The butler/toastmaster allows the audience to realize why it is a treat to hear this speaker, without hyperbole (exaggeration) that the speaker cannot hope to live up to. He is brief without being curt.

The butler/toastmaster makes sure the speaker sticks to his allotted time, and when he has finished, thanks him on behalf of the audience without repeating his speech. It is a pleasant touch to personally thank the speaker afterwards, handing him/her a small gift as well as their fee or honorarium where agreed upon beforehand.

The butler-as-toastmaster remains low key and in the background when not actually speaking. Even if he is wearing a crimson coat, he is not the center of attention or the star of the show. The reason, by the way, for the crimson coat, is so that he can be easily spotted in a crowd and summoned by his employer—or for the hotel butler, the hosting guest. The practice originated, I believe, during the Middle Ages in Italy when a distraught employer couldn't find his butler at a large affair.

So we come to the final point in our review of the hotel butler's world. What follows are the checklists that you can use as the basis for your own checklists to make your work easier.

I wish you much success.

*The following appendices appear in the order
in which they are introduced in each chapter.*

Letter of Introduction to Other Employees

Dear Associate,

We would like to introduce ourselves as the butlers of Haute Hotel.

So you understand the services we provide, they include:

- Personalized wake up service:
  - Drawing of the curtains
  - Beverage of choice
  - Drawing of the morning bath
  - Laying out of the morning clothes
  - Laundry and ironing services as needed

- Complimentary refreshments in our Club Lounge:
  - 7:00 a.m. – 10:00 a.m. Light breakfast
  - 11:30 a.m. – 2:00 p.m. Light lunch
  - 3:00 p.m. – 4:30 p.m. Afternoon tea
  - 5:30 p.m. – 7:30 p.m. Cocktails

- Concierge services, including arrangement of activities and transportation.

- Express check in and check out services.

- Personal valet services, including packing and unpacking of suitcases, laying out of clothes, shoe cleaning, laundry, ironing, etc.

- Arranging for special requests and needs to make guest stays even more enjoyable and complete.

Our purpose is to provide traditional butler service for guests so that their stay here is especially smooth and memorable. We can only do this by working closely with each of you.

What we need from you in order to do our jobs is any information you have on our guests with regard to their likes and dislikes.

We may well contact you for assistance in making a reservation, in fixing or purchasing something for the Butler Service guests, in finding out how the guests enjoyed their service with you. Your timely filling of their needs is always appreciated.

In turn, we would like to hear from you with what you need from us in order to assist these guests. Maybe you need certain types of information, or for us to submit certain forms or follow certain procedures. It's a two-way street, so please let us know how we can make your job easier in servicing these guests.

We can be reached at *butlerservices@hautehotel.com* or at Extension 1234, so please feel free to contact us if we can be of assistance.

Sincerely,

The Butlers of Haute Hotel

APPENDIX 4B
Job Description—Head Butler

JOB TITLE: Head Butler
REPORT TO: Director of Lodging
LOCATION: Butler Department

DATE: _____

DEPT. Lodging

JOB SUMMARY:
This position oversees the daily operation of the Butler Services Department. The head butler anticipates, schedules, and facilitates the needs of both the staff and guests in providing a seamless and exemplary experience for all guests at the resort. This position is responsible for the hiring, training, disciplining, and administration of the butler staff, as well as stepping in and personally servicing guests when needed.

DESCRIPTION OF JOB DUTIES AND RESPONSIBILITIES:
1. Essential knowledge of all direct-report positions, including but not limited to:
   * Greeting of guests and care of luggage
   * Butler specific duties (clothes valet, food services, special requests)
2. Knowledge of LMS, Spa Soft, ARTS, Micro Soft systems.
3. Maintain a constant training schedule for entire department. Track training progress and target areas of deficiencies.
4. Food and beverage knowledge and service standards, including but not limited to:
   * Thorough understanding of room service presentations and menus
   * Working knowledge of all outlet menus and hotel wine inventory
5. Financial control and budgetary review for department, including monitoring and controlling revenues, payroll, and expenses.
6. Review and finalize scheduling of all butler service staffs.
7. Maintain payroll and staffing standards and control overtime expenses.
8. Perform Human Resources functions for all reports including: maintaining vacation and time-off requests, associate reviews (30, 60, 90 day and annual), and counseling of associates.
9. Conduct pre-shift meetings on a daily basis with staff to review occupancy, special requests, assign primary positions as necessary and perform inspections.
10. Hold a weekly meeting with all butlers and coordinators to review the past week's performance, forecast for upcoming room nights and events, arrange schedules, take up any issues, fine tune SOPs as needed, isolate successes, work out ways to promote as well as improve service.
11. Inventory and order supplies for department.
12. Develop and implement policies and procedures to increase and maintain high standards of safety and health controls within the department.
13. Update guest histories and files as necessary.

14. Maintain a hands-on approach to all associate interactions, performing all the tasks as necessary to ensure the smooth operation of departments.
15. Demonstrate an ability to interact at a high level with all managers and staff of all outlets at the resort.
16. Demonstrate an ability to maintain confidentiality and privacy.
17. Demonstrate an ability to interact with aplomb, even when faced with guests who have high and possibly even unreasonable expectations.

ACCOUNTABILITIES:
The head butler is responsible for the seamless operation of the guest experience, from arrival through departure, while maintaining a financially accountable environment. Comment cards, guest correspondence and the percentage of return visitors define guest satisfaction, while adherence to a set budget determines the level of success financially.

QUALIFICATION STANDARD:
The candidate must possess strong interpersonal relationship, reading and writing skills. College level diploma or related schooling/training is necessary. The use of the computer, including Microsoft Office products, PMS system, spa booking system, and CRM system is required. Prior knowledge of the systems in use is not necessary, but a definite plus. A minimum of five years prior experience in related hospitality management fields, including work as a butler, is necessary.

PHYSICAL QUALIFICATIONS AND STANDARDS:
Head butlers must be able to lift in excess of 70-pound loads. They must be willing to work varied hours, including nights, weekends, holidays, and split shifts (according to the needs of the guests). Candidate must also be able to stand for 90% of their scheduled time.

I have received, read, and understand the general requirements of the job.

_____   _____
Signature of Associate   Date

_____   _____
Signature of Manager/Division Head   Date

Job Description — Hotel Butler

JOB TITLE: Hotel Butler
REPORT TO: Manager of Butler Department
LOCATION: Butler Department

DATE: _____

DEPT. Lodging

JOB SUMMARY:

The hotel butler sees to all the personal needs of Butler Service guests. The butler contacts the guests prior to arrival, personally booking all activities and making any special arrangements necessary prior to arrival. Upon arrival, the butler provides formal but friendly butler services and assists the guests in planning their stay while on property. The butler also assists the guests with their folio of charges throughout their stay and coordinates their checkout procedure. The expectation is that the butler will move beyond service to creating extra-special moments for the guests.

DESCRIPTION OF JOB DUTIES AND RESPONSIBILITIES:

1. Contact guests and assist with personalized services (pre-booking spa, dining and activity reservations).
2. Arrange, record, deliver, and charge all special requests for arriving guests.
3. Greet guest at entrance and escort to Butler Service area, touring guests through any elements that are new to them in the lounge and their suite; present keys, and have the guest sign the registration card..
4. Be able to operate, and help guests with, equipment such as Web TV in their suite.
5. Offer personalized services, including packing/unpacking and organization of guest belongings, clothing pressing, laundry management, shoe shining, and description of room amenities.
6. Create extra-special moments for guest at every opportunity, including recognizing and celebrating birthdays, anniversaries, etc.
7. Monitor guest activity while at the resort, including being on call for any special requests or last minute needs, including shopping.
8. Gain a comprehensive understanding of all menus, outlets, and on-site amenities and communicate these to the guests when asked, so they engage in those activities
9. Communicate movement of guest to all resort outlets, ensuring proper service and recognition.
10. Inspect all guest rooms prior to guest arrival, ensuring their excellence.
11. Inspect, present and clear all food and beverage items ordered by the guest.
12. See to any secretarial needs of guests, such as faxing, copying, printing, courier services, etc.
13. Present folio to the guest upon departure. Research and have the front desk clarify any misunderstandings with regards to guest folio.
14. Assist guests with luggage, transport arrangements and bookings, and bid them farewell.

15. Follow SOPs for the White Board, Driver's License, Red Book, computerized Guest Profile upkeep, Food Orders, etc.
16. Maintain a well-stocked pantry so all items needed per SOPs are at hand in sufficient numbers
17. Operate on the basis that service to and the pleasure of the guests is the highest priority.
18. Demonstrate an ability to operate seamlessly with all departments and work well as a team member within the department.
19. Demonstrate an ability to understand guests' service needs and continue to interact with aplomb, even with guests with high expectations.
20. Demonstrate an ability to maintain confidentiality and privacy.

ACCOUNTABILITIES:
Ultimately, the duty of the butler is to forge close relationships with both new and returning guests. The butler's performance will be judged in a variety of ways. Primarily, instantaneous feedback will be received from comment cards. Secondly, the percentage and amount of return business that the butler entertains will be taken into effect as a measurement of success for this position. Accuracy in booking activities, spa, dining, and lodging reservations will also be used to determine job success.

QUALIFICATION STANDARD:
The candidate must possess strong interpersonal relationship skills and be able to maintain excellent professional presentation and grooming. He or she must also possess strong reading and writing skills. High school diploma is necessary. The use of the computer, including Microsoft Office products, PMS system, spa booking system, and CRM system will be necessary. Prior knowledge of the systems in use is not necessary, but a definite plus. A minimum of two years prior experience in related hospitality fields is necessary, and prior formalized training as a butler is highly regarded. All standard work cards are also required.

PHYSICAL QUALIFICATIONS AND STANDARDS:
Butlers must be able to lift in excess of 70-pound loads. They must be willing to work varied hours, including nights, weekends, holidays, and split shifts (according to the needs of the guests). Candidates must also be able to stand for 90% of their scheduled time.

I have received, read, and understand the general requirements of the job.

_____   _____
Signature of Associate   Date

_____   _____
Signature of Manager/Division Head   Date

APPENDIX 4D
Job Description--Hotel Butler Coordinator

JOB TITLE: Hotel Butler Coordinator

REPORT TO: Manager of the Butler Department

LOCATION: Butler Department

DATE: _____

DEPT. Lodging

JOB SUMMARY:

The hotel butler coordinator acts as the relay point between Butler Service guests and the butlers. He or she takes and logs all guest requests, relaying them immediately to the butlers in person or by radio, and then notes when they are done, chasing up any delinquent requests. The butler coordinator also enters data into the computer and onto the White Board on an ongoing basis, as well as assisting with the food service in the Guest Lounge.

DESCRIPTION OF JOB DUTIES AND RESPONSIBILITIES:

1. Take calls professionally, picking up the receiver within three rings and saying "Good (morning, etc.), this is (name) in the butler's pantry, how may I assist you?" Note down the requests accurately and rapidly.
2. Immediately and calmly relay these requests face-to-face to any butler in the pantry, or by radio.
3. When no butler is available to respond immediately, make appointments and relay requests to valets and make reservations at restaurants, activities, etc. for on-board guests.
4. Input the requests into the coordinator's log.
5. Note when the request is filled and draw the butler's attention to any request not filled in a timely manner.
6. Input onto the computer, as well as the White Board, information on guest preferences, activities, arrivals, departures, etc., so as to maintain a running record of the status and known information about guests.
7. Input and print off turndown cards that give guests options for butler wake-up service, and brief them on the next day's weather and calendar.
8. Assist butlers when necessary by making reservations for future guests
9. Help set up and serve breakfast, lunch, tea and cocktail hour in the Guest Lounge.
10. Keep the refrigerator clean and stocked with fresh items, as well as supplies in the kitchen
11. Have an excellent grasp of services, activities, menus, wine and cigar inventories etc. so that you can answer questions accurately and rapidly.
12. When needed, assist butlers with inventory of supplies and order when low.
13. Operate on the basis that service to and the pleasure of the guests is the highest priority. Demonstrate an ability to operate seamlessly with <u>all</u> departments and work well as a team member within the department.
14. Demonstrate an ability to understand guests' service needs and to interact pleasantly and effectively with even those guests with high expectations.

15. Demonstrate an ability to maintain confidentiality and privacy.

ACCOUNTABILITIES:
Ultimately, the duty of the butler coordinator is to bring about a rapid and precise response to guest wishes by making them known in a timely and accurate fashion to the butlers in such a way that the butlers can fulfill those wishes. The butler coordinators performance will be judged in a variety of ways. Primarily, instantaneous feedback will be received from comment cards. Secondly, the percentage and amount of return business that the Butler Section entertains will be taken into effect as a measurement of success for this position. Accuracy in relay of requests, booking activities, spa, dining, and lodging reservations will also be used to determine job success.

QUALIFICATION STANDARD:
The candidate must possess strong interpersonal relationship skills and be able to maintain excellent professional presentation and grooming. He or she must also possess strong reading and writing skills. High school diploma is necessary. The use of the computer, including Microsoft Office products, PMS system, spa booking system, and CRM system will be necessary, including the ability to type reasonably rapidly. Prior knowledge of the systems in use is not necessary, but a definite plus. A minimum of two years prior experience in related hospitality fields is necessary, and prior formalized training is highly regarded. All standard work cards are also required.

PHYSICAL QUALIFICATIONS AND STANDARDS:
The butler coordinator must be willing to work varied hours, including nights, weekends, holidays, and split shifts (according to the needs of the guests).

I have received, read, and understand the general requirements of the job.

_____   _____
Signature of Associate   Date

_____   _____
Signature of Manager/Division Head   Date

Guest History/Profile

The guest profile should contain the following information, using any of the appropriate computer programs:

- Full name
- Whether guest is a celebrity or VIP
- Nationality and cultural traditions observed
- Company name and position if a corporate guest, and contact information
- Who accompanied the guest? (Create a separate profile for each guest)
- Arrival date for each trip and its purpose
- Mode of arrival for each trip, including preferred airline, limo pick up, private aircraft, etc.
- Length of stay
- What activities he/she engaged in while here, restaurants visited, with comments on outcome
- What special requests they have for food, drink, toiletries, etc.
- Smoking/non-smoking room, smoke preferences
- Allergies and medical concerns
- What arriving amenity and turndown, which ones preferred
- Any special configurations of the room
- Preferences in butler and butler service
- Any issues they had with the room, the service, individuals (good or bad), etc. and how resolved
- Guest's general character and emotional tone
- How many times returned

APPENDIX 4F
Butler's Supplies

Supplies Needed	Quantity	Where purchased from:
Band aids		
Birthday candles		
Packing tape—brown		
Packing tape—clear		
Cigar lights		
Can opener		
Laundry forms		
Shipping boxes—large		
Shipping boxes—small		
Batteries—D		
Batteries—AA		
Batteries—AAA		
Batteries—C		
Batteries—9 Volt		
Hair spray		
Hair gel		
Nail buffers		
Toenail clippers		
Fingernail clippers		
Body sponge		
Advil		
Excedrin migraine		

Tylenol		
Tums		
Condoms		
Metamucil		
Baby powder		
Bubble bath		
Bath salts		
Lint brushes		
Shoelaces — black		
Shoelaces — brown		
Shoelaces — white		
Shoe polish — white		
White out		
White board markers/eraser		
Hotel letterhead		
Hotel envelopes		
Letter files		
Hanging folders		
Highlighters		
Legal pads		
Stapler		
Staples		
Tape dispenser		
Tape		
Post-its		

Paper clips		
Computer paper		
Staple remover		
Thumb tacks		
Sharpies		
Rulers		
Three-hole paper puncher		
Scissors		
Glass cleaner		
Furniture polish		
Multi-purpose cleaner		
Extended duster		
Duster		
Broom		
Cordless sweeper		
Floppy & zip disks/CDs		
Flashlights		
Cards with logo		
Folio templates		
Paper cutter		
Tape measurer		
Tool box		
Elmer's glue		
Elmer's wood glue		
Bleach		

Nail brushes		
Hand disinfectant		
Rubber bands		
Clock		
Remote controls		
Emergency candles/holders		
Bud vases		
Trays		
Ring holders		
Pourers		
Double-sided tape for ironing		
Terga cloths		
Etc.		

Names/Phone Numbers of Suppliers and Services

	First	Second	Third
Florist			
Men's clothing stores			
Ladies' clothing store			
Tailor			
Cigar store			
Vintner			
Chocolatier			
Gift store			
Golf/sporting/hunting stores			
Mobile car wash and detailing service (if not done by hotel valets)			
Party supplier			
Fancy dress supplier			
Stills photographer			
Video photographer			
Paramedic (for large, especially outdoor functions)			
Security service (*Appendix 10D*)			
Printers (*Appendix 10J*)			
Etc.			

Ordering and Taking Delivery of Merchandise

Item to be ordered _____

For which guest/employee_____

Requested when? _____

Authorized by _____ When _____

Supplier's name_____

Date of order_____

Ordered by letter_____ phone_____ fax_____ in person_____ e-mail_____

With whom dealt _____

Description of what ordered _____

Quantity/weight_____

Catalog number_____

Quoted price_____

Their order number_____

Delivery date_____

How paid/to be paid (i.e. credit)_____

Running balance with supplier_____

Action taken if late delivery_____

Remarks on arrival_____

Any action taken on receipt_____

Payment entered in Bills Paid Ledger_____

Reimbursement received from guest/guest billed_____

The Butler's Book

The book is mostly computerized, but includes some ancillary hard files. The book is compiled over the years, kept up to date and handed over to any successors.

SERVICE STRUCTURE PROGRAMS

- Guests' needs and wants
- All checklists (such as are listed in this book)
- Job descriptions for butler service personnel
- Schedule of functions for staff
- Programs for the upgrade of the butler service area
- Cleaning and maintenance task sheets
- New staff briefing sheet
- House rules

INTRODUCTION FROM THE TELEPHONE BOOK, including:

- Local Maps
- Underground/bus plan
- Museums and art galleries, etc.
- Libraries
- Theaters, concert halls, stadiums, sports venues, etc.
- Local outings and attractions
- Churches of all denominations
- Sources of information

TELEPHONE LOGS AND COSTS OF LOCAL AND LONG DISTANCE CALLS

CLOTHES

- Clothing standards
- Inventory
- Dry-cleaning and repair record

LISTS AND RECORDS
(by subject, but also cross-referenced as appropriate on the computer's calendar function)

- Telephone message form
- Credit card order format
- Birthday list
- Christmas presents list (with info on presents already given)
- Christmas and New Year cards received/sent

- Forthcoming events
- Long-term Diary Planner
- Religious festivals/seasons, with do's/don'ts and which guests/staff members follow them
- Amenities in stock
- Publications with renewal dates and details of payment
- Wine cellar stock list
- (Shopping) list of foods and dry goods normally stocked
- List of clocks (for power failure/time changes)
- List of files in cabinets and archives
- Menu and Guest Book for special occasions (giving the occasion; date; guests; menu; wines; seating plan; flowers; decorations; dress and jewelry worn by lady guest(s) involved; comments)
- Instruction books, receipts and guarantees for appliances and other purchases (hard copy)
- Rules of the house
- New staff briefing sheet
- WQSB (Navy term for Watch, Quarter, and Station Bill, meaning a large board showing at a glance what everyone's main and subsidiary duties are, when they are on shift, their contact info etc.)
- Rollodex of employees, suppliers, contractors, guests, other hotel employee numbers, etc.

SUPPLIERS

- Addresses
- Phone/fax numbers
- Contacts
- Records
- Account numbers
- Comments

FINANCIAL

- Orders and purchases made and well received
- Bills Paid book
- All financial records, disbursement vouchers, bills etc. in weekly and monthly order (hard copy)
- Monthly and annual summary of accounts
- Inventory (including suppliers and their addresses)

TRAVEL

- Agency information
- Names, addresses and phone numbers of airline, cruise, train, cab and limo companies
- Insurance and emergency numbers abroad

PERSONAL INFORMATION

- Clothes sizes of butler service department staff
- Favorite items of guests, from forms of address to newspapers to drinks to foods/recipes to pastimes
- Family members of guests
- Addresses and phone numbers of all guests
- Cultural, ethnic and religious traditions honored by guests and employees
- Medical concerns, such as allergies, for guests and employees
- Local doctors and dentists, phone numbers and addresses and also at-home doctors and dentists of guests who may experience medical difficulties
- Dietary and drink requirements of guests
- Telephone/fax lists
- Speed dialing lists
- Long distance area codes, time zone map, international dialing codes
- Addresses—all ever used
- Scrapbook of articles on the hotel as well as guests (hard copy)
- Working file for each major function put on (hard copy), with salient points noted as applicable on the computer
- Correspondence (hard copy)

Format for Bills Paid Ledger

Date _____

What purchased_____

_____

Quantity_____

Charge_____

Paid to_____

Paid by:

      Hotel account   _____

      AMEX   _____

      Diner   _____

      Visa   _____

      MasterCard   _____

      Cash   _____

      Check   _____

      Other   _____

APPENDIX 4L
Phone Memo
(Use for calls other than for purchase of merchandise)

Number called _____Date_____

Person spoken to _____Time_____

My request_____

_____

Person's response_____

_____

_____

Action promised by them_____

_____

_____

Action needed by me_____

_____

_____

APPENDIX 4M
Stocking The Bar

BEVERAGE NEEDED	TYPE	APPROX. QUANTITY for 100 guests
Beers	Various	36 bottles
Lagers	Various	36
Bourbon		2
Rye whiskey		2
Scotch	Various Blended	12
	Various Malt	12
Campari		3
Gin	Strong	3
	Aromatic	3
	Popular	3
Vodka	Various	9
Pernod		1
Rum	Light	3
	Medium/dark	1
Vermouth	Sweet	2
	Dry	2
Brandy	3 top brands	6 of each
Sherry	Sweet	2
	Medium	2
	Dry	2
Wines	White sweet	3
	White medium	3
	White dry	3
	Red	10
	Rose	5
Champagne	Pink sweet	25
	White dry	50
	White Medium Dry	25

For a champagne reception, bank on one bottle per person per hour; or if a full bar is available, half a bottle per hour. Then add 25% to that final figure and return any unused bottles. For champagne during dessert, one glass per person + 25% should suffice.

BEVERAGE NEEDED	TYPE	APPROX. QUANTITY for 100 guests
Liqueurs	Selection of all types	1 bottle each
Non-alcoholic wines	Selection of various reds, whites and rosés	5 of each
Non alcoholic beers	Selection of various brands, US and European	42 bottles

Mixes, Sodas and Juices:

Angostura bitters	2
Bitter lemon	12
Canada Dry-Ginger	36
Clamato Juice	3
Various sodas diet	24
regular	36
Lime juice	2
Mineral Water-Carbonated	75
Still	25
Orange Juice	12
Soda water	36
Tonic Water	36
Tomato juice	25

FOODS	APPROX. QUANTITY for 100 guests
Ice, crushed and cubed	10 bags
Maraschino cherries	
Lemon/lime slices/wedges	
Olives	
Cocktail onions	
Nuts	
Horseradish	
Worcestershire sauce	
Salt	

GLASSES TYPE	APPROX. QUANTITY FOR 100 GUESTS
Champagne flutes	300
Sherry (small)	50
Martini	30
Manhattan	100
Cocktail	60
Highball	100
Whiskey	100
Water	100
White wine	40
Red wine	40
Port	25
Brandy	40
Shot	25

ACCESSORIES

Cocktail sticks
Blender
Cocktail shaker
Pitcher and long-handled stirrer
Different types of bottle and can openers
Cutting board and knife
Decanters (for wine, whiskey, spirit and liqueur)
Ice buckets
Ice tongs
Measures
Silver trays
Soda siphons
Wine coolers
Coasters
Long spoons
Purified water
Large fridge
Ice machine
Bar towels

With a hundred guests, it is better to set up at least two bars with a minimum of one bartender at each, and have three waiters circulating with drinks and canapés.

APPENDIX 4N
A Butler's Day In The Life

7.00 a.m. First butler arrives and:
1. Checks with the night concierge or bell staff regarding wake-up calls and any relevant happenings during the night
2. Checks with room service regarding breakfast orders made since 11.00 p.m.
3. Retrieves print-out of all departing-guest folios, places in envelope, and attaches to clipboard ready for presentation to guest at appropriate time
4. Un-forwards phones from night concierge/bell staff
5. Prepares butler wake-up service trays and schedule
6. Reviews weather report on-line and checks for messages

8:00 a.m. to 11:00 a.m.

8.00 a.m. Second butler arrives and:
1. Picks up the arrival sheets for the next fourteen days from front desk or prints from the butler's computer
2. Updates the White Board
3. Both butlers:
- Provide wake-up service
- Deliver room-service breakfast orders
- Early check-out/packing and portfolio presentation
- Print guest itineraries

Club Lounge breakfasts are managed by the butler coordinator

11:00 a.m. to 2:00 p.m.

1. Prepare for guest arrivals
2. Confirm amenities for arriving guests in stock
3. Room inspections as they come available
4. Add the amenities and personalized items
5. Contact future guests fourteen days before their arrival (or as soon as their name appears on the arrivals list if less than fourteen days before their arrival) to do the pre-arrival interview
6. Confirm the appointments and items arranged for guests earlier, are still in place for the fifth day ahead of today. .
7. During slack times, work out specials/upcoming events of interest in liaison with marketing, and contact departed guests via letter and invite to return. Note any sour responses and work out how to handle, and then do so.

2:00 p.m. to 5:00 p.m.

1. Complete room inspections
2. Greet arriving guests in the lobby, tour them as needed and have guest sign credit card slip
3. Unpack as needed
4. Arrange any and all changes/new reservations
5. Ironing of evening clothes
6. Shoes cleaned if needed

3:00 p.m., first butler leaves, third arrives—with enough overlap to turn over ongoing activities for the day
4:00 p.m., second butler leaves, fourth arrives—with enough overlap to turn over ongoing activities for the day

5:30 p.m. to 8:00 p.m.

1. Assist in dinner departures
2. Alert F&B regarding on-site dinner arrivals
3. One butler covers cocktail hours in the Club Lounge
4. Serve dinner to those having room service.
5. Shoes shined as needed

8:00 p.m. to 11:00 p.m.

1. Confirm turndown has been done and provide amenities
2. Provide cordial/drink service
3. Collect and note all wake-up service and breakfast requests
4. Print personalized stationary/business cards for guests arriving next day
5. Update White Board
6. Prepare reports
7. Input data into profiles from daily guest notes
8. Inventory updates

All shifts:
Service all telephoned and face-to-face guest-requests.

11:00 p.m. to 7:00 a.m.

Telephones are forwarded automatically to the night concierge or bell staff if no real demand is expected for butlers.

If guests are still active during these hours, a butler graveyard shift can be created, in which all guest requests are handled, and any incomplete projects are worked on from the first two shifts.

Pre-Arrival Interview Questions

Interviews are on average of 5-10 minutes duration, asking only those questions that are appropriate for the guest. Where the guest has a butler, personal assistant or personal secretary, or even a less-busy spouse, it is best to obtain whatever information is possible from them first.

1. Good morning/afternoon/evening, Mr./Ms. _____. My name is _____ and I am one of the butlers at _____ (or for a repeat visitor, "[Salutation], this is John the butler from (hotel)."

2. "If you have a few moments, I would like to assist you with the calendar and reservations for your upcoming visit."

   - If not, "When may I call back, or is there someone else I should contact?"

3. Number and names of adults and children coming?

4. Confirm dates for stay

5. "Do you have an anticipated arrival time?"

6. "How will you be arriving?"

   - If flying: "May I have your flight information?"
   - "Do you require transportation from the airport?" *(Arrange through Valet Department or if an extremely important guest, you may wish to meet them yourself.)*

   - If driving: "Do you require directions?"

7. "What facilities would you like to use during your stay?"

- If unknown, go through the list:
  o Golf
  o Tennis
  o Sailing
  o Skiing
  o Shooting
  o Spa
  o Equestrian Center (height and weight of any riders required)
  o Fishing
  o Hiking/Biking
  o Hang gliding
  o Parasailing

- Restaurants
- Etc.

8. Ask for preferred schedule for these reservations and an alternative

9. If not already known, "Are there any special needs or requests we should be aware of, Mr./Mrs. ____?"
   - Dietary
   - Medical
   - Room

10. "In the butler wing, we offer a special program whereby regular guests can bring photos and other personal items to decorate their suite as a home-away-from-home, and then leave them with us for safekeeping for reuse during subsequent visits. Some gentlemen like to bring cigars and keep them in our humidors. If you have such items, please feel free to bring them."

11. Unless there is something else you would like to cover, "Mr./Mrs. ____, I would like to thank you for your time. We look forward to seeing you on the ____th of month."

Guest Information Sheet

Guest Name: _____

Phone Numbers: Home _____

Work _____

Mailing Address: _____

_____

No. in Party: _____ Adult _____ Children

Names: _____ _____

_____ _____

_____ _____

Date of Arrival: _____ Approx. Time: _____

Method of Arrival: _____

Date of Departure: _____

Special Needs: _____

_____

Reservations:

Breakfast: _____

_____

_____

Brunch: _____

_____

_____

Lunch: _____

_____

_____

Dinner: _____

_____

_____

Activities _____

_____

_____

_____

_____

_____

_____

_____

Amenities: _____

_____

_____

Notes: _____

_____

_____

_____

Date called: _____ Caller: _____

APPENDIX 5C
Welcome Letter

Dear (Guest title and name),

Welcome to the (butler wing) at (hotel/resort name).

Please take a moment to familiarize yourself with the following services offered by your butlers:

- Personalized wake up service including:
  - Drawing of the curtains
  - Beverage of your choice
  - Drawing of the morning bath
  - Laying out of the morning clothes
  - Laundry and ironing services as needed

- Complimentary refreshments in our Club Lounge:
  - 7:00 a.m. – 10:00 a.m. Light breakfast
  - 11:30 a.m. – 2:00 p.m. Light lunch
  - 3:00 p.m. – 4:30 p.m. Afternoon tea
  - 5:30 p.m. – 7:30 p.m. Cocktails

- Concierge services, including arrangement of activities and transportation.
- Express check in and check out services.
- Personal valet services, including packing and unpacking of suitcases, laying out of clothes, shoe cleaning, laundry, ironing, etc.
- Arranging for special requests and needs to make your stay more enjoyable and complete.

We are here to provide whatever you may require to enjoy your stay. Please do not hesitate to call upon us by picking up the telephone.

Sincerely,

The Butlers of (hotel name)

Appendix 5D
Next Day's Calendar Card

Dear (title and name[s] of guest[s]),

On behalf of the (hotel name) butler staff,

We wish you a very good night.

Tomorrow's weather

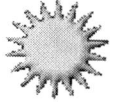   

Sunny   **Partial Cloudy**   **Cloudy**   **Rain/Snow**
(i.e. 30% chance a.m.)

The temperature

High _____   Low _____

Your calendar for tomorrow

10:00 a.m.	Links Golf Course *Please arrive 15 minutes prior*
10:04 AM 10:12 AM	Tee Time for party of 4 Tee Time for party of 4
6:30 p.m.	Cocktail reception at Lafitte Gardens
7:30 p.m.	Seating for dinner and entertainment at L'Oignon de Chef

Please contact the butler station
if you would like to change your calendar.
Thank you

In the event that the weather forecast completely precludes the guest's planned activities, the usual card with their calendar of activities would only rub salt in the wound, so in this case, alternative wording for a different card under the weather-forecast symbols could be:

> *"In light of the inclement weather expected tomorrow, may we suggest any of the following indoor activities?*
>
> *(List them)*
>
> *We would be happy to make the bookings."*

Alternatively, perhaps the guest has no activities planned or booked. The butler could then use a card that suggests activities that might appeal to the guest, whom the butler has already done some homework on to know the likes and dislikes.

> *"The weather will be perfect for a variety of activities at the hotel/resort/spa/villa tomorrow.*
>
> *(List them)*
>
> *We are happy to make any bookings if you decide you would like to engage in any of these activities."*

Butler Wake-Up Service Card

(Hotel Name)
Butler Wake-up Service

Wake-up time: _____

Would you like: How many?
    Coffee   _____
    Tea   _____
    Orange Juice   _____
    Cranberry Juice_____
    Other   _____

If you would like a bath drawn, do you prefer:
    Salts   Bubbles   Plain
  Cool   Med   Med-Hot   Hot

Clothing laid out for your morning activities? Yes   No
Clothing laid out during afternoon for your evening activities? Yes   No

Please give this to your Butler
or leave outside your door for pick-up.

APPENDIX 5F
Suite Inspection
(Sample based on AAA checklist)

Suite #_____

BEDROOMS	Needs Attention/Done
1. Entry door free of dust and marks	
2. Windows and window frames clean and free of dust	
3. Drapery clean and free of dust	
4. Drapery opens and closes freely	
5. Walls and ceiling clean and free of marks	
6. Baseboards clean and free of dust	
7. Vents clean and free of dust	
8. Pictures and mirrors clean and free of dust	
9. Carpet is clean and free of stains	
10. Lamps clean and free of dust	
11. Lamps are set to the light switch and are operable. Bulbs are 3-way where appropriate.	
12. Comforter, blankets, and sheets are clean and free of stains	
13. Bed is neatly made- comforter straight and pillows fluffed	
14. Dust ruffle hangs about an inch from the floor- on all sides	
15. Bed bench clean and free of stains and marks	
16. Carpet clean under bed and furniture-no debris	
17a. All furniture upholstery clean and free of stains	
b. All furniture woodwork clean and free of marks	
c. All drawers clean inside	
18. Alarm clock set to the correct time and operable. The alarm is not set; volume is set to medium-low.	
19. Phone clean and all speed dial buttons work	
20. Trash cans clean and free of marks	
21. Compendium: All pages included and free of	

	Needs Attention/Done
marks and tears, stationary and envelopes, note pads and pen	
22. Ice bucket, tray, and four glasses clean	
23. Two robes hanging in the closet	
24. Two laundry bags and laundry slips hanging in the closet	
25. Twelve hangers: two satin hangers, six pant hangers and four skirt hangers	
26. One blanket and one pillow on the shelf in the closet	
27. Two luggage racks in the closet	
28. Balcony floor (and furniture) clean	
29. Do Not Disturb sign in good condition & placed on inside door knob	
30. Emergency exit diagram in easy view / plainly understood	
31. Safe clean and operable	
32. Two magazines and (hotel) catalog on stand	
33. TV is free of dust, remote control is operational	

BATHROOMS	*Needs Attention/Done*
1. Mirrors and light fixtures clean and free of dust	
2. Walls, ceiling, and vents clean and free of dust	
3. Floors clean and free of debris	
4. Shower walls, floors, and glass free of soap scum and mildew	
5. Brass fixtures free of white chalky mineral build up	
6. Tub free of hair, soap scum, and marks	
7. Four bath towels, four hand towels, and four wash clothes	
8. Two bars of soap, one bottle of shampoo, one bottle of conditioner, one bottle of shower gel, one bottle lotion, and one shower cap	
9. Vanity area clean and free of all debris	
10. Make-up mirror clean and light works	
11. Shower curtain clean and free of mildew	
12. Toilet clean	
13. Toilet holder clean with a full roll of toilet paper	

	Needs Attention/Done
14. Phone clean	
15. Hairdryer clean; cords wrapped	
16. Jacuzzi jets free of mineral or dirt build-up when operated	

LIVING ROOM	Needs Attention/Done
1. Windows and window frames clean and free of dust	
2. Drapery clean and free of dust	
3. Drapery opens and closes freely	
4. Baseboards clean and free of dust	
5. Vents clean and free of dust	
6. Walls and ceiling clean and free of marks	
7. Pictures clean, free of dust, and leveled	
8. Carpet is clean and free of stains	
9a. Lamps clean and free of dust	
9b. Lamps are set to the light switch and are operable. Bulbs are 3-way where appropriate	
10a. All furniture clean and free of stains	
10b. All drawers clean inside	
11. Phone clean and all speed dial buttons work	
12. Trash cans clean and free of marks	
13. Compendium: All pages included and free of marks and tears, stationary and envelopes, note pads and pen	
14. Extra blanket and pillow	
15. Balcony floor (and furniture) clean and neatly arranged	
16. Two magazines and (hotel) catalog on stand	
17. Sofa bed sheets and blanket clean and free of stains	
18. Mini-bar area clean, stocked with drinks, snacks, glasses, ice bucket.	
19. TV is free of dust, remote control is operational	
20. Fireplace and doors free of soot and black build up. Remote control operational if applicable	

APPENDIX 5F-1
Suggested (Guest) Room Checklist

1. Flowers   . _____
2. Sparkling & still water _____
3. Drinks cabinet clean and stocked (lemon, etc.) _____
4. Ice _____
5. Candies and bars _____
6. Fruit (washed and ripe) _____
7. Glasses _____
8. Clothes and lint brush _____
9. Writing paper, pens, pencil and stamps _____
10. Alarm clock (working) _____
11. Radio (working) _____
12 TV and Video and video tapes (working) _____
13. Amenity gift (champagne, chocolates, etc) _____
14. Bathrobes _____
15. Towels, bath mat, flannels _____
16. Toiletries, such as shampoo, soap, toothpaste, toothbrush, his and her deodorants, razor and blades, mouthwash, sun block, hand and body cream, hairspray, all unused or looking unused _____
17. Hairdryer, hair curlers, comb and hairbrush _____
18. Insect repellent, plasters/bandaids, aspirin, analgesics _____
19. Trash cans clean and empty _____
20. Carpets, curtain, furniture cleaned/polished _____
21. Beds clean and made _____
22. Windows spotless _____
23. Bathroom spotless, mirrors, too _____
24. Toilet paper, tissues, cotton buds and balls _____

175

25. If fireplace, spotless, and fire ready laid, with log baskets and coalscuttle full; dry pine for kindling. Use hawthorn, oak, beech if possible, otherwise ash, holly, birch, hornbeam, sycamore or hickory   ———

26. If a shoot or golf, game cards and invitations displayed on the mantelpiece   ———

27. Heating, ventilation, A/C, lights all working and adequate   ———

28. Books, magazines suitable/requested for guest/occasion   ———

29. Playing cards, jigsaw, games (toys for kids)   ———

30. Ashtrays if a smoker (plus favorite smokes, and a lighter   ———

31. Humidors full and serviced   ———

32. Clocks properly wound up   ———

33. Guide books   ———

34. Schedule of events put on by the host   ———

35. Local events, attractions at that time   ———

36. Hyperallergenic pillow assortment   ———

37. Extra blankets   ———

38.   ———

39.   ———

40.   ———

Guest Tour of Suite on Arrival

A. Cover the following points:

1. What is behind each door (i.e. bathroom, closet, etc) to orient the guest.
2. Where the light switches are (explain how to use variable-lighting-level switches if not known).
3. Ask if they will want to use the safe, and if so, show them how it is operated.
4. Show the TV/VCR/Digital players, remote controls, Web access keyboards and game controls and how to use as needed.
5. Show any fireplace control and how to use.
6. Show the bar location, instruct to call the butler for ice or items not in the bar.
7. In the bathroom, point out Jacuzzi, jet safety and controls, and any telephone.
8. Point out the CD/radio/alarm clock.
   - State that some guests prefer their butler wake-up service to an alarm or wake-up call from reception, and indicate the butler-wake-up service card for them to fill out (tea/coffee/juices/milk, etc., newspaper, bath, laundry and laying out of clothes).
9. The telephone and how to reach the butler, who will see to all their needs in the hotel.
10. The folder with resort amenities, activities, safety, restaurant menus, etc.
11. Ordering breakfast in their room—show them the door hanger.
12. Point out the printed copy of the calendar for their stay.
13. Tell them the butlers are available to assist with any needs with regard to their calendar or anything else desired to make their stay most pleasurable.
14. Confirm the address etc. on their registration form, hand them the form, pointing out the type of room and the rate, and ask them to sign. Thank them using the guest's name.
15. Note: If there is no credit card number on file for the guest, ask the guest for a card so you can swipe it at the front desk.
16. Explain the following:
- How many butlers servicing the guest, so will also be serviced by others than yourself.
- Turndown service
- To call butlers if need clothes ironed, shoes cleaned or anything else.
- Likes and dislikes are recorded for future visits.
- The program for personalizing their room with photographs, mementos, humidors on future visits.

B. Ask if any questions.

C. For those guests who are first timers, and if you have not already toured them around the property, make it clear that the hotel has many amenities and activities. You or another butler will be happy to tour them or guide them to specific activities or answer any questions.

D. Offer to bring any refreshments

E. Offer to unpack and/or lay out clothes for their next activity (dinner?), and do as requested.

F. Leave after checking, "Will there be anything else, Mr./Mrs.?"

G. The signed registration card must then be taken to the front desk for filing and any credit card swiped.

H. Return the guest's credit card.

APPENDIX 5H
Butler Wake-Up Service

Late night shift if there is one, or if not, the second shift:
Collects the butler wake-up service cards from guest doors.

7.00 a.m. shift:
1. Collects any other service-request cards and works out the delivery schedule.
2. Prepare trays with bud in a vase, china and silver, etc., and irons the front and back of any newspapers with ink that smudges.
3. Deliver those newspapers to the doors of occupied suites that are not having morning wake-up service or breakfast en suite.

Delivery
Make the tea/coffee ten minutes before each wake-up call time, transferring the tea to a new, hot pot without leaves when brewed. Put enough in each pot for two cups.

1. Knock on the door three times softly. If not answer, knock again slightly louder.
2. If still no response, call the guest on the telephone: "Good morning, Sir/Ma'am. It's _(time)_. Are you ready for your morning (tea/coffee, etc)?"
3. Then return, knock on the door, and let yourself in when invited.
4. Hand the guest the newspaper, saying, "Good morning Mr./Mrs. XXX"
5. Place the tray on the bedside table. If they are having tea or coffee, pour the first cup and place it and the creamer/sweeteners on the side of the tray nearest them.
6. As you walk over to open the curtains, state:
   - The weather is _____ and looks good for your (golf/tennis, etc.)
   - Optional: if they have requested clothing lay-out and you know they have more than one   choice: "Do you have a preference for your (golfing, etc.) clothing, Mr./Mrs. XXX?"
   - Optional: "Shall I arrange for transport to your (activity)?"
7. If they requested a bath, draw it and keep checking the temperature with either a thermometer, or your elbow.
8. Place folded bathrobe(s) with belts drawn through loops at foot of bed if not already there.
9. Clear dirty clothes, place in laundry bags and fill out the laundry slip.
10. Place the clothing for the morning on a chair and the dumb valet.
    - Royal sock fold and placed on top of shoes.
    - Coordinate jacket, trousers, shoes, belt and socks and tie choices
    - Three choices of tie/cravat.
    - Loop the belt.
    - Underpants and undershirt folded on chair top, ties on back of chair with jacket on top, shirt and trousers hanging on dumb valet.

- If evening attire, cufflinks etc. already inserted.
11. Complete the bath and either run the Jacuzzi briefly to distribute the crystals or bring out the bubbles, or do so with your hand.
12. Ensure shampoo, conditioner, shower gel, soap and towel are at hand and the bathroom is neat.
13. Check back with the guest.
14. If finished with tea/coffee, clear the tray.
15. Say: "Your bath is ready Mr./Mrs.___. Will there be anything else, Sir/Ma'am?"
16. See to their needs.
17. Withdraw, taking the laundry bags with you as well as the tea tray.

When you have a moment, file the bottom copy of the laundry slip and call laundry to collect the laundry. Later on,
- Cross check laundry returned against the slip
- Deliver the laundry to the room, preferably when the guests are out, and pack it away. You can leave a note to that effect.

APPENDIX 5J
Breakfast Service SOP

Evening shift
1. Just before 11:00 p.m., picks up breakfast orders left either on the guest's door or phoned in to the butler coordinator.
2. Log onto the White Board.
3. Take hangers and food order forms to room service on the way home.

2:00 a.m.
Bellman picks up and drops off the rest of breakfast orders at room service.

6:00 a.m.
Night concierge drops off any called-in food order forms at room service.

7:00 am shift
1. Butler checks with room service and for any post-11:00 p.m. orders.
2. Room service calls to say they are leaving and brings up breakfast, always on a table with a hot box, with the original hanger/order form, and any bread/muffins etc. un-toasted.
3. Butler makes the tea, toast the bread/muffins etc. and warms the milk while checking the order against the hanger.
Note: Cross out any line asking for additional gratuity and sub-total, and write in the total yourself.

Take breakfast to the guest's suite; knock on the door three times softly. If no answer, knock three times somewhat louder and enter when invited to do so. If still no answer, quickly call the guest to alert them to your presence

Transfer the breakfast from the trolley table onto the guest's table where one exists, or extend the flaps and set one or two chairs at the right points at the mobile table. If the guests want breakfast in bed, this should be known in advance, and bed-trays with folding legs are brought in with the breakfast already on them, and placed above the guests in bed, who should be sitting up by now. Leave the breakfast invoice on the table for signing.

Pour the tea/coffee from the pot.

Ask if anything else is required.

Inform the guest that you will return in an hour's time to clear the table if that is convenient. If not, ask the guest to call when they would like the table removed.

Clear the table from the room after an hour or when requested by the guest, and place in the service elevator, together with the signed breakfast invoice.

In Room Lunch/Dinner Service

1. Butler or butler coordinator takes the order from guest, noting it in writing, with time wanted. Ask for drinks if not mentioned.
2. Relay order to room service.
3. Take delivery of the lunch/dinner cart and check its accuracy.
4. If anything missing or unsatisfactory, call room service immediately and rectify the problem.
5. Place room service note under the tablecloth.
6. Add candle unit (and take a lighter).
7. Add silver condiment tray and place condiments in it.
8. Cross out the "additional gratuity" and "sub-total" lines and write in the total.
9. Remove food from hot boxes and place on cart.
10. Remove the hot box(es) from the cart.
11. Take food to suite.
12. Knock three times and if invited in, walk in and announce, "Dinner is served Sir/Ma'am."
13. If still no answer, knock again slightly louder.
14. If still no answer, telephone and say, "Your Lunch/Dinner is ready, Mr./Ms. XX."
15. Return to the room, knock three times and enter.
16. Roll the table to the space where there is enough room for chairs (or to the dining room table for suites with these tables).
17. Lay the table or place chairs around the room service table.
18. Light the candle.
19. Ask if you can open the tomato ketchup/mustard containers.
20. Leave the room service invoice on the table.
21. Announce, "Mr./Ms. XXX, dinner is served."
22. Remove the covers from the hot plates if they will eat this course first.
23. Pour the drinks.
24. "Will there be anything else, Sir/Ma'am?"
25. Handle as needed.
26. Notify guest that you will return in an hour to collect the cart or clear the table. If this is not convenient, inform the guest that they may call when they are ready.
27. Leave quietly.
28. If you do not hear from the guests, return in an hour to clear the table
29. Take the table to the elevator, replace the hot box(es) and ensure the invoice has been signed.
30. Let room service know the table is ready for pick-up — sending down if they are ready to collect.

APPENDIX 5L
Taking an Order

Record any meal order on a butler's pad (a leather holder for 3x5 index cards) and transfer it afterwards onto a Food Order Sheet; or preferably use a Food Order Sheet to take the order:

Room: Time wanted:	Cover #	
Menu item #	#	Description/Condiments

The Food Order Sheet is a duplicate pad with copies for the butler coordinator to call in the order or to give the kitchen, the copy being kept by the butler to check against what is delivered by room service.

Butlers need to know all of the menus as well as what is not available on the menus that day.

He or she must also know what questions to ask when taking orders: (i.e. "How would you like your eggs/steak, Sir?" and only if the person does not know the options, detail them), what comes with the dish and what side orders are available.

I.e.: Milks: regular, low fat, 2%, buttermilk, goat, soy, rice, half & half, etc.?
Eggs: scrambled, over easy, over hard, sunny side up, hard-boiled, soft-boiled, poached?
If an omelet, how many eggs, anything added: mushrooms, tomatoes, ham, bacon, etc.?

For lunches and dinners, ask questions such as:
* Bread choices, toasted?
* Salad dressing?
* Cook order on meats?
* What type of cheese?
* What to drink?

As a note, present butter and margarine unless the guest specifies otherwise or their Guest Profile indicates a preference.

Do not ask too many questions. For instance,

- Don't ask if they want sour cream, butter, chives or bacon bits on a baked potato. Bring them *all* in small side dishes.
- Same with condiments: bring mustard, ketchup, mayonnaise, etc.
- If you are not sure if they want coleslaw or French fries, for instance, bring both. Extra is better than having to run back for it. When in doubt JUST BRING IT.
- And know their preferences from their profile as well as the pre-arrival interview.

Butler coordinators should have a copy of every menu in a binder at their fingertips for quick reference. Such very smart binders need to be available in the butler's pantry for use when a guest wants to see the menus.

It is optimum if guests preorder breakfast via the time order/door hanger.

APPENDIX 5M
Guest Activity Follow-Up

1. Provide guests with their calendar/weather forecast each night with turndown.

2. Ask at wake-up service whether they need any assistance with arranging travel and provide it if so, by calling the Valet Department.

3. At the expected time of completion of each activity, call that activity and ask if Mr./Ms. _____ have completed their activity. Then ask how their activity went, or if there were any issues. You can also ask how they performed (i.e. three under par or hole-in-one on the 5th or shot 98 of 100 on the shooting range), etc.

4. If there were some issue, find out how it was resolved and whether the guest was completely satisfied. If not, work out with the associate involved what could be done to handle.

5. If the guests are running late, ask the associate involved to tell them that you will call ahead to the next appointment and alert them.

6. Then do so.

7. When the guest returns, ask them about their experiences at an appropriate moment, congratulating them on any good performance.

8. In case of any complaints, apologize and immediately call the associate again and work out a solution with him or her. Present the solution and handle until the guest is happy again.

9. Where the guest speaks highly of a particular associate, let that associate know verbally, and if compelling enough, e-mail or dispatch that person and his senior with the good news.

10. When the guests are out at dinner, if not appropriate before, remove any dirty clothing from the afternoon's activity to the laundry if the guest is not leaving the next day.
    - If they are leaving the next day, then place the items in laundry bags.
    - If the items are wet, then hang them to air dry.

11. Input data into Guest Profile

APPENDIX 5N
Check-out of Guests

1. Ask the guests on the day prior to their departure when they are checking out. I.e. "I know you are scheduled to leave tomorrow, may I offer to:
   - Pack
   - Ship any items
   - Confirm or make travel plans."

2. Do as requested.

3. Over breakfast (or morning wake-up) the following day, hand over their folio and collect it once they have signed it. If guest does not arrange wake-up call or breakfast service, folio could be placed in an envelope and delivered under the door first thing in the morning.

4. If the guest has a problem with the bill, tell the guest that you will inform the front desk so that they may research the problem. You do not want to play piggy in the middle, but you do want to facilitate the rapid and satisfactory resolution for the guest, so as soon as front desk has resolved the issue, bring the new folio to the guest.

5. Ensure whatever transportation needed is ready: Limo to the airport is waiting or guest's car is brought around (cleaned and serviced), etc.

6. Bring down the luggage for the valets to load and leave the folio with the front desk.

7. Escort the guests to their transport. Say your own version of "Is there anything else I can assist you with, Mr./Mrs. _____? We have enjoyed servicing you, and look forward to seeing you again soon at (Hotel name). Have a safe trip."

8. Once the guests have departed:

   - Notify the front desk of the check out;
   - Record updates to their Guest Profile directly into the computer if you have time, or leave in the daily file system for input later that day by the butler coordinator;
   - Take the guest names off the White Board;
   - Place any departure tip in the kitty.

9. Write and send a "Thank You" card with any digital photograph printouts taken of them during their stay, as well as any small hotel-branded items they expressed satisfaction with.

Equipment Checklist for Caring for a Wardrobe

1.   Clothes brush

2.   Lint brush   _____

3.   Steam iron (cordless)   _____

4.   Padded ironing board, or large table, padded   _____

5.   Steamer   _____

6.   Trouser presses   _____

7.   Portable sewing kit   _____

8.   Sets of hog bristle shoe brushes, 2 for each color shoe

9.   Short haired bristle brush to remove mud/dust   _____

10.   Knife and nail brush to remove mud   _____

11.   Kiwi polish of all colors   _____

12.   Meltonian brand shoe creams of all colors   _____

13.   Wren's Dubbin brand shoe waterproofing   _____

14.   Saddle soap   _____

15.   White spirit (to de-crust applicator brushes)   _____

16.   Cotton buds   _____

17.   Small sponge   _____

18.   Cotton rags   _____

19.   Meltonian grease and tar remover   _____

20.   Brasso   _____

21.   Suede fabric shampoo and a weather-proofer   _____

22.   Spare shoe laces   _____

23.   Old toothbrushes   _____

24.   Wooden shoe and boot trees (plastic for travel)   _____

25.   Shoe racks   _____

26.   Hangers (wooden, shaped and unvarnished)   _____

27. Shoe and boot bags for each pair   ———

28. Trouser cuff hangers   ———

29. Plastic hangers for travel   ———

30. Padded hangers for ladies   ———

31. "U" shaped shield to use for polishing

     brass buttons   ———

32. Barbour material thorn-proof dressing   ———

33. Acid free tissue paper (art supply shop)   ———

34. Stickers for hangers, shoe bags, for labeling/

     inventory   ———

35.   ———

36.   ———

37.   ———

38.   ———

39.   ———

40.   ———

Checklist for the Morning Tea or Coffee Tray

NAME: _____

Room: _____ Wake-up time_____

Coffee and type_____

Tea and type _____

Fruit juice and type _____

Cream and type _____

Milk and type _____

Sugar and type _____

Sweetener and type _____

Cereal and type _____

Cup and saucer _____

Doily for cup _____

Spoons for: Coffee _____ Tea _____ Cereal _____

Juice/milk glass_____

Napkin _____

Newspaper(s) and type _____

Flower and type _____

Flower vase _____

Tray_____

Cloth for tray matching napkin _____

APPENDIX 7B
Breakfast Buffet Checklist

ITEM	TYPE	QUANTITY
Coffee		
Tea		
Fruit juices		
Cream		
Milk		
Sugar		
Other sweeteners		
Cereals		
Yogurts		
Fruits		
Eggs		
Toasts		
Rolls		
Croissants		
Muffins		
Jams		
Jellies		
Marmalades		
Butters		
Margarine		

Condiments		
Other dishes		
Sausages		
Bacon		
Tomatoes		
Mushrooms		
Fish		
Kidneys		
Meat		
Mugs		
Cups		
Saucers		
Glasses		
Cereal bowls		
Yogurt/Fruit dishes		
Side plates		
Entree plates		
Knives		
Forks		
Spoons		
Teaspoons		
Coffee spoons		
Tea pot		

Strainer and bowl		
Coffee pot		
Milk jug		
Cream jug		

APPENDIX 7C
Checklist of Items Needed for
a Full English Afternoon Tea

1. Large urn of boiling water
2. Separate pot of tea for each type of tea wanted
3. Teacups and saucers
4. Tablecloth
5. 3" square napkins
6. Teaspoons
7. Castor sugar
8. Sugar cubes
9. Sweeteners
10. Honey
11. Side plates
12. Small knives
13. Small forks
14. Tea strainers and bowls
15. Thinly sliced lemons
16. Milk jugs
17. Hot water jug (to weaken tea)
18. Plate and fork (for lemon slices)
19. Small boxes for leftovers
20. A little of every variety of tea, properly sealed
21. A lot of the usual teas
22. Tongs for sandwiches
23. Cake servers
24. Cream (double and clotted), bowl and spoon
25. Jam bowls and serving spoons
26. Salvers and 3 tier cake stands
27. Doilies

NOTE: You'll need at least three of all plates, cups, napkins, etc. per person.

Checklist for Preparing for a Less Formal
Lunch or Dinner

FOOD

- Appetizers
- Salad
- Dressing
- Soup
- Crackers
- Bread/Dinner rolls
- Meat (Sauce?)
- Fish (Sauce?)
- Fowl (Sauce?)
- Starch/pasta (Sauce?)
- Vegetable "A" (Sauce?)
- Vegetable "B" (Sauce?)
- Vegetable "C" (Sauce?)
- Pudding/Desert (Sauce/cream?)
- Fruit
- Cheese and crackers

GARNISHES

- Appetizers
- Soup
- Salad
- Meat
- Fish
- Fowl
- Vegetables
- Pudding
- Tea
- Coffee

- Ice/ice bucket

UTENSILS

- Place mats
- Knife & fork for entree
- Spoon for soup
- Fork & spoon for dessert
- Specialized cutlery
- Serving spoons/forks etc.
- Serving bowls/platters
- Serving tray
- Napkins
- Soup bowls & plates
- Entree dishes
- Salad dishes
- Side plates & bread plate
- Dessert plates
- Fruit bowl, plates and knives
- Coffee mugs/cups
- Water glasses
- Wine glasses
- Salt & pepper
- Coffee pot
- Butter dishes
- Ashtrays
- Bell or remote bell control
- Candles

APPENDIX 7E
Details of Menu, Including Key Ingredients, Points of Interest

Appetizers_____

Hors D'oeuvre_____

Other course_____

Entree_____

Pudding_____

Fruits_____

Cheeses_____

Breads_____

Sauces_____

Wines_____

Coffees_____

Chocolates/petit fours_____

Brandy/Port_____

Cigars/Cigarettes_____

SPECIAL DIETS

What substituted for which course and for whom:

_____

_____

_____

_____

Checklist of Staff and Material Needed for a Dinner Party

Date and Time_____

Location_____

Time of reception_____ Dinner_____ Time end_____

Special occasion/Theme_____

Guests_____

STAFF REQUIREMENTS

Chefs_____

Kitchen Hands_____

Waiters_____

Sommeliers_____

Others_____

UNIFORMS REQUIRED

Jackets_____

Bow ties_____

Cummerbunds_____

Ladies' shirts_____

White gloves_____

TABLE SETTINGS
(For tableware, flatware and glasses, add 25% to number of expected guests)

Dinner service to use _____

Flatware to use _____

Glasses: number and type: 1)_____ 2)_____

3)_____ 4)_____ 5)_____

6)_____ 7)_____ 8)_____

Tablecloths #_____ Color _____ Sizes _____

Napkins #_____ Color_____

Candles #_____ Color _____ Sizes _____

Printed Menus_____ # Place Cards _____

#/Type Ashtrays _____

#/Type Vases _____

Cruets_____

Salt/Pepper shakers _____

Figurines _____

_____

Flowers for tables_____

For room/entryways_____ For guests _____

Nuts/Chocolates_____

Knives, #/type: 1)_____ 2)_____ 3)_____ 4)_____

Forks, #/type: 1)_____ 2)_____ 3)_____ 4)_____

Spoons, #/type: 1)_____ 2)_____ 3)_____ 4)_____

Other, #/type: 1)_____ 2)_____ 3)_____ 4)_____

Serving utensils: 1)_____ 2)_____ 3)_____ 4)_____

5)_____ 6)_____ 7)_____ 8)_____ 9)_____

Plates, #//Type: 1)_____ 2)_____ 3)_____ 4)_____

5)_____ 6)_____ 7)_____ 8)_____ 9)_____

Circle the following items needed, noting numbers required:

CHINA

Cereal bowls	Luncheon plates	Knife rests
Cheese plates	Oyster plates	Oval platters
Ramekins	Salad bowls/plates	Scallop shells
Side plates	Seafood cocktail sets	Soufflé dishes
Soup bowls	Soup cups and stands	Dessert plates
Egg cups	Napkin rings	Entree plates
Escargot shells	Corn-on-the-cob holders	Finger bowls
Artichoke plates	Flan dishes	Mustard bowls
Fruit plates	Fish plates	Grapefruit
Hors d'oeuvre plates	Ice cream coupes	Sundae glasses
Coffee cups	Coffee saucers	Coffee mugs
Demitasse cups	Demitasse saucers	Irish glasses
Tea cups (breakfast)	Tea saucers (breakfast)	Tea cups-small
Tea saucers (small)	Tea plates	Sugar bowls
Floaters		

MISCELLANY—SERVERS

Asparagus servers	Cake/pie servers	Toast racks
Pastry tongs	Sandwich tongs	Sugar tongs
Decanting basket	Carving knife/fork/board	Fish servers
Grape scissors	Crumb brush and scoop	Kebab skewers
Wine coasters/buckets	Chopsticks	Meat servers
Salad spoon/fork	Salvers/Serving trays	Tea strainer set

FLATWARE

Spoons

Sugar	Dessert	Bouillon	Coffee
Grapefruit	Tea (large)	Tea (small)	Egg
Soup	Ice cream	Jam	Iced tea
Mustard	Soup	Salt	

Tablespoon (dessert and table size)

Knives

Butter	Caviar	Cheese	Dessert
Dinner	Entrée	Fish	Fruit

Forks/Tongs etc.
Lobster picks
Cake/pastry forks
Asparagus tongs
Crab crusher

Escargot fork/tongs
Corn holders
Dinner fork
Table forks

Oyster forks
Fish forks
Entree fork
Dessert forks

SERVING
Baskets (bread/rolls)
Sauce boat/stand
Trifle bowl
Cake plates/stands
Food covers (sml/lrg)
Casserole (oval 3.5 pts.)
Caviar container
Soup tureen
Vegetable dish (un/covered)
Cheese platter
Coffee pots
Sandwich tray

Gravy boat and stand
Breadboard
Sugar bowl (un/covered)
Chocolate container
Round casseroles (.75/2.5/4 pints)
Condiments (salt/pepper)
Jugs (cream/milk)
Marmalade dish
Vegetable tureen
Fish platter
Tea pots

Salad bowl
Cheese board
Fruit bowl
Butter dish

Water carafe
Cheese dish
Jam dish
Pickle dish
Meat platter
Tea tray

ACCESSORIES
Glass towels
Place-card holders

Menu holders
Napkin rings

Tray cloths
Waiter's cloths

Checklist for Organizing a Formal Dinner Party

PREPARATIONS

1. Discover from host(ess):

   - Date and time
   - Venue
   - Guests (names, numbers, B list)
   - Invites
   - Menu (alert to any repetitions for guests)
   - Wines
   - Cigars
   - Seating arrangements
   - Musical chairs
   - Flowers
   - Any special theme
   - Presents for guests

2. If doing invites, complete Printer Checklist (*Appendix 8B*)

3. Contact guests (or their staff) to confirm travel arrangements, any needed facilities at house, special diets or forms of address. Handle any points required

4. See chef to fix alternate recipes and order food

5. Trial tasting for self, chef and host if new or tricky recipe

6. Check bar, wine cellar and humidor and make necessary orders

7. If musical chairs planned, contact/contract photographer

8. Use checklist if hiring agency staff (*Appendix 8G*)

9. Use checklist if valet service needed (*Appendix 8J*)

10. Order special uniforms/fancy dress/decorations as required

11. Draw up and/or print table plan, seating plan and index as required

12. Alert hostess on what worn last time with those guests

SETTING UP THE TABLE

The Day before:

1. Ensure linens, chairs, cutlery, glasses in sufficient number (*Appendix 7F*)

2. Dining room cleaned, including chandelier, replacing any dead bulbs

The Day of the Dinner:

3. Bring all the items for the table into the room, with 25% extra for the sideboard (*Appendix 7F*)

4. Set the table, with a sample cover for staff to emulate

5. Air room if needed; check ventilation and ensure it is adequate for the number of bodies expected

6. Check lighting levels

7. Ensure the sideboard is properly stocked with cigars, cigarettes, coffee cups, saucers, spoons, sugar bowls, finger bowls, chocolates and nuts

8. Cheeses, cream and butter dishes in fridge

9. Ripe fruit in supply

10. Coffee set up

11. Check bar stocks; prepare the port

12. Ensure needed wine is at right temperature, decant as needed

LATE AFTERNOON AND RECEPTION

1. Shower and change

2. Check table, food, wines and drinks; staff and valet present, relevant rooms spotless and serviced (i.e. flowers)

3. Red wines opened, cheeses out of the fridge

4. Staff eat, including sampling the foods and briefing on ingredients

5. Staff inspection and briefing on ground rules

6. Dummy run lines for coats, rest rooms, seats in reception room, bar, ash trays, table/seating plan, easy access to dining/withdrawing rooms. Ensure all posts are manned and staff knows what to do

7. Ensure chauffeur/valet room set up w/entertainment, food/drinks

8. Alert host to any items of interest re: foods/drinks/guests

9. Check w/chef on schedule

10. Fruit dipped in iced water and drip-dried on towel

11. Butter placed on table on ice-filled bases, one per guest

12. Welcome guests; housekeeper/self take coats, announce guests to host if needed

13. Seating plan handed out at reception room; waiters serve drinks, hot and cold canapés

14. If musical chairs, clear with involved guests

15. Keep tight line in between chef and host

16. Phone any late guests and handle as late or no-shows

17. Check with host and likely guest if grace being said

18. Announce dinner and get guests seated

THE DINNER

1. Announce grace as needed

2. Pour fizzy/still waters and remove table numbers

3. Serve the main course and pour the wine

4. Handle any late guests, catching them up to the rest of the party

5. Top up wines and offer seconds if enough to go round

6. Clear condiments and bread with the main course and crumb down

7. CONDITIONAL: If cheese is to be served
   - remove condiments and bread and
   - crumb down after cheese course

8. Serve pudding and clear

9. Serve fruit and clear

10. Put out petit-fours, chocolates and nuts; serve coffee and tea, then clear

11. Serve the port

12. Announce toast and/or speech if to be given

13. Distribute ashtrays, cigars and cigarettes if required

14. Keep cups freshened, the brandy moving and liqueurs etc. offered

15. Clear and clean the dining room, putting away all contents once cleaned and polished

16. Leftovers distributed

17. Guests sign visitor's book, if required

18. Button hole guests staying overnight and make arrangements for the following morning's needs and requests

19. The following day, note all information in the Butler's Book. Send any letters of thanks needed and musical chair photographs

Checklist for Planning a Function

1. Date and time? _____

2. Type of function?
   Champagne Reception   ____   Picnic   ____
   Theater/Opera Supper Party ____   BBQ   ____
   Dinner at Hotel   ____   Restaurant   ____
   Supper and Ball   ____   Home   ____
   Other _____

3. Any theme for function, influencing dress/decor/food?   ____

4. Inside or outside? Marquee required?   ____

5. Number of guests?   ____

6. Names (and addresses) of guests made available   ____

7. Any VIPs who MUST attend?
   (Quickly confirm date/venue is OK via their secretaries)   ____

8. The date does not conflict with any event popular with the
   intended guests?   ____

9. Invitations need to be sent out?   ____

10. Entertainment required?   ____

    Type of Music   _____

    Band/Disco/Cabaret/Chamber/Orchestra/Pianist, etc.   ____

    Film ____   Play ____   Singing ____   Poetry   ____

    Clowns____ Videos ____   Games ____   Fireworks   ____

    Reading ____   Lightshow ____   Other _____

11. Caterers required, or preferred?   ____

12. Outside agency staff needed? What functions?   ____

13. M/C or Toastmaster?   ____
14. Speakers?   ____

205

15. PA system? ＿＿

16. Valet service? ＿＿

17. Limo hire? ＿＿

18. Photographer/Video? ＿＿

19. Guests staying overnight?

   Who? ＿＿＿＿＿＿＿＿＿＿＿＿＿＿＿＿＿＿＿＿＿＿＿

20. Menu? ＿＿＿＿＿＿＿＿＿＿＿＿＿＿＿＿＿＿＿＿＿＿＿

21. Cigars/cigarettes offered? ＿＿

22. Drinks? ＿＿＿＿＿＿＿＿＿＿＿＿＿＿＿＿＿＿＿＿＿＿

23. Wines? ＿＿＿＿＿＿＿＿＿＿＿＿＿＿＿＿＿＿＿＿＿＿

24. Flowers? ＿＿

25. Specific instructions re: special decor? ＿＿

26. Existing tableware and linens to use? ＿＿

27. Special costumes? ＿＿

28. Security and safety (fire/First Aid)? ＿＿

29. Insurance? ＿＿

30. Coat check-in? ＿＿

31. Powder/Men's Room adequate? Portaloos needed? ＿＿

32. Gifts for guests? If yes, purchase selection from shops
    on sale-or-return basis, or procure catalog ＿＿

33. Total budget? ＿＿

34. Access to finances for running costs, guest for consultation? ＿＿

NOTE: Refer to appropriate checklist to accomplish each step.

Printing Checklist

1. Determine: size, paperweight, color, print style, motif, design and contents for the following:

    -   Invitation cards
    -   Place cards
    -   Menus
    -   Table index, folded, wallet size for each person (alphabetical names with seat and table noted [could have a table plan with seat numbers noted, on back page])
    -   Seating plan (couple of large ones outside dining room, with each person listed at table sitting at)
    -   Table plan (couple of large ones outside dining room giving floor plan of tables and the entrance)

2. Contact printing company and ensure they can manage the job on time

3. CONDITIONAL: If unknown, check quality of earlier products and ask for referees to ensure reliability

4. Ensure they can accept changes on printing the seating arrangements up to the day of the event, and that they will print on that day

5. Have the invitations sent out six weeks ahead (eight weeks over a holiday period). Use a secretarial service if printing company cannot send out the invitations

6. Keep on hand a list "B" of close friends/family who do not mind being invited as back up at the last minute, to cover no show guests

7. Finalize the seating arrangements with the printer, and have him print the seating information on the morning of the event

Booking an Off-Site Restaurant for Dinner

1. Investment tip made beforehand as needed.

2. Give the manager your a photograph of the hosting guest and clear the plans for the dinner with him.

3. All drinks at bar put on the bill, with barman asking host what guests want to drink.

4. Then guests given menus without prices, and host given the one with prices.

5. Barman checks again with host re: drink refills.

6. Head waiter draws attention to stellar foods available and waiter takes orders up to main course.

7. Party called to eat, with host seating people according to conversational optimum.

8. Once seated, host given wine list with prices and decides.

9. Butler can sit in for host if he is delayed. When host arrives, a new cover is put down and butler leaves.

10. Butler pays for meal next day, and tips manager in cash. If needed, the manager can be left a credit card as security that night. Check for and query any obvious discrepancy in the bill.

Appendix 8D
Booking Another Venue for a Function Checklist

1. Contact the banqueting manager of the guest's desired event venue and arrange an appointment.

2. Confirm the following:

   - Adequate space to handle required numbers

   - Supervised and ticketed cloakroom

   - Clean, adequate and accessible restrooms for number of guests involved

   - Cleanliness, especially in the kitchens

   - Menu planned, quality, portion sizes

   - Wines, aperitifs and after dinner drinks

   - Cigars and cigarettes

   - Flowers on tables and around rooms — state what

   - Linen, glasses and cutlery of adequate quality and quantity

   - If not, get him to hire some and check them

   - Spare table set up nearby in case of additional guests

   - Sound and PA system of adequate quality

   - Adequate stage, electrical points; room for artists to change and stay in

   - Adequate dance space

   - No late charges

   - Tips included

   - Staff ratios of 1:6 waiters and 1:10 sommeliers, with the latter briefed to help waiters when not engaged in serving drinks, cigars and condiments

   - Place for cars; valet service included

   - Complimentary suite for guest if staying overnight

- Complimentary tasting for guest and self (paid for if booking subsequently canceled)

- Total cost with no hidden extras (bar wines, drinks and cigars separately billed per consumption)

- Take pictures for guest

3. Brief guest, show pictures to illustrate items of interest.

4. During tasting, check for taste of food, presentation, color, appeal, preparation, wine combination and service.

5. Negotiate any changes needed and any reduction in price for same services. Then confirm booking with the venue, fax confirmation and receive acknowledgement from the banqueting manager. Send any needed advance payment and the fax original.

6. Confirm final guest numbers three days before event and arrangements all in hand

7. On day of dinner, ensure everything is proceeding according to plan, sampling food

8. Announce guests as they enter the event hall

9. Ensure guests happy and event running smoothly; check with host

10. Announce speakers.

11. When banquet is over, send final payment with letter of thanks and recommendation, and a small present to the banqueting manager

APPENDIX 8E
Hiring A Marquee Checklist

1. Contact company and ensure marquee of choice is available at prescribed time

2. If so, set up a meeting and iron out the following:

   - Necessary tents available
   - Portaloos
   - Ground covering
   - Furniture, stage
   - Electrical outlets
   - Insurance coverage, in writing
   - They obtain necessary fire, police and local council authorizations
   - They provide someone during the event to service their equipment
   - How long to set up, and when to set up by
   - When take down?
   - Restore turf, make up any damage, remove their trash
   - Complete cost quoted, no overheads
   - Pictures provided, and referees
   - Contract drawn up

3. Obtain guest authorization and contact the company with any needed changes; negotiate a reduction in price for same service

4. Fax new agreement, and once acknowledged, send any needed advances

5. Should marquee remain unused an extra day, propose to guest and hotel management he allow its use by a charity or club (a business opportunity for the hotel). If acceptable, contact the charity, etc., let them know the do's and don'ts; and have a legal agreement drawn up that clears the guest & the hotel of any liability for any phase of the activity.

6. Five days before the event, phone the marquee company to re-confirm

7. When the men arrive to set up the marquee, show them the locations and keep an eye on their progress

8. Ensure they use their Portaloos; supply them with refreshments

9. Buttonhole the person who will be remaining behind and ensure he or she is able to:

  - Handle any emergency, such as fire, tent collapse, etc
  - Electrical maintenance
  - Plumbing and servicing of the portaloos

  Ensure he/she has:

  - The needed tools
  - Smart uniform
  - Schedule of events
  - Badge or other marking to be easily spotted from a distance
  - Cell phone

  Ensure he/she knows:

  - Where his food and base will be
  - To contact you if any problems
  - There's a gratuity if all goes smoothly

10. Confirm police, security, fire, insurance, council/city government permissions obtained

11. Ensure take-down occurs as promised, and any damage made good

12. Send check and letter of thanks/recommendation plus small gift, if appropriate

Hiring a Caterer Checklist

1. Phone appropriate caterers to determine availability

2. Arrange meetings and iron out the following:

   - Menu and numbers involved (+25% on portion control)
   - Experienced waiters, not students
   - Waiters/chefs uniforms
   - Flatware
   - Crystal/glasses
   - China
   - Linen
   - Condiments and their containers
   - Furniture (tables must be lockable to prevent the legs from collapsing)
   - Arrival of materiel the day before
   - Staff arriving first thing to clean, polish, set up
   - Use/non-use of home kitchen/equipment
   - Tasting for client and self (free if booked)
   - Total costs, without hidden extras
   - Obtain references and pictures of past dinners if caterers are new
   - Obtain written quote and statement of intent

3. Verify references, arrange and hold tastings with guest

4. By phone, go over any required changes, negotiate to discount the price for same services, and then fax new agreement. Once acknowledged, send original of final fax, plus any advance needed

5. Three days before the event, confirm staff and supplies have been arranged

6. Ensure arrival and set-up in plenty of time; sample food and have any corrections made as needed

7. Assign own staff as liaisons for the caterers

8. Brief all staff on schedule, ensure they know where everything is and are ready for the evening

9. Staff shower if needed, change and eat

10. Staff inspection and briefing on food contents as needed

11. Rove around during the event, ensuring guests are happy and everything is running smoothly in the following areas:

    - Bar tending, bottle opening
    - Drink distribution and top-up
    - Glass, ashtray, napkin and trash collection
    - Canapé distribution
    - Buffet set-up and running/table set-up and laying
    - Plate/silver service
    - Clearing tables
    - Taking coats w/tickets
    - Checking rest rooms (sign-posted)

12. Ensure clean-up, and later take-down, occurs rapidly and smoothly

13. If all went well, tip the person in-charge

14. Send check and letter of thanks/recommendation, and present if appropriate

15. Thank/reward own staff

APPENDIX 8G
Hiring Casual Agency Staff Checklist

1. Determine what staff are needed and how many of each:

   - Chef

   - Sous-chef

   - Kitchen hand

   - Waiter/ress

   - Cloakroom Attendant

   - Sommelier

   - Bar staff

2. Determine:

   - Time period:

   - Location:

   - Occasion/dress:

3. Contact agencies, arrange for staff to be hired

4. Check two days before that those trained staff are confirmed

5. Five hours before the event, call roll, introduce yourself, instruct on schedule, menu and drinks; their food arrangements, rest rooms, shower and uniform provisions; parts of house out of bounds, tips (and wages, if needed). Assign duties and drill

6. Have them help with preparations and polishing of glasses, flatware, etc. (for dinner, show them a cover, and have them set them up)

7. Let them eat, shower and change as needed, and then do final inspection

8. Supervise the staff at work

9. At end of day, retrieve uniforms, any cutlery, gloves, linen, etc.

10. Give wages/tips as indicated

11. For any good staff noted, take their names and addresses, for future casual personnel pool, or future staff, if interested (remember to give the agency a commission if you do take one of their current staff)

12. Send check and letter of thanks/recommendation to agency

13. Next time you use that agency, negotiate a discount

APPENDIX 8H
Hiring Uniforms/Linen
(In the event that caterers or staff agency do not have correct items available)

1. Determine items, quantity and sizes needed of:

   - Jackets, shirts and bow ties (color?)
   - Gloves (color?) (five per person)
   - Special theme uniform
   - Chef's uniform
   - Other
   - Table cloths
   - Tray cloths
   - Napkins
   - Waiter's cloths
   - Glass cloths

2. Place the order, to arrive two days before the event itself

3. Upon arrival, check for dirt, tears, missing or wrong-sized items and have supplier correct immediately if any found

4. After the event, ensure all items are collected, checked for damage, and returned with payment and letter of thanks

APPENDIX 8J
Valet Service Checklist

1. Contact companies to determine availability

2. Arrange meetings with those available to iron out:

   - Adequate resources (three drivers per ten cars)
   - All drivers insured and properly licensed
   - They find location for cars and properly patrol locations
   - All drivers uniformed
   - Two-way radios between house and car park
   - Two vans for transporting drivers back to car park
   - Cleaning of cars during the event, if host would like that courtesy for the guests

   - Total cost, without hidden extras
   - Negotiate discount without reducing service
   - Procedure they follow; ensure it aligns with your hotel guest's needs

3. Fax agreement; once acknowledged, send original and any needed advance

4. The day before the event, ensure all drivers will be in place one hour before event

5. When drivers arrive, show them their room with television and refreshments; brief them on the event and the schedule

6. Check with the foreman on insurance, licenses, vans and two-way radios; check over procedure they will follow, and what they will need

7. Check over drivers for uniform, attitude, manners, and correct via foreman as needed

8. Check over selected ground for parking, correct any problems; give foreman a list of VIP cars that may stay on the grounds

9. When guests have arrived, arrange for roster of drivers not engaged in security or cleaning, to return for food and relaxation

10. Before guests start to leave, alert foreman to send drivers back

11. Where possible, alert foreman of those about to depart for minimal delay in delivery of their car

12. As remaining number of guests dwindles, allow some of the drivers to leave

13. Tip the foreman when all done if gone smoothly

14. Send check and letter of thanks/recommendation to the company

Appendix 8K
Hiring a Security Firm Checklist

1. Contact firms and check (if unknown):

   - Availability
   - Referees and credentials
   - What services they provide
   - Any insurance
   - Bonded and experienced personnel only
   - Small walkie-talkies, with one for you
   - Complete price, no hidden extras; negotiate reduction
   - Fax confirmation
   - When acknowledged, send any needed advance with original of the fax

2. Two days before the event, phone to confirm

3. Ensure they have food/beverages, rest rooms and base set up, if needed

4. They arrive beginning of the day, show them round, brief them on sequences, guest names and vehicles, staff expected, locations, VIPs.

5. End of the day, tip and return walkie-talkie

6. Send check with letter of thanks/recommendation

Appendix 8L
Checklist for Engaging Entertainment

1. Unless the hosting guest names specific artists, track down requested type of artist by word of mouth and yellow pages

2. Discover when and where they are playing and go look and listen: video or tape the performance if possible; check for professionalism in performance/dress/conduct; determine overall attitude, communication ability, adequate equipment. Judge whether they conform to your guest's requirements

3. If applicable, play video/tape to guest and make proposals for back-up performers

4. Contact managers and ensure the performer(s) picked are available on the event day (meaning the key artists, not fill-ins)

5. If so, hammer out contract as follows:

    *   They arrange economy travel to city, billing you on arrival
    *   You arrange local travel
    *   Bed and breakfast only at motels/hotels (mini-bars and other items like phone calls not covered)
    *   You feed them
    *   What do they need in terms of electrical outlets?
    *   They provide all equipment, but changing room, rest rooms and stage provided
    *   What is cancellation fee?
    *   Insurance covered by themselves; get what, in writing
    *   Failure to perform clause
    *   Non-alcoholic beverages; no eating/drinking on stage
    *   Total fee, free of any hidden extras

6. Fax the agreement to manager and receive acknowledgement

    *   Iron out any problems
    *   Follow up by sending him original of final fax and any advance

7. Draw up a list of actions to implement the points brought up in (5) above, and get it done

8. Check with manager that everything is going according to plan one month and again one week ahead

221

9. On arrival of artists, brief them on outline of the event; its schedule and purpose

   - Show them their rooms and facilities, where to go for food, etc.
   - Introduce them to staff member looking after them (if not self), and to relevant contractors

10. Find out any further needs and wants and satisfy them if appropriate

11. Have artists set up beginning of day

12. Ensure everything is smooth for the artists before and during the performance and audience appreciating them

13. At the end, give tip, ensure travel arrangements set and they are happy

14. Send final check to manager with letter of thanks and recommendation, and some gift/memento, if appropriate

Appendix 8M
Checklist for Miscellaneous Services
Needed for Functions

1. Arrange for the following as needed, using hotel resources where they exist:

    • Florist

    • Gardner and landscape gardener

    • Electrician

    • Vintner

    • Grocer

    • Butcher

    • Fishmonger

    • Stills photographer

    • Video photographer

    • Paramedic

    • Trash collector (for extra pick up) and Portaloo services

    • Fire Marshall (for standby truck)

2. Contact and confirm those companies available, briefing them on what is needed and wanted. Arrange for them to visit

3. When they visit, do full planning, work out agreement, negotiate discounted fee and pay any needed advance

4. Confirm by phone two days before

5. When they arrive, groove them in and ensure they have everything they need to produce. Show them their "office," including food and restroom arrangements

6. Ensure they are doing their job during the function

7. Send letter of thanks with check

APPENDIX 8N
Champagne Reception Checklist

1. Ensure sufficient bottles in cellar, or purchase one bottle per person per hour on sale-or-return basis

2. Order three fluted champagne glasses and two china plates per guest as well as serving plates and trays, to arrive the day before

3. Arrange with chef or caterer for the purchase and making of fifteen eye-appealing canapés per person

4. Staff arrive day before or beginning of day and are briefed on the event purpose, schedule, highlights, tips and out-of-bounds areas; arrangements for their own food, rest and changing rooms. Give each a specific function, which you run them through the motions of, and make sure they know what everyone else is doing

5. Glasses polished and checked for breakage

6. Three hours before event start, oversee final clean-up and set-up, including champagne chilled in fridge for at least two hours

7. Drill the staff on the procedure and iron out any snags

8. Staff fed and changed into uniform one hour before

9. Final staff inspection for appearance & cleanliness of nails, face and hands twenty minutes before

10. Champagne poured fifteen minutes before first arrivals

11. Sequence: valet service; security service if needed; two people taking coats, with tickets; toastmaster introduces guest to host while clicking a counter to check numbers arrived

12. Guests file through pink-jacketed waiters on one side, with pink champagne, and white jackets/champagne on the other side

13. The front waiters peel off, replenish and join the line at the back, the other waiters moving forward one

14. Others circulate arrived guests, topping up, "May I freshen your glass, Sir/Madam?" Only change glass if champagne now warm

15. Canapés available, and also distributed with another waiter in tow with clean napkins

16. When most of guests have arrived, assign waiters at the entrance to top up (no tray used), canapé rounds, trash policing, clearing glasses, checking rest rooms. Ensure all areas of the grounds are covered if guests outside

17. Bar tenders give away no unopened bottle

18. Chill more bottles if needed, twenty minutes upside down in ice water is the fastest way

19. If guests request non-champagne drinks, then waiter ascertains where guest will be and brings drink to them

20. As guests leave, decrease number of bottles being opened, and toward end, your authorization is needed to open any more (to prevent waste of partially used bottles of champagne)

21. If an (urgent) call comes through for a guest, track him or her down in a low-key manner—no tannoy/PA system announcements!

22. Rotate staff for breaks as needed

23. Ensure clean up and set-down rapidly and smoothly done

24. Ensure return of glasses, trays and china

25. Staff thanked and paid upon return of uniforms

26. If the event continues into the night, give a couple of trusted staff a bonus, taxi fare home, some nice food and drink and extra time off, and have them stay overnight to make the place spotless by the morning

27. Secure left-over champagne and return, or keep if good quality

28. Extra food given to staff to consume there and then

29. Send checks to staff agency and caterer, with letters of thanks and/or recommendation

Theater-supper Party
(Use in conjunction with checklists 7E, F and G)

1. Briefing from hosting guest to include:
   - Guests by name
   - Date (possibly subject to any VIP's availability)
   - Theater and performance
   - Menu, including drinks (motif'd on the play?)
   - Intermission drinks

2. Invitations printed and sent out

3. Purchase tickets, programs, souvenir brochures; find out about the schedule. (If guests not able to be seated together, purchase in twos at least and let hosting guest allocate seating.)

4. In the event that tickets have been sold out, contact concierges, ticket agencies and touts and pay over the odds according to your hosting guest's expectation

5. Book limo service as needed *(Appendix 8U)*

6. Alert chef to the required menu

7. Check stock levels of food/drink, and order/purchase as needed

8. Order and have (Belgian) chocolates delivered

9. Phone guests to determine how arriving, special diets, preferred drinks for intermission (unless guest has specified which drinks to provide)

10. Alert chef to any food needed for chauffeurs, limo drivers, and also special diets for guests

11. Have menu copies and place cards printed off for each cover

12. Set up entertainment rooms for chauffeurs

13. Day before play, see the head bartender at the theater, order and pay for drinks, arrange their location, and pay him a tip (if any drink choices are not known, arrange to phone the orders through after asking the guests before dinner)

14. On the day before the event, confirm:
    - Limo
    - Food is in
    - Drinks are in
    - Chocolates are in

15. Using the dinner checklist (*Appendix 7G*), lay the table for the first two courses

16. As needed/required alert the hostess to what she wore last time she went to the theater/opera, and entertained same guests

17. Staff and rooms inspected

18. Limo drivers arrived, briefed on schedule and on confirming arrival and departure at theater by phone; limos numbered if required

19. Tickets in envelopes with guest's name on and their limo number, and placed ready with brochures, programs, chocolates

20. Welcome each guest, take coats

21. Give aperitif, circulate with dinner board giving the seating arrangements and information on their neighbor(s); ask for intermission drink choice if unknown and phone through to head bartender at the theater

22. Ensure dinner starts on time, and keep host informed of the time

23. Serve first two courses

23a. CONDITIONAL: If guests not eating very fast, ask if food is to their liking. If yes, then tactfully alert to deadline

24. Give tickets to host to hand out

25. Give chocolates to the ladies, "Compliments of (hostess)"

26. Give programs and brochures (and tickets, if sitting individually) to the men, "Compliments of (host and hostess)"

27. Remind them of the limo numbers on their envelopes, and to return in same limo

28. Tell the host where the drinks will be placed during the intermission

29. Check (visually or verbally) that they all have their tickets if they do not leave straight away with them

30. When they have gone, air the room, completely clear the table and re-lay for the dessert etc. (seat assignments will be random on their return)

31. On their return (heralded by call from limo drivers), greet them at the front door, take their coats, programs, brochures and remaining chocolates and use their old place cards to identify which items belong to whom. Ask: "Did you enjoy the show, Sir/Madam?"

32. Show them through to their suite, and serve up dessert/wine

33. Meanwhile, pay off limo drivers, ensuring nothing has been left in limos

34. Serve after-dinner coffee, liqueurs

35. On departure (either home if locals or to their suites), ensure guests take their brochures, etc.

APPENDIX 8Q
Checklist for a B-B-Q

1. Go over menu with chef or caterer; based on this, work out food needed, plus 25%

2. Have chef or caterer order food or do so yourself

3. Work out and order drinks, plus 25%

4. Glasses, cutlery and plates ordered

5. Portolets/Portaloos and BBQ gear ordered

6. Supplies in 1-4 above all arrived on time

7. Staff arrived five hours before the event and briefed on schedule, event, menu, drinks, their duties; as well as their food, drink, rest room, shower, changing and uniform arrangements; house out of bounds; tip

8. Have the staff:

    *   Polish cutlery and glasses
    *   Set up tables and chairs
    *   Establish pits
    *   Move food, drinks, ice chests, charcoal, lighters and tools into place, as well as napkins, plates, cutlery, glasses and wet-wipes
    *   Erect signs showing locations
    *   Erect lanterns if night event

9. Staff eat, shower and change into uniforms (chef uniforms for pit attendants) and final inspection done

10. Valet service in place and operating

11. Coats collected and tickets given

12. Butler introduces guests to host on arrival

13. Guests offered any drinks they would care for

14. Canapés served

15. Start cooking; queues will form as smells permeate

16. If any line is overlong, have less busy chefs cook that item and let guests in long lines know about alternative lines

17. Staff circulate in all areas, collecting dirty glasses & dishes, replacing with new; providing drinks as needed; servicing portaloos

18. Ensure clean up done swiftly and smoothly. Pay a couple of staff extra, if late at night, to make everything spotless

19. Staff thanked, tipped, and given leftover food

20. Double-check everything spotless first thing in the morning

21. Agency/caterer sent check and letter of thanks/recommendation

Note: Variations on barbeques can be as exotic as spit roasts, Hawaiian pits and large Paella pans.

Checklist of Items Needed for a B-B-Q

- Grates
- Bricks
- Lighters
- Charcoal
- Tongs
- Spatulas
- Lanterns
- Torches
- Napkins & wet wipes (five per person)
- Very thick cardboard plates (three per person)
- Knives/forks/spoons (three per person)
- Quality plastic glasses (three per person)
- Trash bags
- Chef uniforms
- Portaloos
- Fire blankets and extinguishers (one per pit)
- Tablecloths (three per table)
- Locking tables   (so they do not collapse)
- Chairs
- Balls
- Frisbees
- Boules
- Volleyball and net
- Horseshoes
- Other games:

Checklist for an Outdoor Event, Such as a Picnic

1. Find locations, such as an old barn for a shoot, a pretty place for a picnic; draw clear map on how to get there and distribute copies to different drivers before leaving

1a. Find an alternative location in case of rain or other problems, such as mosquitoes, etc. so the event can continue

2. Obtain phone numbers and addresses/map of doctors, hospital, police, veterinarian, garage, hotel, rest rooms, etc in the area. Contact and ensure open that day

2a. Ensure any necessary permits are obtained, including permission to serve alcohol

3. Use four-wheel drive wagon for supplies; dress appropriately

4. Obtain needed supplies:
    - Foods that are easy to eat and serve
    - Thermos for hot/cold soups and drinks
    - Ice chests and ice for drinks
    - Plates
    - Cutlery
    - Cups
    - Napkins and tablecloths
    - Seats and tables
    - Cheese board
    - Trash bags
    - First aid kit, fire extinguisher
    - Primus stove and pan
    - Golf umbrellas
    - Change of clothes and towels
    - Wet wipes, kitchen rolls
    - Portable phone
    - Games for picnic (balls, volleyball, frisbee, etc.)
    - Hampers (individual ones for kids maybe)
    - Bug and bear sprays
    - Plastic sheeting, blankets

5. Precede party to the location and set up

6. Serve everyone with drinks to start

7. Give everyone plate and cutlery wrapped in a napkin

   Note: For a shoot, use butler service; for a picnic, buffet service would be more appropriate

9. After meal, collect utensils (check they're all there, if valuable)

10. Collect up trash (one bag for paper, one for food)

11. At home, unload, wash and store everything

12. For a shoot:
    - Prepare drying room for wet/muddy clothes
    - Clean clothes and boots
    - Ensure guests have their pheasant brace (male and female) wrapped in newspaper before leaving
    - Do not serve same food type for dinner as the items shot, unless specifically requested

13. If it rains, cover food with plastic sheets while family takes shelter. If it thunders, move everyone into cars straight away

Christmas

PREPARATIONS
BETWEEN JULY AND SEPTEMBER

1. In July, contact guest and determine what he/she needs and wants:
   - Number of family, guests, how long to stay? (And secondary list of guests to cover any no-shows)?
   - Travel/pick up for family/guests, who to pay?
   - Meals where?
   - Timetable of events?
   - Presents to be bought, for whom and what (refer to earlier gifts bought)?
   - Payment arrangements

2. Xmas tree, decorations, Father Xmas, Magician, disco, dance, other?

3. Printing of invites, special Xmas cards, Thank you cards, menus, schedule of events, local events?
   - Commissioning of special presents?
   - What gifts in room, stocking gifts?
   - Special themes, i.e. staff in seasonal costume?

4. Book as needed:
   - Restaurants
   - Theater, concert
   - Flights
   - Limos
   - Temp agencies for waiters, extra valets/maids/drivers
   - Father Christmas, other uniforms/costumes
   - Conjuror/magician
   - Marquee in hot climates
   - Disco/cabaret/band
   - Caterers

5. Draw up checklists for staff use

6. Hold meeting with chef and housekeeper; brief them and give them their checklists; adjust checklists according to their input

7. At the next weekly staff meeting, brief the staff on Xmas plans and schedule (and bonus!).

8. If any staff really cannot make it, cover with agency staff/contacts you have

9. Determine and arrange any special transportation/accommodation needed for staff, and iron out any further problems or objections, enlisting their superiors or those they look up to, for assistance in resolving

10. Chef to propose menus for whole period, including staff meals

11. Guest's approval obtained

BEGINNING OF SEPTEMBER

12. Order, or ensure those responsible have ordered::
    - Food
    - Wine
    - Non-alcoholic drinks
    - Spirits
    - Dry goods
    - Specially commissioned works
    - Flowers (call florist in to advise)
    - Printing job
    - Videos
    - Confectionery
    - Xmas tree
    - Christmas crackers

BY OCTOBER

13. Purchase:
    - Decorations for trees, rooms, outside house
    - Wrapping paper, ribbon, bows, tape, tags
    - Games to play
    - Presents (or arrange purchase of) according to the guest's wishes

BY NOVEMBER

14. Send invitations to guests at the beginning of the month

15. Check all suites and ensure any needed upgrades/re-decorations are done

16. Investigate Church, community, cultural activities, listing out on a schedule basis, with details and addresses
    - Add to proposed schedule of events for Xmas
    - Obtain guest's approval, make necessary reservations
    - Have schedule printed

17. Ensure Maintenance has serviced refrigerator, freezer, extractor fan, all electrical, gas and fire appliances

18. Confirm all orders and bookings and handle any problems

19. Contact all guests who have not yet responded, confirming arrival and departure times, special diets, and needs

20. In the event of any guests unable to come, confer with guest and contact the secondary guest list as needed

PRE-CHRISTMAS

21. Decorate tree

22. Ensure arrival of:
    - Drinks
    - Food
    - Flowers
    - Printed menus, schedule, etc.
    - Presents
    - Tickets, etc.
    - Dry goods
    - Costumes
    - Confectionery
    - Decorations
    - Videos

23. Presents put under tree, stuffed into stockings

CHRISTMAS EVE

27. Guests arrive, unpacking done, toured as necessary.

28. Put on a buffet dinner as most convenient for guests arriving at different times

29. Put out Christmas stockings

30. Set-up breakfast, tea and lunchrooms (prepared and cleaned)

CHRISTMAS DAY

31. Give staff a very good breakfast before nine in the morning

32. Do the usual morning teas, etc, with some Christmas twist

33. Breakfast is a leisurely affair, with a very wide selection. During the meal, show the guests the lunch menu, and take note of any special requests, letting chef know of them as soon as possible.

34. Father Xmas then comes in, presents are distributed and unwrapped.

35. The guests go their different ways: take walks, play, Church, etc., and are offered refreshments when they appear at random

36. While the breakfast room and tables are cleared and laid for tea, the lunchroom is laid for lunch

37. Half an hour before lunch, punch is served hot, with a fruit punch for the children

38. At lunch, serve the wine first, and accept yourself, if pressed. Lunch is also a very leisurely paced meal

39. When the bird or roast is ready for the main course, dim the lights and have the chef present it to the host, hostess and guests, and then carve it after letting the hosting guest do the initial carving

40. Warm the (good quality) Brandy, pour it over the Christmas pudding and bring it in ceremoniously, all a-fire

41. Staff do their performance

42. Serve mince pies, cream, port, brandy, cigars and nuts

43. Washing up/clearing of tables done on all-hands basis, and lunchroom set up for dinner buffet while guests go for walks, etc.

44. Very informal tea served, buffet style at 4.30 p.m., then cleared away

45. Dinner buffet set up (no leftovers, please), with first course at both ends so no bottleneck. Chef stands by to carve. Ensure plates and cutlery are swiftly cleared when anyone goes up for more/new course

46. Bring out the cold/iced puddings once main course is wrapped up and place them on empty buffet table

47. Announce that coffee will be served at the table

48. Once all guests have gone, clear and clean suite and prepare for next day

49. Ensure thank-you cards are sent on behalf of the guest for presents received

APPENDIX 8U
Checklist For Hiring Limousine Service

1. Contact limousine companies in your area and arrange a visit. _____

3. Check their offices, the vehicles, the drivers and dispatchers, and determine if they are well-organized, well groomed/ uniformed and professional in demeanor. _____

    Verify that
    - Their resources are adequate _____
    - All drivers are insured and properly trained and licensed _____
    - They have cell phones for communication between house and car _____
    - Procedure they follow; ensure it aligns with guests' needs _____
    - Total cost, without hidden extras _____
    - Negotiate discount without reducing service _____

3. Narrow down the best three limo companies and enter them into your butler's book _____

4. When a limo service is needed, contact your chosen limo companies and book the one that is available. _____

5. Fax an agreement and once agreed upon, send original and any needed advance _____

6. The day before the event, ensure the drivers will be in place one hour before event _____

7. When drivers arrive, review their instructions for the day/night/trip, give them your cell phone number and tell them to call you at significant points in the trip (i.e. when they reach the destination, or if they need any assistance). Write down their cell phone number. _____

7. At the same time, confirm their appearance and attitude and correct on the spot or ask for a replacement _____

9. If the driver is picking up someone and you will not see them, then do step 7 above at the same time as step 8 _____

10. When the limo driver has completed the trip, check with the person being driven how the trip was. Pick up and resolve any problems so they are happy. _____

11. Ensure nothing has been left in the limo and then tip the driver _____

12. If the guest was mistreated or unhappy, take it up with the limo company (or the driver, if minor). _____

13. Build a file of reliable drivers and ask for them when ordering service, or keep them in mind if you need to hire a chauffeur _____

14. Send check and letter of thanks/recommendation to the company _____

Spa Guest Pre-Arrival Interview

In asking these questions, you may need to delve by asking additional questions if the guest brushes off the questions or is hesitant about answering. It is best to ask these questions at the end of the standard question interview, as the person should be in smooth communication with you. If it is obvious the person is not in a calm and safe environment to talk about personal issues, then make an appointment to call back.

1. "Have you been to a spa before?"

2. "What did you like about that experience?"

3. "Was there anything you disliked about that experience?"

4. "Do you have a goal for your visit with us?"

5. (If not already stated) "What changes, if any, are you hoping to make?"

6. "Are there any specific spa services that you would like to undergo?"

7. (If not already answered) "Is there any specific spa methodology that you achieved results with before and would like to repeat?"

8. "Do you have any allergies or medical conditions we should know about?"

9. "Are you following any particular nutritional plan?"

10. "Would you like to follow any such plan while staying with us?"

11. "Do you have a specific spa specialist you would like to be serviced by?"

12. "How can we support you in achieving your spa goal?"

13. "Are there any specific resources you need in order to make this experience work for you?"

14. "Would you like to be in contact with anyone during your stay about your spa experience?"

15. "Will anyone be traveling with you?"

16. "Should I contact them about a spa visit?"

By the end of the interview, the butler should know what type of spa guest the interviewee is.

APPENDIX 9B
Spa Guest Room Set-up

1. Has the suite been refreshed by opening the windows if clean air exist outside, or by smudging or spraying aroma mists? _____

2. Are natural elements present in the guest suite, such as plants and waterfalls? _____

3. Is relaxing and pleasant music playing in the suite? _____

4. Are beeswax or soy candles ready and available to be lit? _____

5. Are healthy living magazines or literature available for guests? _____

6. Are the foods offered natural and/or organic, and water or herbal teas provided? _____

7. Have the phone ringers been adjusted to their lowest audible volume?_____

8. Is the light in the space soft yet adequate? _____

9. Have harsh corners been camouflaged? _____

10. Is the furniture comfortably inviting? _____

11. Are the sheets and linens fresh, clean, and soft? _____

12. Are the robes, towels, & linen fresh and soft? _____

13. Are robes, towels, & linen displayed in an inviting way for the guest? _____

14. Is the footwear the right size and comfortable for the guest? _____

15. Are the amenities offered and presented in a beautiful way? _____

16. Are ceilings pleasantly engaging for a guest to view? _____

17. Are safety instructions clearly stated for in-room sauna or steam? _____

18. Is a digital thermometer present in the bathroom for therapeutic baths?_____

19. Is floor space available for an exercise mat for such as Pilates? _____

20. Overall, does the guest suite portray peacefulness? _____

Bath Choices Questionnaire

Time:_____ A.M._____ P.M._____

Bath types:

Rose petal _____

Lavender _____

Milk _____

Milk and honey_____

Mint _____

Hibiscus_____

Citrus_____

Mineral bath_____

All baths include appropriate relaxation music, candles, warm towels, warm robe, warm slippers, and one of the following beverages:

Red wine_____

White wine_____

Champagne_____

Chamomile tea_____

Warm milk_____

Evian_____

Other _____

Hydrotherapy Treatments

These supplement spa treatments and can be expected to produce immediate results for the conditions being addressed.

CONDITIONS	TUB TREATMENT EFFECTS	NUMBER OF TREATMENTS & FREQUENCY	PRODUCTS USED IN TUB
Cellulite	Breaks down toxins	6-12 Twice weekly	4T (tablespoons) algae powder (seaweed that assist in detoxification) 20 drops of drainage essential oil
Water retention	Eliminates excess fluid	6-12 Twice weekly	4T algae powder 20 drops of detox essential oil
Lack of skin tone	Tones and firms	4-6 Twice weekly	6T algae powder 10 drops each of detox & serenity essential oils
Dehydration	Re-mineralizes cells	2-4 Twice weekly	6T algae powder 10 drops each of hydrating & serenity essential oils
Anxiety	Soothes calms	As needed or once a week	4T algae powder 10 drops each of anti-stress and serenity essential oils
Sports injury	Reduces inflammation and swelling	As needed or once a week	4T algae powder 10 drops each of serenity & deep-heat essential oils

Lack of energy	Invigorates and awakens	As needed or once a week	6T algae powder 10 drops of vital energizing essential oil
Thick ankles	Eliminates fluid retention stored in tissue	2-4 Twice weekly	4T algae powder 20 drops of detox essential oil
Sleeplessness	Soothes & calms	As needed or once a week	6T algae powder 10 drops each of serenity & anti-stress essential oils

Spa Treatment Shower Instructions

Name	Temperature and Duration	Drying	Effect
Cleansing	Begin at 100°F. Gradually raise temp. to tolerance, 110-115°F. Hold 2 Minutes. Cool rapidly to 90-85°F	Friction with towel, fan with sheet.	Cleansing preparation
Refreshing	Begin at 100°F. Quickly raise temp. to tolerance, 110-115°F. Maintain 1-3 minutes. Gradually lower to 100°F Maintain for 3 minutes. Then lower to 94°F. Client should not feel cold.	Dry with some friction. Guest should be in a state of heat conservation.	Cooling, not tonic or stimulating. Should not feel cold at any time.
Tonic Pick-up	Begin 100°F. Hot phase—110-115°F, 1 minute. Cold phase—97 or lower, 1 minute. Three cycles. End neutral.	Dry with friction. Vascular exercise	Vigorous tonic
Sedative Relaxing	Begin at 100-102°. Drop steadily to 97-94°F. Hold 3-5 Minutes.	Dry without friction or fanning.	Sedative Relaxing

Tools of the Trade for the Twenty-first Century Butler

- Pantry
- Computer, with laser printer with graphics
- Software for calendar, book keeping, word processing, data base and rolodex functions
- PDA and cell phone with computer hook-up capability
- Digital camera
- Fax machine
- Xerox machine
- Large safe
- Table board for table settings
- Petty Cash Disbursement Vouchers
- Furniture polish & brushes
- Hogs hair bristle brushes for different ceramics/metals
- Pony hair fitch for gilded items
- Plate brush for silver
- Cotton and plastic gloves
- White gloves for serving
- Goddard's silver dip; Long Term Impregnated cloth; Long Term Silver polish.
- Hygrometer
- Thermometer
- Acid free tissue paper
- Superonic-N or other silver dip
- Brown wrapping paper
- Envelopes, large & small
- Letterhead
- Gift wrapping paper, matching tags, ribbons & bows
- Office supplies

- Boxes for presents and also cakes, chocolates, etc.
- Small tool kit

See also the clothes checklist, Appendix 6

WHAT A BUTLER CARRIES ON HIS/HER PERSON

- Personal Digital Assistant
- Cell phone
- Several pens
- Note pad
- Paper handkerchiefs
- Keys
- Butler's friend
- Coins and bills
- Credit card
- Phone cards
- Cigar cutter/gas-lighter combo
- Small digital camera (can be part of a PDA or a pen)
- A portable translator (if dealing with foreign speaking guests)

APPENDIX 11B
Outline of Actions for Assuming a New Position

The following sequence of actions followed will enable you to discover the hotel structure and insert yourself successfully into the team. As may be clear by now, it is vitally important that you compile a written record of the information unearthed in doing these steps, adding them to the Butler's Book, so that the information is not just verbally stated and then almost immediately lost. The profession has suffered in the past from a lack of written materials at all levels — whether in the form of textbooks or written records. The result has been non-uniformity and lost technology, both of which have conspired to undermine the profession. By keeping records, you will make it easier not only for yourself, but also for your successor.

1. Introduce yourself to each of the staff, let them know about your title, duties, and roughly what you might need from them to carry out your duties. Find out what they need from you to carry out their duties. Make sure they understand what you have said, and feel fine about your being there _____

2. Find out the existing service standards and policies for the hotel.   _____

3. Find out the preferences and likes/dislikes of key guests:

    *   food   _____
    *   drink   _____
    *   entertainment   _____
    *   manners   _____
    *   forms of address   _____
    *   customs and observations   _____
    *   taboos

4. Determine any already existing schedules, programs and plans for the year ahead and start to work on those still valid   _____

5. Contact each supplier/service person, and let him/her know of your duties. Let them know what you need from them. Make sure they are happy and provide them with anything they might need from you to do their jobs properly   _____

6. Work hard to provide each guest, employee and supplier with what they need from you   _____

7. Have them provide you with what you need from them to do your job   _____

8. Purchase needed items per *Appendix 11A* ____

9. Review this book for ideas on what else can be implemented to improve service to your guests ____

The following would be done by the head butler:

10. Inspect the security situation at the hotel and bring any weaknesses to your senior's attention for broaching with security. ____

11. Do the same for matters of hygiene ____

12. Do the same for fire safety and first aid ____

13. Hire more staff if below complement ____

14. Work to improve staff issues such as morale, health, discipline and ethics, understanding of their jobs ____

15. Improve administrative matters, such as computerizing the accounts (with a view to streamlining paperwork, rather than increasing it) ____

16. Complete an inventory; make sure that all valuables are insured ____

17. Inspect and submit a program to upgrade the butler area ____

Addendum

The following supplementary articles (and one speech) were published (or delivered) in various industry magazines and newsletters.

THIN RED LINE OR RED INK?
DETERRING TERRORISM

The likelihood that any single hotel will be the target of a terrorist act is very small indeed, given the number of hotels in the world. The risks increase with the size of the hotel, its location, it being a trophy building or the destination of guests whose views are antipathetic to those of any of a variety of terrorist groups. Or perhaps the fact that it is an easy, soft target and offers a way of doing what terrorists do best: destroy buildings and lives, undermine the peace of mind and economies of whole nations. So how safe does that make any hotel?

While the hospitality industry is experiencing lower occupancy rates since that pivotal day in September 2001, it is at the same time being forced into spending money on higher insurance premiums and/or greater security measures. Perhaps not vast sums of money in the overall scheme of things, but certainly insurance rates doubling in three years is at odds with the need to reduce expenses. The JW Marriott in Jakarta didn't hesitate to do the right thing, however, instituting more stringent security procedures and so saving the day. Not the lives of some of its security personnel, but certainly of the majority of its guests and the integrity of the building itself, which was structurally intact after the car bomb exploded on that day in August 2003.

In August 2004, the hotels on the Strip in Las Vegas (including 18 of the 20 largest hotels in the world) were accused of withholding from the general public the fact that Al Queda low-lifes had been "casing the joint." There was concern reportedly that a public warning might hurt tourism or increase legal liabilities. The casino hotels apparently did increase what was already arguably the tightest security in the industry, but their experience and systems were designed for criminals, not terrorists. One thing is certain, their approach resulted in a PR flap that did little to enhance their image. The fact that these hotels also handed over names and other information on quarter of a million guests to the FBI over the New Year's Eve celebrations 2003/2004 may not have endeared them to those and future guests, either. Dealing with the threat of terrorism isn't easy and was certainly not covered in any great depth during any hospitality training for American hoteliers.

For a look at effective anti-terrorist measures in the hospitality industry, Sea Island provides a better example during the G8 summit in June 2004. A tour-de-force in terms of electronic gadgetry and armed security forces, it was the government not the hotel that drove (and paid for) that security event. Nice if you can get it, but hardly within the budget of any hotel, and certainly the

253

siege mentality was not conducive to the ambiance that generally draws guests to hotels.

So where does this leave hotels? Certainly, terrorists do not make it easy, presenting the prospect of any of a number of ways of creating their effects via an unknown individual at an unknown time. As the homeland security advisor to the governor of Nevada is reported to have said, "We have so little information. We pray a lot." Not to argue with the power of prayer, but a concrete plan would probably sit better with guests, insurers, owners, and employees alike.

Fear is a third-rate motivator employed by weak individuals, so perhaps a better approach to this whole subject of combating terrorism is to view it as a challenge to our intelligence and resourcefulness. Our purpose as an industry is to provide comfort and pleasure to our fellow man and woman. Maybe our goal in providing adequate security, then, should be the retaining of our freedoms and joys, not the fighting of psychotic individuals or the purveying of fear. This may seem like an extraneous piece of philosophy, but any lesser goal on our part lets the terrorists set the rules, makes us play their miserable game.

What's the Problem?

Perhaps the first point to establish is, what is one protecting against? Ill-intended individuals or groups coming onto the grounds and into the premises in any of a variety of ways: by stealth as overnight guests, day guests, guests of guests, convention attendees, vendors and service personnel, employees, ex-employees, on business (whether as reporters, law enforcement, or any number of guises); or by brute force as a swarm of invaders or behind the wheel of a truck or car—the favored method of the terrorist. And what is one concerned they may do once they have access? The most obvious is use explosives, or weaponry. Then there is the possibility that they may use biological or chemical weapons.

How would these elements be brought into the hotel space? By people on their person, in their luggage or vehicles, or via packages delivered. The next question then is, how does one ascertain that these routes are clear of threat without a) invading privacy and upsetting guests, b) inordinate expense, c) creating a siege mentality and ruining the ambiance, d) delaying guests or tying up employees with added tasks.

The task for security then is to monitor these routes for these harmful elements in a way that is not only effective, but does not interrupt the flow of guests arriving and deliveries being made, and which maintains the ambiance of the hotel. If we were being real smart, we'd find a way to turn the need for security to advantage for guests, possibly even making it fun.

What's the solution?

Let's consider a possible ideal scenario based on existing resources in the market and industry. When guests arrive, their vehicle drives over a simple wireless camera system with infrared capability that beams the license plate and picture of the driver to the security office, while also surveying the undercarriage for bombs attached. The guests disembark at a slight remove from the hotel structure, where bollards have been placed to prevent vehicular access, and are given their favorite beverage served on a tray. They walk through a metal detector at the front entrance (or even part of it) without even noticing it, and through a detector that can sense explosives carried in the plume of hot air that wafts upward naturally from their warm bodies. Their bags are removed from their trunk and the seats of the vehicle and carried up to their room via a scanning machine such as is seen in airports, as well as one that detects the possible presence of biological or chemical weapons or explosives. The valet then inspects the trunk and under the hood before parking the vehicle. Those dealing with the guests are trained to look unobtrusively for tell-tale signs of explosive belts, shifty guests, etc.

Impact on guests? Improved service. Impact on hotels? Slightly larger payroll with more personnel hired to cover valet parking and bellhop, and a better rating for security and service. A bite out of the budget initially for the detection equipment.

What about the employees and ex-employees? Set up parking away from the hotel and institute an ID card that has to be scanned, together with the employee's face, before entry to the grounds/hotel is authorized. These scans are recorded and transmitted in real time wirelessly to the security office.

And tradespeople? Set up a similar procedure that requires their vehicle undercarriage be scanned as covered above at a distance from the hotel, and then a security employee inspects the cargo container (again, this can be done using a camera system with infra red and wireless capability, so unlit areas can be viewed at a command center removed from the truck being inspected). And only then have the driver bring the vehicle to the hotel building, where he or she can be asked to scan his driving license into a machine that snaps a photo of his face and sends both images to a command center. Invaluable for determining that any unexpected or unusual driver is legitimately at the location on behalf of the company he claims to represent.

Looking for Eyes and Ears

When the terrorist alert was raised in Las Vegas, taxi cab drivers were given photographs of wanted terrorists. That was a good idea and capitalizes on the basic truth about all law enforcement: the police cannot possibly maintain the law without the cooperation of the populace. Which means they rely on the general public's eyes and ears to be law enforcement's eyes and ears.

255

So why not take this one step further? Let guests and employees be kept up to speed on law enforcement needs, as well as public service announcements? Similar to the reality TV shows that highlight *America's Most Wanted* and *Unsolved Mysteries*. Imagine then a TV screen embedded in a piece of equipment positioned strategically in a hotel lobby or staff entrance, that shows terrorists and felons, provides Amber Alerts, the latest updates from Homeland Security, and when those are not being broadcast, which shows PSAs (such as hurricane alerts) or ads. Ads, incidentally, which can pay for the equipment. How about if that piece of equipment also provides two-way intelligence? If it took images of people coming and going and relayed these wirelessly to a security office. They could check these against data bases, especially where an individual behaved suspiciously (such as hiding his face and walking away rapidly) when he noticed the images on the screen.

How about a similar machine that was also a cell phone charger, and which a guest could also stand in front of, call a family member who would log onto a Web site and then be able to see the person calling on his cell phone from the hotel lobby (or convention space)?

This kind of wireless, 2-way intelligence equipment is coming onto the market now, driven by the need to use technology to respond to the threat of terrorism at home. This equipment goes beyond the old security cliché of stringing wires to multiple cameras and hoping to catch someone in the act.

The common denominator of these solutions is an intelligent use of technology to ferret out not just terrorists but also criminals. The smarter rationale, however, is one that preempts or discourages anything destructive from occurring by being more overt or obvious. What self-respecting criminal or terrorist would walk into an environment in which his physiognomy was likely to be flashed in a hotel lobby or staff canteen, or snapped in real time and compared within seconds to a data base which he has the misfortune to be featured in? In other words, the real desired product is incident-free days, more than thwarted terrorists. The intelligent approach also solicits the cooperation of guests and employees alike, not because they are frightened, but because they are informed and even pampered a bit.

It takes surprisingly little green in the long term to build a thin red line around a hotel when one goes beyond the idea of snooping cameras, bollards and personnel as the weapons available. It is certainly better than drowning in red ink because guests are sufficiently unimpressed with antiquated or invisible security systems to look for safer ports of call—or because terrorists perceive a soft target in their sights.

September 2004

BUTLER'S PROFESSIONAL CODE OF ETHICS

INTEGRITY
Always act in the best interest of your employer. Placing their interest above your own, perform and maintain the highest level of professional standards in all relationships and duties.

CONFIDENTIALITY
Keep all confidences regarding employer, guests, and other employees.

SERVICE
Serve the guest as the guest chooses to be served.

LAWFUL BEHAVIOR
Be knowledgeable of and ensure compliance with all applicable local and national laws. Abide by the highest ethical, moral and legal standards.

DEDICATION
Perform your duties diligently, impartially and responsively, to the best of your ability. Activities outside working hours must not diminish confidence in you or your ability to perform your duties.

PERSONAL DEVELOPMENT
Endeavor to improve and enhance both personally and professionally. Strive to increase your service knowledge and improve your skills through training, study and the sharing of information and experiences with your peers.

RESPECT
Work towards achieving a strong foundation of mutual respect between the employer and other employees. Educate and instill a healthy respect for all persons and property associated with the employer and guests.

PROFESSIONAL RELATIONSHIP
Strive to maintain appropriate relationships and boundaries in all aspects of service. Avoid discrimination based on age, disability, gender, sexual orientation, race, national origin or family politics.

PROMOTION
Commit to the promotion of superlative service, through personal and professional example, mentoring, establishing industry standards, and consistent, active involvement.

Summer 2001

THE INDOMITABLE BRITISH BUTLER

Unabridged text of a speech delivered at "Restoring the Art" Conference hosted by Starkey International in Denver, Colorado, USA, on March 9-11, 2001

Thank you very much for your vote of confidence. I'll take this applause as an advanced payment and hope that I may do it justice in the next hour. I plan for our time together to err on the side of pleasurable and if I fail in this mission, feel free to walk out. I, for one, would lose too much sleep knowing that anyone here had dislocated his or her jaw executing an overly ambitious yawn.

If I happen to use a word or say something that you cannot decipher, either because I mumbled or someone coughed or my accent was intolerably un-American, please feel free to wave a hand so I can clarify my meaning. It is important that you track with me at all times, otherwise we'll drift apart and you will not be saying anything polite or even printable about me when you leave.

Mrs. Starkey, a wonderful lady, has asked me to talk to you about that strange noun and verb, "butling," British style. She suggested that I read from my book, *The British Butler's Bible*, and while that is terribly flattering, I have a better idea—that you'd be better off getting you money's worth when you purchase the book (which Mary also suggested that I encourage you to do), because then the information would be pristine to you, and not second hand.

And my message, Archduke, ladies and gentlemen, is quite simple. I'll leave it to you to determine what it is, and perhaps you can do me the courtesy of clarifying for me at the end of our time together, what that message might be.

What is a British butler? "Officially," and I quote from *The British Butler's Bible* here, because I couldn't have put it better myself, "according to dictionary consensus, the Butler is "a male servant and head of the household." The Oxford English Dictionary breathes some life into the word with the tidbit that two thousand years ago, "buticula" meant "bottle" to a Roman.

Presumably, after enough bacchanalian orgies, the bottle became synonymous with the person bringing it around to the average reveler; and even though the word evolved from Latin, through French and into its current English form of "Butler," the idea has remained essentially the same: a Butler is a person who caters to the needs and pleasures of the wealthy.

Let us flesh out this definition, however, to arrive at a more complete understanding of the "British butler."

To understand any fact at all, it is necessary to compare it to a datum of comparable magnitude. It would be hard for an aborigine of 17th century Australia, for instance, to understand a car in the absence of a datum of comparable magnitude, such as, let us say, a series of pictographs showing a canoe on wheels that paddles itself much faster than a kangaroo can bound. With this understanding, rather than view this new wonder as some embodiment of an evil spirit, the Aborigine might be more inclined to venerate it in the same way that most Americans do, today.

Similarly, let us draw upon Mrs. Starkey's technology to review a Day in the Life of a butler in the average 12th century castle in England, just after the arrival of William the Conk, as he may have been known by those whom he conquered in 1066. For this window overlooking our past, I am indebted to Joseph and Francis Gies, authors of *Medieval Life in a Medieval Castle*, published by Harper & Row. Personal service, obviously, is not a recent phenomenon, so let's immerse ourselves in the roots and see where doing so takes us.

During the Middle Ages in England, most domestic staff were men, usually themselves of "gentle" birth, working for the nobility as part of their training for court and other activities. As a note, for those who may be wondering, the only women who worked in households were washerwomen, nurses, and "gentlewomen" who waited on the ladies of the castle. The Butler worked under the direction of the steward and was basically responsible for the care and serving of wines. The steward, whom we would now call a Butler Administrator or Household Manager, supervised the domestic affairs of his master's castle, such as the service at the table, directing the staff and managing the finances.

The wine was mostly imported from Bordeaux, which the English ruled at the time. In the absence of any effective technique for stoppering containers, the wine would not keep beyond a year and so had to be drunk young. Vintage, therefore, was not an issue, and the idea of inhaling the bouquet and savoring the taste was still several hundred years away, as Peter of Blois notes in a letter describing the serving of wine one day at Henry II's court:

> "The wine is turned sour and moldy—thick, greasy, stale, flat and smacking of pitch. I have sometimes seen even great lords

served with wine so muddy that a man must needs close his eyes and clench his teeth, wry-mouthed and shuddering, and filtering the stuff rather than drinking."

This challenge to his professionalism notwithstanding, the butler would receive wine in barrels and decant it into jugs. Some he would spice and sweeten for the final course.

Local brews made from barley, wheat, and/or oats by an alewife, were drunk mainly by the servants and were not the domain of the butler. Part of the reason brewing was left to women was the view held at the time that beer was as much a food as a drink. Perhaps the reason the nobles suffered the wine is because, as the noted authority, Peter of Blois, again describes, "the ale is horrid to the taste and abominable to the sight."

With the most important guests at the high table, the loftiest place reserved for an ecclesiastical dignitary, the second for the ranking layman, a procession of servants would enter after Grace had been said. First came the pantler with the bread and butter, followed by the butler and his assistants with the wine, and beer for those who desired.

Guests were served at dinner with two meats and two lighter dishes. Between courses, the steward would send the servers into the kitchen and see to it that they brought in the meats quietly and without confusion.

Ceremony marked the service at table. There was a correct way to do everything, from the laying of cloths to the cutting of trenchers and carving of meat. A trencher, by the way, is a wooden platter for the serving of food and meat. Part of a squire's training included learning how to serve his lord at meals: the order in which dishes should be presented, for instance, where they should be placed, how many fingers to use in holding the joint for the lord to carve, and how to place trenchers on the table. Not too far a cry from table etiquette today, I think.

The solid parts of soups and stews were eaten with a spoon, the broth sipped. Meat was cut up with the knife and eaten with the fingers. Two persons shared a dish, the lesser helping the more important, the younger the older, the man the woman. The former in each case breaking the bread, cutting the meat, and passing the cup.

Etiquette books admonished diners not to leave the spoon in the dish or put elbows on the table, not to belch, not to drink or eat with their mouths full, not to stuff their mouths or take overly large helpings. Not surprisingly, in light of the finger-eating and dish-sharing, stress was laid on keeping hands and nails scrupulously clean, wiping spoon and knife after use—forks were not used at that time—wiping the mouth before drinking, and not dipping meat in the salt dish. Contrary to legend, Medieval man loved baths and took them regularly in what were called "stews" — large tubs filled with hot water in which one stewed for a while. Hard soaps had just appeared from Spain, luxury articles made of olive oil, soda, lime, and aromatic herbs (hence the modern Castile soap). These replaced the soaps made in the manorial workshops out of mutton fat, wood ash and natural soda, and were greatly appreciated by the butlers of the time.

While butlers could be counted upon, then, not to be too recognizable by their musk, they could be considered hirsute for the very good reason that shaving was difficult, painful, and infrequent. The soap didn't lather and the razors were nothing more than small carving knives, often old and dull.

Haircutting scissors were similar to grass-trimming shears and pulled mightily. As for halitosis, it was another century before even the lord and lady of the manor had access to tooth brushes. The butler had to make do with rubbing his teeth with a green hazel twig and wiping with a woolen cloth.

Does this trip back down the butler's genealogical tree help us appreciate his roots? Possibly not, although I am sure our appreciation, for everything from proper-stopping techniques at vineyards to toothbrushes aplenty on supermarket shelves today, has grown immeasurably.

However, like the dusty vats of malmsey (a sweet wine) that he so lovingly looked after in the cobwebbed cellar, the Butler has matured over the centuries into a richer, rarer and more complex figure in the household.

As the middleclass took to hiring more staff during the industrial revolution —did you know that the lower rung of the middle class was redefined in London to include anyone who could afford only three servants— and as downsizing impacted the large English household in the 20th century, the Steward and his duties were gradually assumed by the butler, who became, as the Oxford dictionary so correctly states today, the head of the servant household. Let us leave England and discover what the American butler was engaged in after the country was granted its independence by dear, mad, King George.

A Mr. Roberts laid down the vital points a butler should know in his *The House Servant's Directory of 1827:*

· The benefit of early rising
· Trimming & cleaning lamps
· Setting up the candles
· Regulations for the pantry
· Regulations for the dinner table
· Setting out the dinner table
· Waiting on dinner

261

·Extinguishing lamps and shutting up the house
And lastly,
·Address & behavior to employers

As we can see, the butlers skill-set had extended in America to the candles as well as the pantry. And what is his skill-set today, now that we rarely use candles and few architectural plans include a pantry? I am reminded in this, by the way, of the story of the wealthy English landowner who, upon checking employee records, called a longtime employee into his study.

"Peter," asked the landowner, "how long have you been with us now?"

(*Devonshire accent*) "Arlmowst tweni foive yeer," replied the employee, at which his employer frowned.

"According to these records, you were hired to take care of the stables," the landowner pointed out.

"Thart's c'rrect, Sur," responded the veteran employee.

"But we haven't owned horses for over 20 years," declared the landowner.

"Roit, Sur," replied the old retainer. "Whart werd yer loik mee tu do next?"

I know of no butlers at this time who can boast such a relaxed work schedule, but before we look at Butling as she is did today, let's anticipate the household environment we can look forward to enjoying in the very near future.

As a writer, I have the opportunity of conducting interviews with highly interesting and diverse groups of people, and one particular group I have had the fortune of hobnobbing with is that ethereal, forward-looking minority of beings whom we call, for want of a better moniker, Futurists.

They do not have to go too far out on a limb to draw bizarre-to-our-ears scenarios, because science and technology are advancing at such a rapid pace that we no longer have to wait a lifetime, for the Dick Tracey, two-way audio-visual monitor-on-a-wristwatch to become a reality. We are only a few years away from the growth of computers—not in terms of growth in production or capacity, which we already enjoy, but in terms of computers existing at the cellular level, being grown in Petrie dishes.

So when I tell you that we can look forward to domestic help in the form of R2D2s, you may well say, "Oh, we've been hearing about that since the 1920s." And I won't deny it.

But you may like to know that one Dutch supermarket chain already has robot cleaners in service, machines called Sinas and built by Siemens. Nicknamed Schrobbie, the robots carefully navigate around obstacles and, if an obstacle happens to be a human, will politely ask them to step aside with the words, which I translate into English for the benefit of those present, *(robovoice)* "Excuse me, I'd like to clean here." It's not bad for a robot. Of course, a real maid would know not to disturb guests with her chores—in fact, she would have been let go without references two centuries ago—but this is a restriction that robots no doubt would find most illogical. Now you may laugh, but when Schrobbie isn't scrubbing and vacuuming, he (or she) is distributing mail, conducting inspection rounds, and transporting passengers and goods. If you think change over the last five years has been rapid, better not blink during the next five.

Sony corporation has already built a 10-pound human robot that can kick a soccer ball, walk, wave, and dance. Within a few years, the company expects this robot to perform household tasks. Honda wants to give it voice-recognition capability and the ability to identify faces—with a master plan of assigning them to Honda car showrooms to help salespeople. Obviously, Japanese car salespeople are unlike their American counterparts, as they seem to have difficulty recognizing people and speaking to them, otherwise Honda would not be looking further a-field for its "personnel."

By the way, always being somewhat intrigued by derivations, I looked into this word "robot" and discovered that a Czech dramatist coined it in 1920. He was looking for a name for the artificial creatures in his play. Originally, he proposed the word "labors." His brother suggested "Robota," which means "work" in various Slavic languages. Both provide a clear indication of the destiny man envisions for his robots. Let's hope that, in playing God, we have the foresight to allow them at least one day off a week, or the next thing we know, we'll have Robot unions, go slows and walk outs. Now, why will we see more, not less, robots—apart from the natural proclivity of man to tinker with machines? Not because we will ever run out of those people willing to do the jobs we ourselves eschew. But because we constantly look to control our environment, and robots are imminently more predisposed to obeying orders than humans, who tend to have their own ideas. And that is *exactly* why we will continue to see butlers and other household personnel very much in evidence in households. Because we can think for ourselves and we are alive.

There are, however, some employees who act as if they are robots, needing to be controlled instead of acting under their own direction. They can be exhausting to have around. If even human robots are the bane of households and organizations, then surely the constant inability to ORIGINATE action that is intelligent and out of the norm, will drive employers to consign most of their robots to the back of the golf cart garage, and bring in real people.

Although I do not consider robots the universal panacea that some manufacturers hope for, there is no doubt in my mind that we will be seeing more of them. And used intelligently, they do have their place.

NEC, another company, is building a home robot that can recognize household objects with its two camera eyes and remotely control TV sets and other appliances. By watching points on its owner's face, it can tell whether he or she is happy, sad, frustrated, angry, confused, or apathetic. Something most butlers have a finely honed sense for, as a matter of self-preservation.

NEC's robot even has a built-in video camera for recording video messages. When it sees the intended recipient of the message, it says *(robovoice)* "Hi, I have a message for you" and plays the video. One hopes it will have the intelligence to note that, when the human's face looks angry, it's not the time to play that message from the bank president about the question of the overdrawn account. Or that when the Mrs. is present, the Mr. doesn't want to see that message from his latest secret dalliance.

For those who may not have the time to look after pet messes, vet bills and the daily walk regimen, there is now Robodog from Sony — the electronic pet that will fetch, play, and bark. And more recently, RoboCat was created who, like its cleaning-maid cousin, is also capable of interacting with its owner, needing love and attention and developing his or her own specific feline personality. Just like a real cat, she has emotions, purrs when stroked and sleeps whenever — and wherever — she wants. Microphones let her recognize her own name and react by turning her head and blinking. You'd think that with 58 million dogs and 66 million cats in the US alone, the need for metallic substitutes would be somewhat contrived. However, they do represent the fuzzy and warm end of the robot spectrum. More utilitarian are the robots being created at the Edmonton Research Park in Alberta. Robotics experts there are working on creating teams of cheap, disposable robots to achieve complex tasks without communicating with each other, based on research of, yes, you got it, ant colonies.

It is far cheaper and easier to build a large number of simple robots, apparently, than to build one expensive, complex robot to do the same job. The question is, who wants a colony of metallic ants underfoot in the house, that you can't even plug a name into? Pass the RAID, please.

While robots will appear a handful of years up the line, we are already beginning to see the following.

Automation in the house that includes microwave ovens that read a pre-packaged food's bar code, download recipes from the company's web site and follow instructions for preparing the meal.

A system called *Aware Home* senses inhabitants and responds to voice commands. Another system uses a small pendant that watches for and responds to gestures that control appliances. Make a drinking motion and the water purifier may start up, for instance. But then again, maybe the fridge door will open and milk and beer will be ejected, too. Humans will no longer have a monopoly on misreading messages.

There used to be a time when bespoke tailors behind Bond Street were the Mecca for the nattier dressed man, when pure Marino wool sweaters were the smarter additions to one's wardrobe. The smart clothing to buy now, it seems, is "intelligent clothing" — meaning clothing that sports small built in computers — trousers with mobile phones, shirts with walkie-talkies. Researchers are working on a keyboard made out of smart fabric that can be sewn into trousers or, for those women working in businesses who still wear them, skirts. To use it, they just sit down and start typing on their lap, making this the first truly laptop computer. The keyboard, by the way, is washable, shockproof, and even ironable. The company is now working on a necktie that functions as a mouse, and I wonder to myself, where are they going to put the monitor? Did you know, by the way, while on the subject of clothes, why men's shirts have the buttons on the right and women's blouses have the buttons on the left? It's not to differentiate the gender of the intended wearer, as commonly supposed.

Buttons were relatively expensive during Queen Victoria's reign and so were generally worn by the wealthy. Ladies who were able to afford buttons were also invariably dressed by servants, most of who were right handed. Do you see the picture? The buttons had to be on the lady's left for right-handed servants. Most gentlemen, on the other hand, while they had valets to lay out their clothes, tended to dress themselves — so their buttons were placed on the right side of the shirt.

The tailors who made shirts for those who could afford buttons, but not servants, copied the style of the wealthy, and so women's buttons have remained stubbornly on the left, even though most women are right handed and no longer need assistance in dressing. Such is the logic of tradition.

Which reminds me, if you will excuse another digression, of another fascinating story, attributed to Professor Tom O'Hare at the University of Texas and written for the delight of engineers. The U.S. standard railway gauge (which is the distance between the rails) is 4 feet, 8.5 inches. This gauge is used because the English built railroads to that gauge and U.S. railroads were built by English expatriates.

Why did the English build railroads to that gauge? Because the first rail lines were built by the same people who built the pre-railroad tramways, and that's the gauge that they used. Why did those wheelwrights use that gauge? Because the people who built the horse-drawn trams used the same tools that they used for building wagons, which used that same wheel spacing. Why did the wagons use that odd wheel spacing? For the practical reason that any other spacing would break an axle on some of the old, long distance roads with well-established wheel ruts. Who built these old, rutted roads? The first long distance roads in Europe were built by Imperial Rome for their legions. The initial ruts were first made by Roman war chariots, which were of uniform military issue.

Thus, we have the answer to the original question. The United States standard railroad gauge of 4 feet, 8.5 inches derives from the original specification for a Roman army war chariot. A specification, by the way, is the technical order that engineers are given to follow in building something.

Let me break briefly from this story to remark that specifications and bureaucracies live forever, it seems, neither of them are popular with crusty engineers. I say this to soften the blow of the good professor's closing remarks:

So, the next time you are handed a specification and wonder what horse's ass came up with it, you may be right on target. Because the Imperial Roman chariots were made to be just wide enough to accommodate the back-ends of two warhorses. Tradition and precedent can be two-edged swords, as any Butler who has had to wear tails in the great Florida outdoors, during a summer afternoon, can testify.

Returning now to the 21st century, clothes, it seems, have joined the multi-functional bandwagon, being fashioned to alert us when we have forgotten the house keys, to play music that fits our mood, and, lest we forget, to cover our derrieres and other assorted body parts. Maybe my tone smacks of the same indignation British buckle makers must have felt when the shoestring finally put them out of business at the close of the 18th century. But we have gone from quality, natural clothes to permanent press finishes that require no ironing, to the latest advance: a new fabric under development, according to the American Chemical Society, that kills pathogenic and odor-causing bacteria, not to mention a few viruses. So now we need not wash our clothes, either?!

We are a long way from the butlers of the 12th century with their mutton-fat soap and sour wines. But at least they knew they had to work for a living and for a standard of living. What about that other treasured domain of the butler—food? Here, technology is crowding him out again. Stick-on food patches are the 21st century cuisine of choice, romantically named the Transdermal Nutrient Delivery System—I can see it now, "TNDS" stalls right next to the TCBY stalls in airports. The "system," which doesn't even have the marketing sense to call itself a cuisine, transmits the vitamins and nutrients needed to maintain the human body, through the skin.

Considering the average person ingests a ton of food and drink each year, that's an awful lot of stick-on patches to stick wherever one sticks them.

Not that first aid is the purview of the butler, but, to round out the picture of the changes ahead, it used to be that when you lost a body part, that was it. Lately, one has been able to sew in a spare from someone else's body. But even this won't be necessary anymore, as the technology is refined for growing body parts from stem cells cloned from one's own cells. Maybe somewhere between this technology and Dolly, that famous English sheep, lies the Fountain of Eternal Youth, the Holy Grail that has galvanized many into ardent action since before the 12th century — my reference being Monty Python, I am sure.

So is there a message amidst all these ramblings? I would hope so. While the British butler represents a great tradition, while he has techniques and technologies for looking after a household in grand style, he will not fare well, and more to the point, nor will his employers, if his forte is the proper techniques for extinguishing candles or reviving sour wine — or even the 20th century equivalents. If he (or she, because women have been butlers in households for several hundred years) considers that there is only one right way to do something, the way that Mr. Smudge, who worked his way up from Third to First Footman to the Queen before he expired in an untimely fashion, used to insist upon, then obviously there's a reality gap. Which brings me to another suggestion that Mrs. Starkey made — that I elaborate upon the pros and cons of the British butler in the American marketplace.

Today's British butler cannot rely upon his old skills. In the immortal words of Vice President Gore, he has to keep reinventing himself — hopefully, less self-consciously than our dearly departed VP.

And I'm tempted to cheat here and give you the gist of the message I want to convey today: that whatever the duties were, are or will be, the British butler will need to move with the expectations and technologies of the time. He will have to adapt to the country he finds himself in. But as long as he realizes that there is one fundamental that will NEVER change, he will always be a success, and his employers invariably satisfied with his performance. This fundamental concerns the tricky art of living for decades on end in someone else's house, when even family and friends stink after three days, as the saying goes. It's quite a trick, when you look closely. I *would* like to look more closely, therefore, not at the tricks of the trade, not at the way an American household Manager wakes up the employer, compared to how a British butler does it. These are peculiarities that can be learned at schools like The Starkey Institute and then refined according to the employer's wishes. I would like, instead, to focus in the time we have remaining, upon the characteristics that make the British butler, one who his worth his salt — which expression, I hasten to add, derives from the medieval practice in wealthier households that could afford salt, of positioning the salt cellar in front of the master.

To his left sat his wife and the other members of the household and to his right sat the guests, placed very carefully in order of wealth and merit. This table etiquette was known as The Order of the Salt, from which we now have the idioms, "worth his salt," "below the salt" and "right hand man."

Attention to detail and a caring to strive for perfection make the British butler the ideal employee for the wealthy, most of who care greatly about their hard-won possessions and enjoying the level of quality that they have attained in their lives. Maybe not the same kind of perfectionism that Leonardo Da Vinci displayed when he painted four completely different versions of Mona Lisa on the same canvas before he was satisfied, but a professionalism closely resembling it. A story I have always liked is the one about the novice at the monastery on Mount Serat in Spain. One of the fundamental requirements of this religious order is that the young men maintain silence.

Opportunities to speak are scheduled once every two years, at which time they are allowed to speak only two words. This particular initiate was invited by his superior to make his first two-word presentation upon completion of his first two years at the monastery.

"Food terrible," he said.

Two years later the invitation was extended once again. The young man used this forum to exclaim, "Bed lumpy." Arriving at his superior's office two years later he proclaimed, "I quit."

The superior looked at the young monk and said, "You know, it doesn't surprise me one bit. All you've done since you arrived is complain, complain, complain."

So while this story may be narrowly focused on the error in complaining, the truth is that over and above keeping his own counsel, the British butler works efficiently to remedy situations, without troubling the employer with the details. He doesn't waste his breath complaining about something that is essentially within his own power to resolve.

We all know that butlers persevere. In fact, the title of this lecture is, "The Indomitable British Butler." An *interesting* choice of word, which I confess I had no part in selecting, "indomitable" means "strong, brave, determined and difficult to defeat, subdue or make frightened."

While I often pose like a body builder in front of the mirror, and strut about like Anthony Robbins, cajoling myself into assume these very qualities, I seem to find the only thing that is indomitable about myself is a Falstaffian belly with ever-expansive ideas of it's newfound role in my life.

"Indomitable" is derived from a Latin word meaning "not to be tamed," and while I have learned a healthy respect for people with "abs of steel," I am not sure that British Butlers as a whole find themselves so endowed.

But I digress again. There is something indomitable about British butlers, and I imagine you'd like to know what it is. Is it the persistence shown by Stevens, the butler in Ishiguro's masterful work, "The Remains of the Day"? Stevens is a character who stands by his employer through good times and bad. Loyal to the point of self-denial, he does not even allow his own father's death to interfere with his duties. Perhaps it is this loyalty that we admire in the doting, old retainers of yore.

My idea of indomitable in relation to butlers is somewhat more insouciant, however, focused on winning with a sparkle in one's eye, not enduring. Take the time Nicolo Paganini was performing with a full orchestra before a packed house in Italy. His technique incredible, his tone beautiful, his fingers flying over the strings, he enthralled the audience. Suddenly, in the midst of an unbelievably complex and fast moving composition, a string on his violin snapped and hung limply from his instrument. Paganini frowned briefly, shook his head, and continued to play, improvising beautifully. Then to everyone's surprise, a second string broke, and shortly thereafter, a third. Instead of leaving the stage, Paganini calmly completed the piece on the one remaining string...

It is the command of all things in the household, a certainty of performance and a determination to carry through with dignity, which marks the British butler as the Indomitable One. As an aside, the strange preoccupation of murder mystery writers with the butler's guilt is perhaps not so far-fetched if one consider that the butler knows more than anyone else about the household, and this knowledge, coupled with impure motives, might well make him the number one suspect. In the same way, the term "knows where all the bodies are buried," was first used in the 1941 film, *Citizen Kane*, when Kane's estranged wife suggests to investigators, in reference to the butler. "He knows where all the bodies are buried." How true. And about all the skeletons in the closet, too. But about all these things, his stiff upper lip is remains permanently sealed. In returning briefly to the concept of dignity, perhaps I can draw from words Ishiguro puts into Stevens' mouth.

"Lesser butlers will abandon their professional being for the private one at the least provocation. For such persons, being a butler is like playing some pantomime role; a small push, a slight stumble, and the facade will drop off to reveal the actor underneath. The great butlers are great by virtue of their ability to inhabit their professional role and inhabit it to the utmost; they will not be shaken out by external events, however surprising, alarming or vexing. They wear their professionalism as a decent gentleman will wear his suit: he will not let ruffians or circumstance tear it off him in the public gaze; he will discard it when, and only when, he wills to do so, and this will invariably be when he is entirely alone. It is, as I say, a matter of 'dignity.'"

In addition to "indomitability" and "professionalism," I'd like to throw some other long words at you, taken from *The British Butler's Bible*, because like this lecture today, I was running out of time earlier this week when preparing this talk and needed something to crib, nowadays done by the simple expedient of cutting and pasting from one document to another. Being a book, the information is delivered with greater intensity, so please excuse the change in style while I rattle off the basic attributes of a butler. You won't need to take notes, as you'll be acquiring a copy of the book later—or so my astrologist assures me.

Trustworthiness is the most basic trait that characterizes a British butler. An employer relies on honesty and reliability when he hands over his house, family, finances, and possessions to a Butler. He doesn't want his possessions disappearing, chores left undone, family sickened from food poisoning or funds being diverted. He does not want to be talked about behind his back or slandered to family and guests, nor to see his name in print via the Butler—so loyalty is another key ingredient, as covered earlier. He does not wish to be upstaged by the Butler, or big emergencies made out of small ones. So the Butler is always in the background, smoothing things over and seeking to make his employer's life as pleasurable as possible. To "butle" successfully, one has to be willing to cause things quietly and let the boss take the credit; or conversely, take the blame in public for a boss's goof, without becoming defensive. One is, in essence, an actor on the stage, playing a part to perfection. As long as one keeps this in mind, the occasional indignities become part of the script and not a life-and-death matter. The employer would like to feel that his Butler really cares for his welfare and that of his family. He wants his Butler to be helpful and willing—a "can-do" type who wants things to work out for the family and who helps them wherever possible.

The Butler has to have some social graces—tactful when confronted with tricky situations so that family and guests are not made to feel uncomfortable. He knows and follows the accepted manners and customs; he keeps track of likes and dislikes of family and guests ("*Favorites*" in the Starkey parlance) and obliges them accordingly; he treats each person individually and with equal dignity, no matter how bizarre they may appear.

In time, he becomes almost as well loved as the rest of the family, but only when he conducts himself as if he is not; because there is an invisible line that he cannot cross. Today, especially, the upstairs and downstairs division (or "back" and "front," as it used to be known in country houses, in contrast to smaller, city dwellings) reflects a familial boundary, more than a societal one. Caring is therefore felt and shown, but always with a certain measure of decorum. Familiarity breeds contempt in the long run, so a British Butler maintains a professional demeanor at all times. It is a matter of actually caring, while maintaining a certain friendly formality in his actions. Being chummy and being impersonal are two extremes, neither of which work for a stranger allowed into the closeness of the nest.

By keeping track of his employer's penchants and moods, he can predict and provide the item or environment that his employer needs before being asked for it. The Butler's attitude is "I am going to do whatever I can to make my employer comfortable and happy." It's a game he plays and the rewards are pleasing to both himself and the employer.

A fundamental distinction is that a good Butler serves, but is not servile. He is there to provide a service that he enjoys delivering. He is willing to accept criticism, and if not justified, to let it ride, or correct it where and when appropriate. But he no longer owes his continued existence to his employer and so can walk tall, if discretely! Whereas he is flexible about the amount of time he works, he is most punctilious about timing, never being late. With regard to other staff in the household, he is also friendly without being too familiar. He is firm about the amount and quality of work done. He cares as well for the staff, that their lives are running well, remembering birthdays and the like.

He is a good organizer, who can manage many people and activities according to a schedule, while keeping up with all the paperwork. As covered earlier, he pays great attention to detail so as to achieve high standards and so essentially communicates an aesthetic message to his employer, the family and any guests. For instance, breakfast could be some greasy overcooked eggs served on a cracked, cold plate by an unshaven, unkempt Butler with a cigarette stub sticking from his lips and a body odor more in place at a zoo. Or it could be a plate of perfectly fried eggs, bacon, mushrooms and grilled tomatoes as the third course in a breakfast that is served on a sunlit balcony by a Butler in morning coat and pinstripes. He offers more hot coffee and the morning's newspapers and all the while, music is playing softly in the background. That's the level of creativity the good British Butler deals in: the making of beautiful moments to put people at their ease and increase their pleasure. At the same time, he has to deal with the raw emotions of upset staff, imperious family members, discourteous guests, indignant bosses, shifty contractors and the best-laid plans falling apart at the last moment—all the while maintaining his composure, his desire to provide the best possible service, and ensuring events turn out satisfactorily. He is much like the proverbial sergeant in the army—the one who organizes the men and actually meets the objectives, sometimes despite the commissioned officers. And at the end of the day, the good Butler still has the energy and humility to ask, "Was there anything I could have improved about my service today?"

There is a bit of the British Butler in everyone—the honesty, the creativity, the caring, the social graces, the phlegmatic; it is rare to find someone with all these qualities, who is able to keep them turned on, day in, day out, despite all the reasons not to. All of which reinforces the value of the British Butler in all his various manifestations and no matter where he finds himself serving.

It is worth pointing out that the Butlers most people see on the silver screen do not usually demonstrate many of the qualities listed above. When Blackadder makes disparaging and scathing remarks to the Prince of Wales' face or behind his back, he may be funny, but he is not being an honest-to-goodness British Butler that any employer would keep for very long—possibly because employers are never quite as naively daffy as they are made out to be in the various media, despite what the following stereotypical story illustrates:

"The wife of a newly-rich Silicon Valley millionaire checked into a hospital for some minor surgery. When the anesthesiologist told her she was going to have a local anesthetic. Her reply was, "Oh, my husband can afford it, order something imported."

To be sure, a British Butler will meet many a situation that challenges his idea of what is sensible. The first Duchess of Marlborough, for example, economized on ink by not dotting her i's or using full stops. Does it need to be said that a sensible Butler will be sensible in dealing with such peccadilloes—that he will refrain from pointing out that the one penny saved each year in ink is uncomfortably offset by the thousands of pounds lost from upset recipients of her letters who no longer want to do business with her, or her husband, because her strange vocabulary and run-on sentences make her sanity somewhat suspect?

So, in closing, I would like to offer an idea for a basic drill to acquire the key characteristics of the British Butler. You don't have to be British, your lip does not have to be any stiffer than normal, and mustaches are optional.

I am referring to the ability to confront or face up to life's situations. A person whose attention is dispersed, thinking of problems or day-today affairs, is not at home, to speak. His (or her) observation of the environment is lacking, because his attention is turned inward, even if to some slight degree. If he cannot observe, he cannot compute properly because he lacks the relevant information on the environment he should be computing upon. And therefore he cannot act appropriately.

Additionally, the ideal condition for a butler to be in, is interested in the environment and others. If he is being interesting, his attention is on himself, trying to attract attention to himself. I am sure you can see the distinction, one first made by Mr. L. Ron Hubbard.

I think you will find that the mastery of the situation, the unflappable panache of the British butler, is entirely dependent upon Being There as the starting point. The movie of that name gives some idea of the magic that "being there" can awaken.

As we draw to the end of our allotted time together, I would like to spend a few minutes practicing this little drill. Please team up in pairs, and turn your seats to face each other.

Now, just sit comfortably and look at or observe the other person. There is no need to be interest**ing**. You are interest**ed** in the other person. There is no need to smile, entertain or impress the other person, or exhibit any social graces. You are just concerned with being there. It's a simple but powerful truth. Let's try it for a few minutes!

….

Very good. How did you do?

[Historical note: Three of the sets of people who did this exercise out of the hundred people in attendance reached a level of equanimity with their randomly selected partner that they struck up a close personal relationship subsequently. Not that this is the goal of the drill at all (it was developed by. Mr. Hubbard as the first step in communicating effectively – see http://www.scientologyhandbook.org/SH5.HTM), but it shows what can happen when one just sits down and is interested in, rather than trying to be interesting.]

And so ends this presentation.
If anyone has any questions, I'd be glad to take them. If you have any comments, I prefer to take them with a stiff upper lip rather than on the chin.

Archduke, ladies and gentlemen, it has been my pleasure. Thank you.

A DUTY TO THE PROFESSION

Much media has occurred of late concerning Mr. Paul Burrell and his book, **"A Royal Duty,"** excerpts of which have been run in the sensationalizing *Daily Mirror* tabloid. In addition to using his own observations while serving the Princess, he has drawn upon private letters sent to and from her. Mr. Burrell has stated, "My only intention in writing this book was to defend the princess and stand in her corner." He also stated it was "nothing more than a tribute to her."

From a logical standpoint, this raises some questions:

1. Is anyone actually besmirching Princess Diana's name, as Mr. Burrell claims? Does anyone actually think badly of her, that Mr. Burrell should feel compelled to intercede? My understanding is that she is one of the most popular women in the world. So why is Mr. Burrell tilting his lance at this windmill?

2. How does revealing the details of Princess Diana's private life make people think better of her?

3. Would Princess Diana welcome the effect Mr. Burrell is creating on her sons, who have stated of Mr. Burrell: "... abuse(d) his position in such a cold and overt betrayal. It is not only deeply painful for the two of us but also for everyone else affected and it would mortify our mother if she were alive today. And, if we might say so, we feel we are more able to speak for our mother than Paul."

From other statements made by Mr. Burrell, he published his book because he was angry at the Royal Family for not helping him during his time of need while undergoing trial (for taking items belonging to his former employer). His anger may or may not be justified, but the way he chose to remedy the situation was not the path a true butler would have chosen.

From an ethical standpoint, Mr. Burrell (whom I have shared the stage with on a couple of occasions and found to be a very likeable fellow, so I have no personal axe to grind with him) has unfortunately broken the written and unwritten code of conduct of a butler. If every butler made public the private life of his employer, nobody would ever hire a butler.

Put another way, if Mr. Burrell hired a butler, would he feel aggrieved or satisfied if that butler later wrote a book revealing every intimate detail of his private life? It's the old golden rule at work.

It is for this reason that I feel compelled, in the light of the barrage of media concerning Mr. Burrell's actions, to reaffirm the basic principle and ethic of butling. It is based on trust and confidence. Writing a book may pay in the short term with wealth and fame, but the profession is weakened with each such book, as is the author. Without maintaining our standards, we will cease to have a profession. This may not concern Mr. Burrell at this present time, but it does impact the rest of us, as well as existing and potential employers. I believe it is important, therefore, that whenever we have an opportunity to comment, we put forward the same message as above.

As for Mr. Burrell and his threat to keep on revealing Princess Diana's and the Royal Family's secrets, if he truly feels that he is "the keeper of these (Diana's) secrets," then I invite him to do as he says. I also invite him to make up the damage he has done to our profession in some way that will restore trust and peace of mind among employers.

October 2003

Ask Not What The Butler Did, But What He Can Do For Your Hotel

The Hotel Butler - Recognizing the Value Butlers Bring to the Bottom Line

We all know the cliché, but what did the butler do that made him so uncharacteristically the focus of attention? In movies and board games, he generally is the one the police want to question further. In the hotel environment, the butler has turned out to be either a failed and somewhat embarrassing experiment, or the ultimate offering in Guest Services that helps keep high-rack occupancy rates at 100%.

Where the butler concept fails, it is because he (or she) is cast in (frankly) degrading-to-the-profession roles such as "bath butler," "fireplace butler," "technology butler," "baby butler" (who provides rocking chairs and watches children), "dog butler," "ski butler," and "beach butler." The idea being, apparently, that anything offering superior service in some small area is called "a butler" in an effort to siphon some of the prestige of the profession. At best, the idea is myopic, at worst, self-defeating.

At least when the term valet was extended to "dumb valet," that furniture item upon which one lays out clothing for the following day, there was no pretence that this was the real item. Fortunately for the profession, the public were not fooled or taken in by these "dumb butlers" and the practice has faded relatively rapidly—hopefully before it soured guests on the value of being serviced by (real) butlers in hotels. And fortunately so for the butlers working in top hotels around the world, who do justice to the profession, and the hotel managements who have recognized the value butlers bring to the bottom line and the repute of word of mouth for their establishments.

In an industry that is completely premised on the idea of service, and in which service is a key differentiator, it's a no-brainer to institute butler service. Butlers have always represented the pinnacle in service quality. After the initial required training, the running of a butler service is not much more expensive to provide than regular service, yet it allows rack rates to be raised and creates a loyal following of repeat visitors, as well as enhancing word of mouth and thus new business that make the investment most sound.

Instituting butler service can be done gradually, perhaps instituting it on one floor, and at not such a great cost, especially when considering the return on investment. Fifteen rooms can be well serviced by four butlers on three shifts, for instance, with one of them assigned as Head butler. If service is to be 24-hour, then a fifth butler would be needed.

Assuming an owner or manager decides to institute butler service, the next question is, "How?"

The first step is to bring on board the most service-minded of your employees to undergo training. The second: Bring in one of the handful of butler trainers who can train hotel butlers (as distinct from butlers in private residence, as the hotel environment is very different and requires fewer and different skills than the traditional butler).

In putting together a training program, it is important to know the four main elements that hotel butler trainees and hotel butler programs need in order to succeed.

First of all, there are the mechanical actions, the skills that butlers need, such as how to clean shoes, how to greet guests and tour them around their suite, how to arrange events for their stay, how to draw baths, pack suitcases, etc.

Then there is knowing and adopting as second nature the psyche or mindset of the butler. In order to do something effectively and with conviction, one has to be able to be the role that one is playing fully. This is obvious when watching a great actor in a movie. But it is also true in life, too. Unless a trainee butler has the right demeanor, attitude and approach as a starting point, he or she will never be able to carry off the role convincingly or handle guests and even fellow staff with the aplomb that makes butlers such quintessential service professionals.

This is why the training has to include the history, rationale, characteristics and communication skills of the traditional butler, and enough drilling-in of these elements so that when the novice butler is faced with a tricky or embarrassing situation, he or she is not left tongue-tied, upsetting guests, or proving that he is not the smooth, low-key character that guests expect in their butlers. When friendly American hospitality employees chatter endlessly and over-familiarly with guests and follow mantras about always greeting the guest by name at least three times within so many minutes, they are presenting ingrained training patterns that do not add up to the butler experience. This is not to say that the butler is not friendly, but there are other ways of expressing it than by well-worn phrases and compulsive chatter.

Thirdly, having covered the theory and done copious drills on applying the skills in a classroom environment, the trainer needs to move out with the butlers and expose them gradually to guests in the actual areas they will be providing butler service. By this is meant that trainees use each other and then senior staff as guest guinea-pigs, and they then service known-to-be-easy guests, and finally are allowed to service VIPs and known-to-be-difficult guests. The trainer should correct them on an internship or apprenticeship basis until the trainees can confidently do their duties.

Finally, for training to be practical and workable, it needs to tie the general actions of butling into the specific hotel environment in which they are working. This means the trainer has to work with hotel management and butler trainees to adapt existing SOPs (standard operating procedures) and propose new ones that align with existing SOPs.

It is workable to develop such SOPs during the early training steps and then drill them and correct them as needed during the apprenticeship period, fine-tuning against the hotel environment until they are smooth and effective. The result is best compiled into a butler manual that can be referred to as needed by the butlers, and which can also be used to train more butlers. The program will probably expand based on the successes of the initial pilot. That has certainly been the experience to date—one owner even building a whole new hotel at $1.5 million per-room-cost just to be able to expand on the butler service pilot he had run.
It is also possible that there will be some attrition or turnover, but to date, hotel butlers that have been trained as above have proven happy enough with their situation to politely decline the inevitable offers from guests to return home with them and run their private households or yachts.

The end result of the whole program as outlined above is generally employees with high morale who competently carry out their duties, wowing guests and resulting, as stated before, in higher-than-usual occupancy, a high rate of return visits, and the opportunity to increase rack rates while enjoying stellar word of mouth.

Perhaps it would be better to ask then, not what the butler did, but what he (or she) could do for your hotel.

August 2004

THE NEW RENASCENCE SPA
OF SPA BUTLERS & BUTLER SPAS

Nearly two-thirds of affluent travelers surveyed in a Pepperdine study last summer stated they set their sites primarily on being pampered—luxury and premium service being key elements—when deciding where to stay while away from home.

This is good news for those hotels and resorts with spas that have invested in the latest industry concept of spa butlers, introduced a few months ago to the spa and hospitality industries in HotelExec.com and the latest issues of *Spa Business* and *Spa Management* magazines). For spa guests, the total immersion experience made possible by the fusion of these two service pinnacles creates a lasting impression. Why? Because the model handles the key drawback with every spa experience, which invariably ends abruptly as a guest leaves the spa to return to his or her suite. For hotel/resort/spa management, the Renascence Spa model represents the next generation of hospitality experience and somewhere to go when you have already traveled as far as the road leads in pampering guests.

This symbiotic liaison between spa and butler programs makes the butler service an extension of the spa experience, wherein butlers providing their usual high-end service on the hotel side are then trained further in the methodologies in play at their spa, with the goal of continuing the spa environment in the guest's own suite.

From the guest's perspective, she (or he) occupies a serene/mellow/invigorated world after being pampered, prodded, plucked, sweated and doused in the spa. It's a destination and transformation she seeks when she thinks about and ultimately walks into a spa—and more often than not reaches. Yet the world that greets her as the spa doors swing shut behind her runs on different agreements: people rush around, lost in thought, stressed. When she reaches her suite, it seems lifeless, out of synch and unsympathetic to her new state. If she is experiencing a catharsis, detoxification, or crisis, or if she just wants to have a sounding board or a ready ear, she is on her own.

Now imagine a butler who knows how guests can react to their spa experience and how to assist them with understanding and empathy. Knowing a guest's spa program, he can converse about the guest's experiences with good reality, should the guest so desire, and can also take actions to enhance that program, be they therapeutic baths, showers, or simply a much needed glass of pure water to preempt dehydration.

The spa butler acts as the main point of contact before, during and after the guest's stay. Translated into the real world, this program means the butler asks and cares about the guest's goal in coming to the spa, giving accurate and convincing explanations of treatments to the guest (and for that important bottom line, upselling). He ensures the guest's room reflects the guest's needs and wants, such as providing Pilates mats, preempting allergic responses, and smudging or applying aroma mists (*Smudging* is the Native American practice of burning sage and/or cedar to eliminate odors and so purify a space. In this case, the idea is not just to eliminate unpleasant smells, but also synthetically derived fragrances that are sometimes employed inside guest suites).

The spa butler supports the guest by being a sounding board and conversing with understanding and empathy. He introduces the guest to the people, places and services she will be experiencing at the spa. He smoothes the preparations for each spa experience and helps her through the ramifications of each spa treatment with follow-on services that help her land gracefully from her spa experience.

This means, for instance, the spa butler being on the lookout for indicators of physiological shifts occurring in the guest that may require action by the butler to help settle the guest where he or she is experiencing discomfort. Some key indicators are:

- Emotional tone changing
- Rapid eyelid fluttering
- A shift from shallow to deep breaths
- Being spaced-out as opposed to being aware of the environment
- Twitching
- A shift in energy flow, such as from much motion to lethargy
- Change in skin temperature or color.

Generally, the body is a self-regulating mechanism that will bring about optimal functioning when provided an environment of support to do so — which defines what is required basically of the spa butler.

Often, the butler can act without seeking permission or agreement, because he can see what is happening to the guest and knows what to do. An offer of a drink of refreshing water, for instance, to a guest who is obviously somewhat dehydrated, doesn't require words or permission.

More than a Number

On the spa side, a recurring complaint is addressed in this butler/spa collaboration by cross training spa personnel on the butler mindset: the complaint being the tendency for therapists to treat guest, especially irregulars, as a commodity. The main focus of the training being giving the spa personnel the ability to be in the moment, able to be there fully for the guest, communicating when the guest desires it (how many therapists chatter endlessly when the guest would rather savor the moment?) in a way that enhances the guest experience, rather than principally entertaining the practitioner. The subsidiary focus is on achieving the same level of grace as, and service mindset of, the butler.

In dealing with guests, the butler maintains an attitude of respectful curiosity, conducting himself (or herself) professionally in a way that never compromises a guest's dignity or privacy. The spa guest may well be impressionable to the suggestions of the spa butler. He, therefore, has an ethical obligation to maintain integrity, tell the truth, and create and uphold an environment of trust and confidentiality so as bring about a safe space for a guest that allows him or her to focus on fixing his or her world. This is not new news to the spa industry and the many therapists who adhere to these principles, but staying in the moment and following through with every guest can be a challenge. This spa-side element is by far the shortest to bring about, taking a few days, rather than the weeks it takes to train butlers first as butlers and then as spa butlers.

The Physical Component

The ultimate spa experience will be blemished, despite the best efforts of spa butlers and "butler spas," where consumables and suite design are out of kilter with the goals of the spa and its guests. Chloramines and fluorides in the water, mite and insect excreta, dust and allergens in the air are counterproductive. So are the use of MSG in the kitchen, neurotoxic sweeteners such as aspartame, and other chemical food additives, such as preservatives, coloring, pesticides, fertilizers, and irradiated and genetically modified foods. As for PCPs (personal care products), the contents of the most expensive and exclusive, which generally tend to be provided in high-end settings, read like a chemical laboratory experiment, with spa guests among the guinea pigs.

A mere handful of the 60,000 chemicals in our air, water and food supply have been tested for their impact on the human body. It is impossible to test the effect of the almost infinite combinations of these chemicals. This makes the exponential growth of chemicals in our lives a giant experiment over the last half-century that may be behind the alarming increases in diseases, obesity, etc. Whether or not they are, an increasing number of individuals are not willing to take the risk and are looking for and even insisting upon pure spaces and ingredients.

Not all spa guests will be concerned about these points, but as spa guests *are* concerned about their health and long-term physique, the likelihood is that many are aware of the chemical onslaught in the environment and would prefer to find in their spa and its hotel/resort, a sanctuary. For those who may not be concerned currently, a leadership position adopted by the spa hotel/resort may well stand them in good stead with their guests in later years. But in any case, having the option available for organic food, stevia for non-sugar sweeteners and the likes of a rich cup of Teechino as a coffee substitute, for instance, for those who *are* concerned, can only win friends. Cleansing the air with ozonators and ionizers, and the water with top-of-the-line filtration systems, will not find any complainers among the skeptical, and plenty of support from believers. High-quality PCPs that contain natural ingredients do exist and likewise could be offered those who care.

Lastly, the guest suite needs to be made spa friendly, whether by Feng Shui methodology or other design, so as to move it beyond the prosaic and into the realm of the ethereal, the calming, the nurturing.

The second presidential suite in Miami's Mandarin Oriental takes just such an approach, creating a "luxury spa haven for total pampering pleasure. It's most unique and outstanding feature is a spa 'serenity room,' a one-of-a-kind sanctuary offering the ultimate in-suite spa experience…a tranquil Zen-like environment with warm color tones, bamboo accents and Mexican river stones accented by Spanish marble tile and a breathtaking view of Biscayne Bay. The spa serenity room features Japanese-style Tatami mats, an infinity-edge soaking bath with color therapy lighting and tear drop ceiling fountain and relaxation area … and ESPA spa amenities, salts, body and bath oils."

Although this room was created for in-suite spa services, maybe it would be a good idea for all rooms catering to spa guests to be designed with the same thoughtfulness in mind?

Pampering is the name of the game and the Renascence Spa concept is the new way to attract these travelers (and locals) to your hotel or resort.

May 2005

So What Is a Butler Anyway?

Rare is the week that goes by without word of some upscale hotel offering butler service as a way to improve service and retain or gain that coveted 5-star or diamond status. That's as it should be. But then consider the industry veteran Horst Schulze's declaration in the Wall Street Journal that Capella, his future line of hotels, will have a *six*-star rating. What does he specify as the criteria for such an august label? Private swimming pools. And personal butlers.

It seems butlers are really not just for the wealthy in their private estates, but also for their convenience when they travel.

So, in providing butler service, a pertinent question might be "What exactly is a butler?" Or more to the point, "What are butlers in a hotel setting?" They obviously are more than the dog, beach, computer, baby, and bath butlers that rushed out fully armed from marketing departments during the 1990s and beat a hasty retreat in the face of public disdain.

The answer is very clear to those hotel executives who have brought in any one of a handful of trainers able to teach their personnel how to "butle." Anyone who has read *Hotel Butlers, The Great Service Differentiators*, will know that there is a technology and mindset to butling. It is something that *can* be learned to jump-start an individual in the Middle East, the Far East, the East Coast or the West Coast of America, the Caribbean, and anywhere else in the art of butling British style.

In addition to the dozen-or-less trainers working on site at hotels, there are a dozen-or-less schools around the world teaching strangers to the art of butling the skills and panache needed to fulfill their roles with sufficient aplomb. There is no shortage of resources for anyone wanting their employees trained to the high standards of service that the butler exemplifies.

In recognition of the increased demand for butlers, and the subsequent need to train butlers, and even non-butler staff in the mindset of the butler so as to raise service standards throughout hospitality venues (be they hotel, resort, spa, or private villa), the International Institute of Modern Butlers was founded.

The Institute purpose being to promote training in the butler model, to act as a clearinghouse for butler training resources around the world, and to help set and raise standards in the profession. It being recognized that, like any profession, butlers need standards and a standard-setting body to prevent the profession from becoming less than it should be.

And in the case of butlers, there is the additional requirement that a model be constructed of what the butler is and does in both the private and hospitality settings in the 21st Century. The ideal being, perhaps, a modern butler with the core values of the early-20th Century butler, rather than a mannequin with the outward trappings and motions of the butler and no mindset to back it up.

One important program the Institute is championing is an apprenticeship program for butler school graduates, whereby they apprentice under butlers in private estates or work in butler departments in hotels to hone their skills and add substance to their training. This represents a handy and cost-effective personnel pool for private estates, as well as hotels intent on offering butler service, or wanting to add butlers to their department without investing in bringing a trainer on board. It also allows butler school graduates to break into an industry that can be quite closed to neophytes knocking at the door.

While a trainer working with trainees on site is the optimum way to slam-dunk a butler department into place in a hotel, an alternative is to bring in butler school graduates and have a trainer visit briefly to fine-tune and provide quality control—an important element given that butler schools focus on the basics of butling and few provide hospitality-centric training.

Which brings us back to the original question: what is a butler in the hospitality setting?

The cinema and various books create stereotypical butlers whom we find amusing for their restraint and biting wit in the face of monumental stupidity; and endearing for their willingness to work behind the scenes while their employers blithely strut across the stage, playing out their own pre-ordained roles. Yet, whether answering the telephone or dealing with difficult situations, there is something about the attentive and slightly aloof British butler that has a place in today's modern hotels as much as in the 19th Century British stately home.

Maybe it is their low-key approach to service, in preference to the maestro-center-of-the-stage performance so characteristic of many American service professionals.

A butler is a frame of mind rather than a status or a series of duties. It is a mindset that anyone can adopt in any situation in life to very satisfying results, because it is founded on the truths that it is better to serve than be served, and that life can be rational and serene when one assumes responsibility for all things.

In almost every person, there is a penguin-suited figure dying to emerge, to bring a surprising level of equanimity, order and happiness to the lives of those around him or her. This may seem far-fetched in a world of hard-nosed corporate executives, self-centered guests and screaming, obnoxious children as sometimes parade through the hospitality world, but what does win in the world of service, funnily enough, is complete devotion to providing service. Anything less is transparent.

Butlers are superior service professionals. Their model has value. It is the future of service.

October 2005

THE FUTURE HOSPITALITY PROFESSIONAL

As adventurous as it may be to predict the future, there is no doubt in my mind that we stand today at the same point as Dick Tracy when he conversed through a two-way, walkie-talkie video wrist-watch to a remote caller six decades ago. In other words, the prediction that hospitality professionals of the future will read the minds of guests may sound a far-fetched fantasy and possibly even ludicrous, but it will come to be. Why? Because it has been done to some extent for centuries by that quintessential service provider, the British butler, when in top form; and because the technology to bring all service professionals to that pinnacle already exists.

Here, we are not talking some corporate formula for guest interaction that too often results in canned phrases and plastered-on smiles; or a consultant guru's mantra for superior guest services that seeks to put a datum where intelligent observation and action should be. We are talking information relay followed by drilling on the "how to's" resulting in an ability gained. It's nothing mystic and has no relationship to any psychological mumbo-jumbo, but down-to-earth application of workable principles resulting in guests being properly assessed and treated in a way that they find pleasurable, which always leaves them feeling better than before the service was administered.

Such guest service employees of the future will be closer to Life Consultants than room service and will care as much about guests as their mothers. So says the crystal ball. Predicting the future can be fun. Take the "Future Holiday Forum" held in London, England recently for leaders in travel, technology and design. Their "2024: A Holiday Odyssey" according to a Forbes.com report predicted the future hotel for remote destinations as a foldable/ transportable, self-sustaining, low-environmental-impact pod on stilts in which guests could choose the images to be projected on the walls. The technology for such hotels already exists.

The line-up of future hotels that will similarly soon be with us includes underwater hotels and airship hotels that permit scenic views as one travels leisurely to one's next destination. Resorts in space no doubt lie in the future, incorporating spinning rooms for all the comforts that we have come to expect from living with gravity.

As for space-age technology addressed at specific hospitality issues, we already have 3-D hologram teleconferencing for hotels specializing in conference services. We will soon see smart cards containing all information on a guest, including likes and dislikes, as well as credit card information that will no doubt make check-in and customized servicing of guests easy.

Other technologies to be introduced into the hospitality sector include robotics for cleaning and check-in; biometric security such as retina scans for entrance to rooms and access to safes. Then there is nanotechnology (manipulating and manufacturing at the molecular level). While we are close to imprinting electronic equipment onto our clothing and even skins, there is talk of using nanotechnology to reconfigure rooms per guest wishes, transmogrifying the furniture, fixtures and decorations at the push of a button (so to speak).

However, notice that the talk of the future is invariably in the realm of gadgetry and machinery. Whatever happened to the human element? Are we giving up on our fellow man? Are we just using him or her until some machine can replace him not just on the factory floor but also in the giving of service? Just as Astounding Science Fiction moved beyond machines to focus on the human element regarding things from outer space during the 1930s, so I believe we need to move into improving the human element, rather than always focusing on the mechanical and even trying to substitute machines for humans. And by improving the human element, I mean moving beyond formulas and mantras to increase employee intelligence and ability to act self-determinedly, rather than other-determinedly by rote.

Butler as Future Service Standard

Whether or not Mr. Horst Schulze, former chairman of Ritz-Carlton, was serious when he announced his plans to introduce a six-star hotel chain that was defined in part by private butlers, he was signaling a recognition of the value of a certain something that classic British butlers bring to the guest experience.

So what's the connection between the British butler of the past and present, and the future hospitality professional? How does one move service employees from transient lower-paid wage earners to professional service providers acting with pride and knowledge, more akin to Life Consultants than room service and caring as much for guests as their own mothers?

Try the code and standards of the traditional butler: trustworthiness, loyalty, attentiveness to guests predicting what they want and attention to detail in providing it before they even know they want it. Always calmly smoothing events into a successful conclusion with a can-do attitude and real caring for the guest; social graces, treating each person with dignity; the soul of discretion; never crossing the invisible line between friendliness and familiarity, attitude free; a superb organizer who always achieves targets set; able to deal with the raw emotions of upset staff, imperious or discourteous guests, indignant bosses, shifty contractors and suppliers and the best-laid plans falling apart at the last moment—all the while maintaining his composure, his desire to provide the best possible service, and ensuring events turn out satisfactorily. Who finally has the energy and humility to ask, "Was there anything I could have improved about my service today?"

That's the basic butler persona and mindset. But beyond that, we need something more to create the service provider of the 21st Century.

Current Best Practices in guest services result in an industry effort to have all guests greeted cheerfully or enthusiastically. That's fine for employees who are naturally cheerful or enthusiastic. But how fake the result when they are not. And is it really appropriate when every guest is so greeted when they are neither cheerful nor enthusiastic at that particular moment nor even as a general rule. One size does not fit all.

What is needed is an understanding of the human mind and character, how their emotions dictate their attitudes, and what they will find acceptable to talk about, consequently, and at what emotional tone.

Anyone who thinks that "emotion" is the opposite of "rationality" won't be tracking with the above. "Emotions" actually refer to the measurable wavelengths emitted by an individual as an expression of his or her like or dislike for various subjects. Some men are enthusiastic about football or conservative about receiving that promotion. Some women grieve over the loss of a relative or dissolve in raptures over a friend's new hair-do. The exhilaration of an individual who has just won the Lotto can be contrasted rather handily with the apathy exhibited by an individual who has nowhere else to go for help and has given up. Or take the boredom a man might exhibit during a business conference as it enters its fourth hour, or the covert hostility (the equivalent of the phrase "passive aggressive") exhibited by a woman as she smiles crookedly while saying "What a lovely dress. I saw one just like it in the thrift store yesterday."

These are emotions. Pegging a guest's (or boss's or co-workers) emotional tone allows one to read their mind and predict their behavior. This technology already exists.

There is more, though: being in the moment or now with guests. Presenting a guest with an attitude, or dealing with them while one's attention is elsewhere, completely misses the boat when it comes to making them the most important element in a hospitality setting. So the question is: how does one anchor employees in the now? It's easy. If you know how.

And when you have that licked, you will find employees will be there enough to observe what is right in front of their faces, compute intelligently, and then act effectively to predict and cater to guest needs, and more importantly, read their mind.

And that is why the future of hospitality lies with the ancient butler tradition, married to the latest in "mind-reading" technology to better read and serve guests. Fit that into the equation, and we will find those floating or space-based hotels, as well as the regular landlubber hotels of today, better serviced and continuing to attract guests who prefer the human touch. Robots for humans is about as satisfying as petting a Sony RoboDog instead of your loyal, lively and loving Lab.

May 2005

WHY GOOD EMPLOYEES MAY BE HARD TO FIND

I believe we have a crisis in the hospitality industry—a dwindling pool of service-oriented individuals—which is making it difficult for HR and management to provide the level of guest service required at high-end properties. Obvious causes, such as low wage scales, could be identified at first blush, but an unlikely source has emerged recently as the real culprit: the marketing and selling of worry to well Americans who are sold psychiatric drugs to resolve that cleverly crafted worry. Half the US population is on these drugs now. The relevance being that the side effects of these drugs include woodenness and disassociation at the less dramatic end, through frustration and anger outbursts, to suicide and murder at the extreme end—none of which are particularly conducive to guest satisfaction.

The issue has been increasingly in the media, lead by British doctors who have forbidden first children and now adults from taking "antidepressants." Court cases and media have at the same time exposed inadequate testing and altered results to hide bad outcomes. Even the FDA, long beholden to the interests of the pharmaceutical lobby, is begrudgingly following suit in the US, hence those black box warning labels appearing on many psychiatric prescriptions. Suicides are the main worry, but the many heinous crimes hitting the airwaves over the last decade (mothers butchering their children, children shooting or torturing their parents or other children, to name just a few) have added to the list of outcomes when people take these drugs.

A book just released, *Selling Sickness: How the World's Pharmaceutical Companies Are Turning Us All Into Patients* (Ray Moynihan and Alan Cassels) and the recently released movie based on John le Carre's fictionalized book, *The Constant Gardner*, both point to a motivational shift by pharmaceutical companies: away from curing sickness to making vast amounts of money; the main strategy being to bring drugs to market by pathologizing life's normal fluctuations and the creation of "lifestyle medicines." Premenstrual tension, for instance, is now a "mental illness" called "premenstrual dysphoric disorder" requiring a psychiatric drug to "manage" (not cure) it.

Instead of relying on evidence to determine a disease and assess the risk/ benefit of a medical intervention, doctors are prescribing drugs based on corporate sponsored "public awareness" campaigns that create "illness." If this seems just fine, then might I suggest re-reading the preceding sentence? We have marketing and PR departments, and executive boards salivating over the bottom line, inventing diseases and then persuading people they have them.

As described by Vera Hassner Sharav of Alliance for Human Research Protection, "The selling of sickness and the birth of a blockbuster drug follows a familiar pattern: the marketing division of a pharmaceutical company identifies a wedge condition, and a set of symptoms or "risk factors"; the company hires a PR firm to come up with a "disease" name, either something catchy (e.g., SAD) or something connoting a serious biochemical deficiency; the company either develops a drug, or recycles an existing one for this new condition; and begins massive marketing to physicians and the public. An advisory panel of experts defines the "disease" broadly enough to include as many previously healthy people as possible, and issues guesstimates about the prevalence of the "disease"; the media pick up the story, suggesting that the 'new' disease is greatly "under-diagnosed and poses severe health hazards if left untreated; the stage is set for the birth of the next blockbuster."

The roots of this travesty can be found in sentiments such as those expressed three decades ago by Merck's chief executive, Henry Gadsden, who wanted to expand his market by making drugs for healthy people, not just sick people.

It is necessary to grasp the reality of this trend in order to understand a previously unrecognized undercurrent that HRs have been hitting up against in finding and keeping good staff.

We have been hearing the complaint "Good employees are hard to find" for a few centuries now, but now it just might be true. While running a workshop on service for a large group of employees at a four-star facility recently, I was fascinated to see a full 50% of them had no interest whatsoever in the subject, one of them even settling down to read a newspaper during the presentation. Their attitude and lack of caring was evident in the lackluster service they offered guests (hence the workshop being arranged by an anxious management), and was also a source of upset for those staff who did care to care and who did derive new insights from the workshop.

The problem is that there is no way for consultants, HR, or management to reach and inspire these people until they are taken off their drugs and the drug residues detoxed from their system (there are ways to do this). Until then, they will continue to manifest a "bio-chemical personality", the antithesis of service.

If the US Armed Forces do not accept recruits who have taken psychiatric drugs, then there may be a lesson to be learned here in our industry. The

Defense Department has learned from experience that such citizens do not make reliable and effective personnel or teammates.

Maybe the hospitality industry could benefit from examining this factor (the drugging of its personnel pool) in trying to create a team of service-minded personnel who actually *do* care for guests, and care to service them well. Maybe the paucity of service-oriented individuals is *not* just the result of genes or some such wild theory, but an artificial condition created by morally bankrupt individuals and out-of-control corporations. In other words, maybe we can do something about it.

September 2005

THE HIDDEN DRUG MENACE

A recent article I wrote (*Why Good Employees May Be Hard to Find*) elicited quite some responses, some of them downright upset. I completely understand the upset, but cannot change the facts. Half of the US populace is on psychiatric drugs, and the vast majority of them do not need to be. But having taken these mind-altering drugs, they develop a biochemical personality that cuts them off from others, either making them wooden and unemotional; or causing great discomfort, making them into walking time-bombs who blow up from time to time (sometimes with disastrous consequences to those around them).

The hospitality industry is based, well, on the concept of hospitality, a word that comes to us from Latin *hospitalitem*, meaning "friendliness to guests." It is hard to be friendly to anyone when one feels half dead, drugged, or when one is seething with upset. It is hard to be genuinely interested in the welfare of another, a basic prerequisite to good service, when one is struggling internally.

The argument that people need these drugs because they have such issues as depression, is putting the cart before the horse: whatever issues a person had before taking a psychiatric drug, they were often quite simply explained and susceptible to a) proper medical treatment (for hernias, allergies, etc.), b) proper diet and exercise, or c) counseling to get through some of life's inevitable roadblocks emotionally, hormonally, etc. This is the regimen the National Health Service in Great Britain has ordered its doctors to follow, instead of prescribing psychiatric drugs. By not isolating and treating these real-world issues, one condemns these individuals to continued problems stemming from those issues. By also inventing a "mental illness" to account for the symptoms, and prescribing some very powerful, mind-altering drug, one merely deadens the symptoms as well as the individual. Then one *does* have a mental issue!

A groundswell of protest by those in the medical and even mental health professions, governing bodies, and those mistreated by such sanctioned drug addiction, gives weight to my observations and contentions. Any Internet search will uncover it, but most recently, Ms. Jeanne Lenzer added the prestigious British Medical Journal to the discussion when she stated in her June 19, 2005 article entitled *Bush plans to screen US for mental illness*, "President Bush established the New Freedom Commission on Mental Health in April 2002 to conduct a 'comprehensive study of the United States mental health service delivery system.' The commission issued its recommendations in July 2003... and found that 'despite their prevalence, mental disorders often go undiagnosed' and recommended comprehensive mental health screening for 'consumers of all ages.'.... The commission also recommended 'Linkage [of screening] with treatment and supports' including 'state-of-the-art treatments' using 'specific medications for specific conditions.'"

As I pointed out in my own article in the BMJ in response to Ms. Lenzer's, "I find I have no argument with senior members of the psychiatric community when they admit to having no clue about the cause of or cure for mental illness.

"'We do not know the causes (of psychiatric disorders). We don't have methods of 'curing' these illnesses yet.' *Director of the U.S. National Institute of Mental Health, Rex Cowdry, 1995.*

"'The time when psychiatrists considered that they could cure the mentally ill is gone. In the future, the mentally ill will have to learn to live with their illness.' *Norman Sartorius, president of the World Psychiatric Association, 1994*

"This is not the forum for detailing exactly why psychiatric drugging is junk science, but suffice to say, if it were not, it would obtain some positive results. Yet study after study not paid for by pharmaceutical companies pushing their own drugs, shows harmful effects and less positive outcomes than sugar pills.

"While we have heard plenty recently about skewed statistics during drug trials carried on by pharmaceuticals eager to rush their latest drug to market, it is telling that no statistics are kept anywhere in the world on improvements brought about in real life by psychiatric drugs. That is, except for King County, Washington (including Seattle), which is the only government organization wanting to know how well its citizen's money is being spent and interests served. About $30 million was spent in 2000 on psychiatric drugs in King County, with the following outcomes: Of 7,831 patients, 6,949 (88.7%) showed no improvement, 597 (8%) showed some improvement, 295 (4%) regressed, and 4 (.05%) recovered. Who would take their car to a mechanic who successfully fixed one in every 2,000 vehicles that passed through his doors?

"In a nutshell, the main problems with the psychiatric theory of a chemical imbalance in the brain as the cause of behavioral disorders are that no tests exist to determine the chemical status of a person's brain while he is living (so how could one recognize an imbalance?); and no delivery system exists to replenish any supposed 'prozac deficiency,' for instance, to a specific part of the brain.

"But this doesn't discourage psychiatrists from misdiagnosing tens of millions of people as having these 'diseases.' Or pharmaceutical companies from making psychiatric drugs to treat these made-up diseases."

If the British medical community has tumbled to what is going on with over-prescription of pharmaceutical drugs, why have we heard so little about the government's plans to medicate the other half of US citizens not already on psychiatric drugs? Perhaps because, as the American Psychiatric Association boasts on its web site, "The BMJ story [by Ms. Lenzer quoted above] has gained some traction in derivative reports on the Internet, though mainstream media have not touched the story, in part thanks to APA's work, for which the administration is appreciative." Interestingly enough, Ms. Lenzer's article was the most downloaded article in the history of the BMJ. It manifestly struck a nerve with a public wary of doctors and politicians whose pockets are lined with drug company money. But for the majority of people in the United States who do not visit the BMJ's august web site, the APA made sure the story did not reach them.

So to return to the hospitality profession in particular, we hear that good personnel are hard to find. Certainly, there are many very competent individuals in the industry who are wonderfully hospitable, but they are the ones who keep the guests wowed, and the ship afloat and off the rocks. Their job is made much harder by the mistakes made by people who are not quite tracking with the rest of us and by the upsets they cause by their attitude, lack of awareness and caring. If you find yourself dealing with employees like this, then realize there is a hitherto hidden influence at work: such employees may well be legal drug addicts. We don't allow street drugs in the work place, so why do we allow psychotropic drugs that are classified as Schedule II drugs (same as cocaine) by the U.S. Drug Enforcement Agency?

So how does one handle this situation and move on? Are such employees dead losses? Absolutely not: If they recognize they are in trouble and want help, then all they have to do is see a competent medical doctor or alternative health practitioner who is not sold on the marketing campaigns by the pharmaceutical companies, for a full and searching physical exam. They may need to fix some physical condition or allergy, change their diet (from junk food high in sugars, synthetic sugars such as the killer aspartame, and empty calories, to nutritious and proteinaceous foods), possibly start some exercise regimen, or have some counseling from a competent and caring individual. They can also do a detoxification program that will remove the residues of the psychiatric drugs so they do not keep releasing into the their blood stream long after the individual ceases taking them.

In the meantime, what does HR do in a hotel environment? First off, research this whole subject for yourself. Otherwise you'll just think the author full of something unmentionable and will continue to miss this important dynamic in your organization. You may also want to consider the impact such psychiatric programs and agendas are having on health care coverage as the cost of health care spirals out of control. It was not so long ago (2001, pushed heavily by pharmaceuticals and psychiatrists) that the Mental Health Parity Act tried to compel businesses to cover mental health insurance (i.e. psychiatric drugs) to the same dollar amount as physical illnesses. Now we have TeenScreen, designed to screen and put the 50 million children in this country on psychiatric drugs as the first step of the President's Orwellian-named New Freedom Commission on Mental Health in drugging all Americans. Once you realize there is a clear and present danger, I am sure you have enough understanding of HR issues to work out how to proceed in your organization.

Sorry if this is all new and bad news to you, and even more so if anyone finds it upsetting: but the truth is that nothing will work short of the truth in the long run. Good luck.

December 2005

NOT ALL BUTLERS ARE CREATED EQUAL

In an industry that is completely premised on the idea of service, and in which service is a key differentiator, increasing numbers of high-end hoteliers have decided to institute butler service. So far so good for a number of reasons, such as raised rack rates, customer loyalty, enhanced word of mouth and, on the employee side, greater retention and raised standards facility wide.

But the reality is somewhat different, as anyone who has experienced butler service in a number of hotels and resorts, can attest. Not all butler departments have been created equal. Sometimes the butlers are invisible; sometimes they are simply pool attendants with a new name badge: "Pool Butler." Or any of the myriad of other inventive ways marketing departments and managers have devised to siphon some of the prestige of the profession. While real butlers appreciate the recognition afforded their profession when offerings of superior service are personified by a butler figure, they are not themselves served well in the long run by this cheapening of their profession. More importantly, guests can recognize a gimmick when they see one and are left in a poor frame of mind at being handed a Mickey Mouse version of the service they had expected and paid for when booking into a facility.

Where butler departments are established, they enjoy varying degrees of success based on their adherence to the basic purpose of butling: the providing of a superb and seamless service that knows and anticipates guest needs. The sources of failure, then, include anything that cuts across this goal. Such as: not selecting proven service professionals for these positions; not training them on the persona, mindset, communication skills, and service skills of the butler in a hospitality setting; not launching the butler program to the rest of the employees in such a way that they support it, rather than viewing it as a threat to their income stream; trying to cut costs by cutting service, resulting in harried butlers providing an irreducible minimum of service to too many guests; not organizing the butler department in such a way that it can run itself, with butler coordinators, runners if needed, head butler, a deputy and supervisors.

As the standard setter for the profession, the International Institute of Modern Butlers, based in Florida, has therefore formulated a rating system that parallels AAA and Mobil ratings but which is focused on butler service in hospitality venues. The purpose of the rating is to help guests make informed decisions about the nature of the butler service being offered by a venue they may be considering; and to assist management and butler employees of those venues in improving their butler offering.

The ratings range from "No Butler" to "Five Butlers" and while assessments are being made initially on a self-assessment basis mixed with assessments by butler trainers around the world, the intention is for the assessments to be made ultimately by the traditional organizations that travelers turn to for information on venues they are planning to visit.

A brief overview of each level (the specifics of these levels run to thirteen pages, so are not the subject of this article) are as follows:

No Butler
The butlers are called such, but have no training or understanding of the nature or skill-sets of a butler, often having a modifier in front of their title, such as "fireplace butler" or "technology butler" or "baby butler."

One Butler
There is literally one butler on the floor, rushing to service guests who are kept waiting or improperly serviced. There may be more than one butler, but training on the skills of the butler or the grace of a butler are lacking, even though some of the service is being provided.

Two Butlers
The butler-to-guest ratio is still too strained, so guests are kept waiting or not fully serviced, but basic elements of butler service are performed and the butlers have been trained in their profession either in schools or on site. No night butler on duty and no butler coordinators to connect guests with butlers.

Three Butlers
There are enough butlers in shifts to manage guests, including night butlers, butler coordinators, and a head butler. The Butler department exists as its own department, not under Housekeeping, Concierge, Room Service, F&B, or any other department. Guests are offered a good range of butler services and these are satisfactorily executed. Butler service has been established and fine-tuned with the assistance of trained professionals.

Four Butlers
Butlers provide excellent, often invisible service to guests who are wowed by the attention to detail. Includes a full complement of butlers who have sufficient presence with the rest of the employees that they have raised their level of service and can obtain instant service for guests. Butler Department personnel receive ongoing training and quality control to keep them sharp and there is a Deputy for the Head Butler who facilitates this training and other organizational steps to keep the Butler Department running smoothly.

Five Butlers

Guests have their own private butler to attend to their every (legal and ethical) needs and desires, including accompanying them on excursions as chauffeur and guide. In the case of guests lacking companions, this level of service may extend to the butler being a companion for a guest, even being skilled enough to play such as golf or tennis (but sufficiently diplomatic always to let the guest win by a narrow margin—and never crossing the line). Where spa service is offered, the butler may also be the spa therapist or so knowledgeable in spa methodology that he or she presents a seamless experience for the spa-going guest.

Expect to see these ratings in use increasingly as the better hotels and resorts recognize the value of making their level of butler service known. If those facilities seeking to ride on the coattails of the butler profession then become earnest about their levels of butler service, then both they and their guests will benefit.

September 2005

THE INTERNATIONAL INSTITUTE OF MODERN BUTLERS
HOSPITALITY BUTLER SERVICE RATING SYSTEM

The International Institute of Modern Butlers has worked with other butler-training professionals to create a rating system based on "Butlers" that parallels ratings such as those of AAA's "Diamonds" and Mobil's "Stars," but which is focused on evaluating butler service in hospitality venues. The purpose of the rating is to help guests make informed decisions about the nature of the butler service being offered by a venue they may be considering, and to assist management and butler employees of those venues in improving their butler offering.

No Butler

The butlers are called such, but have no training or understanding of the nature or skill-sets of a butler, often having a modifier in front of their title, such as "fireplace butler," "technology butler" or "baby butler."

One Butler

There is literally one butler on the floor, rushing to service guests who are kept waiting or improperly serviced. There may be more than one butler, but training on the skills of the butler or the grace of a butler are lacking, even though some of the service is being provided.
The following services are offered as a minimum:

- Butler in a recognizable and appropriate uniform with name tag
- Inspection of the suite before guest arrival to ensure everything clean and working. The alarm clock not set, volumes on radios and TVs set low.
- Knowing which guests are coming and greeting them cheerfully and warmly by name on arrival. Smoothing their way through check-in and escorting them to their suite.
- The en suite telephones have a butler speed dial button
- Attending to guest requests when asked
- Following protocol for entering or not entering a room to maintain guest privacy
- Cleaning shoes when requested to a basic standard
- Returning dry cleaned and laundered clothes to closets
- Keeping a sharp eye out for defective equipment or items and having them fixed as rapidly as possible or the guest changed to another room smoothly

- Assisting with guest departure by confirming travel arrangements, liaising with Front Desk for the bill, Bellmen for the bags, and Doorman, and personally seeing the guest(s) off with a "thank you" for staying.
- Butlers have a sense of decorum and interact with guests and staff alike with refined speech, body language and manner, meaning no slang, swearing or colloquialisms

Two Butlers

The butler-to-guest ratio is still too strained, so guests are kept waiting or not fully serviced, but basic elements of butler service are performed and the butlers have been trained in their profession either in schools or on site. No night butler on duty and no butler coordinators to connect guests with butlers.

In addition to those services of the One Butler facility, the following are offered as a minimum:

- Keeping a rudimentary record of guest preferences and using it to personalize the guest experience
- Greeting guest at front door and touring them around the facility and their suite, if desired, and handling of guest check in en suite
- Offering to unpack and pack suitcases and doing so professionally
- Cleaning shoes, steam or iron clothes in need when requested
- Returning laundered & dry cleaned clothes to the right places in the closet
- Providing a morning wake-up beverage service
- Presenting food en suite, checking that what was ordered was delivered and all needed items brought up by Room Service
- Taking care of guest entertainment and activities, making reservations.
- Bringing the bill to the guest and returning it signed to the Front Desk, sorting out any issues.
- Checking the room after guest departure to ensure nothing left behind. Forwarding it if so.
- Butlers understand that, while still being friendly, they are there to serve, not to be interesting or intrude upon guest space.
- All butlers connected with a two-way radio and discreet earpiece
- Radio etiquette followed, including removing bud when servicing guest.
- Fresh flowers provided and wilting ones removed before they become noticeably sad.

Three Butlers

There are enough butlers in shifts to manage guests, including night butlers, butler coordinators, and a head butler. The Butler department exists as its own department, not under Housekeeping, Concierge, Room Service, F&B, or any other department. Guests are offered a good range of butler services and these are satisfactorily executed. Butler service has been established and fine-tuned with the assistance of trained professionals.

In addition to those services of the Two Butler facility, the following are offered as a minimum:

- A reasonably thorough electronic record (backed up regularly) of guest preferences based on their stays that is used to prepare for guest returns.
- Pre-arrival interviews are pleasantly and efficiently conducted to determine guest needs. All reservations are made and confirmed either by mail, fax, e-mail or telephone. Pick-up arrangements are made.
- Pre-arrival checks are made of the suites before guest arrival to ensure everything clean and operational, with a basic amenity provided
- Guest greeted at the door with a basic beverage and napkin
- Following up on guest activities to ensure service is being and was well delivered.
- Turndown by Housekeeping and checks by the butler are made while guests are out to dinner to ensure everything is ready, neat and clean for guest's return. A basic amenity is provided.
- Providing a wake-up service, menu including beverage, newspaper, drawing of bath, laying out of clothes.
- Laying any table for room service ordered, announcing the meal is served and if there will be anything else
- Providing and either pointing out or explaining the list of butler services for guests when they first arrive with an invitation to utilize the service
- Cleaning shoes, steaming or ironing clothes to professional standards when noticing that they are in need of such, leaving a note to that effect upon returning them.
- Providing a guest itinerary at start of stay, and an updated daily one each evening at turndown
- Morning wake-up service includes cluing guest in on the weather as it affects their activities for the day, and what their activities are
- Basic afternoon snack provided
- Basic fruit bowl and flower arrangement provided
- Removing plastic wraps, clips, safety pins, labels and other laundry/dry cleaning bric-a-brac when returning clothes to closet, and transferring dry cleaning from wire hangers to the wooden/cloth ones available for guests
- Offering a basic travel care package the day before departure and placing it in the departing vehicle just before the guest enters
- All speed dial buttons on the telephone go to the Butler Coordinator (BC) (except an emergency one if desired)
- BC picking up by the third ring latest and greeting guest by name and courteously
- BC logging all requests and relaying them immediately
- BC chasing up to ensure guest requests are filled
- All butlers connected via two-way radio with a dedicated band for the butlers
- The White Board is kept up to date to manage guests

- Butlers are very professional in their behavior, observing the emotional tone/body language of the guests and responding appropriately
- All butler personnel discreet, quietly observing and acting to service guests
- Butler uniforms are sharp and well conceived, yet appropriate for the environment. Butler grooming is impeccable, with regular inspections by the Head Butler
- Guest follow-up, inviting to return based on some event that aligns with their preferences.
- A generally favorable opinion exists among fellow employees, management and guests of the Butler Department and its personnel, resulting in support from these other personnel, and vice versa.

Four Butlers

Butlers provide excellent, often invisible service to guests who are wowed by the attention to detail. Includes a full complement of butlers who have sufficient presence with the rest of the employees that they have raised their level of service and can obtain instant service for guests. Butler Department personnel receive ongoing training and quality control to keep them sharp and there is a Deputy for the Head Butler who facilitates this training and other organizational steps to keep the Butler Department running smoothly.

In addition to those services of the Three Butler facility, the following are offered as a minimum:

- An electronic record of guest information that includes much information gleaned through unobtrusive observation during their stays, from pre-arrival interviews, and from follow-up communications.
- Arrival amenities are tailored to guest preferences or celebration of occasions, and varied between visits
- Arrangements made for limo pick-up as needed, with a care package for guests to freshen themselves on the way to the resort/hotel.
- Guest greeted at door with either a preferred complimentary beverage or, if not known, a refreshing one characteristic of the local area, finely presented on salver.
- Turndown amenities are always varied
- Choice of afternoon snacks provided in rotation, with possibility of guest request for a specific one
- Fruit bowl provided and updated, with knife, plate, napkin for each guest
- Full table service provided for suites with dining rooms, using either butler service or synchronized service.
- Following up on guest activities to ensure service is being and was well delivered. Handling any upsets or concerns to satisfaction of guest; supporting those who serviced guests well
- Folding cleaned laundry and placing in drawers
- When cleaning shoes, replacing old or frayed laces

- Offering a menu of items for a travel care package the day before departure, including food and drink, and placing in vehicle in a small insulated bag just before guests climb in
- While being interested in guests, rather than trying to be interesting to them, butlers also are able to carry off their duties and interchanges with guests and other employees, even in the most tricky of situations, with a degree of panache
- Extra special touches are made to wow guests, based on their preferences
- All guest requests handled within minutes, or responded to within minutes and then worked on, if the handling is not short and simple
- BCs follow up on and escalate guest requests if not attended to within half an hour
- Butlers able to satisfy secretarial/technological/business centre service requests
- All butlers connected by a PDA that also allows them to input and retrieve information in real time on guests
- Butlers make a point of noting down all data of interest in serving guests
- Guest follow-up includes personal touches such as Holiday Cards
- The Butler Department is considered an asset by management and the rest of the employees, and supported in terms of being kept established, given the tools it needs, and in servicing the guests

Five Butlers

Guests have their own private butler able to do anything (legal) required, including playing golf, tennis, chauffeuring, or whatever activities the guest may have available locally and want to engage in with the butler as a companion. Where spa service is offered, the butler is also the spa therapist or so knowledgeable in spa methodology that he or she presents a seamless experience for the spa-going guest.

In addition to those services of the Four Butler facility, the following are offered as a minimum:

- A very detailed record of guest likes and dislikes that is followed meticulously on subsequent trips, including personal and familial information
- Guest greeted at the airport or harbor by the butler and whisked away in a limo while a chauffeur retrieves the baggage and brings it to the suite.
- Arrival and turndown amenities are of interest/value to the guests
- Departing amenity personally presented on behalf of management
- Afternoon snacks are to order
- Fruit and flower arrangements provided according to guest preference and adjusted according to guest demand
- Food is served en suite by the butler
- Food is served anywhere else by the butler, such as a picnic elsewhere

- Accompanying guests whenever needed or desired, to ensure their activities go very smoothly—includes playing games against them when requested, (and letting them just win overall).
- Handling paparazzi so they do not intrude upon guest pleasures
- Screening of calls if desired
- Restocking the mini bar
- Making and serving drinks en suite
- Sending cards and gifts to mark various events, from birthdays to anniversaries, etc., and maintaining a supportive line with guests as appropriate
- Returning shoes in shoe bags if not already, and organizing for broken or otherwise degraded shoes to be mended at a cobbler
- Guest requests and all phone speed dials go to the butler's cell phone/Blackberry
- BCs exist to expedite guest requests for the butler as needed, and coordinate personal butlers in full servicing of guests
- Butlers are so attuned to guest needs, and so consummate at judging moods and desires, that they can anticipate needs and act accordingly.
- Escorting guests back to the airport/port or other departure point

END NOTES

(1) *"Etiquette, A Guide to Modern Manners,"* Emily Post (Harper and Row, NY, 1922)

(2) *"The English Domestic Servant in History,"* Dorothy Marshall (George Philip and Son, Ltd., London, 1949)

(3) Samuel and Sarah Adams, *"The Complete Servant,"* 1825

ABOUT THE AUTHOR

Having worked in personal service and the hospitality industry in England many years ago, Steven Ferry decided to train as a butler in one of the schools offering such an education and then worked in the United States as a butler.

It was during these years that his path crossed with many other British butlers and he founded the Guild of Traditional Butlers to pool knowledge and experience and offer assistance to each other. By drawing on his own training and experience, as well as those of his peers, and ransacking research libraries and old bookstores in London, he wrote the first industry text, *The British Butlers' Bible*, followed by *Butlers and Household Managers, 21ˢᵗ Century Professionals*.

Teaching engagements followed at The International Butler Academy and in private estates. While teaching subsequently at hotels, spas, resorts and private villas, it became evident that a new text was needed to address the issues and needs of hospitality industry butlers, and so came about *Hotel Butlers, The Great Service Differentiators*. Additionally, another avenue for adding value to the hotel butler became evident for hotels and resorts with spas—by understanding spa methodology, butlers would be able to improve dramatically the spa guest experience—and so a chapter was devoted to this subject.

In 2004, Mr. Ferry established the International Institute of Modern Butlers to act as a clearing house for information on butler training resources around the world, and to help maintain standards for the butler profession and raise standards for the service industry as a whole through the butler model.

Steven Ferry is based in the United States, where he indulges in his passions of writing and photography between training and consulting assignments.

He is happy to answer any questions or concerns you may have.

(813) 354 2734
or via *www.modernbutlers.com*

334097

Made in the USA